SOVIET FOREIGN POLICY
THE BREZHNEV YEARS

Soviet Foreign Policy
The Brezhnev Years

★

ROBIN EDMONDS

Oxford   New York
OXFORD UNIVERSITY PRESS

Oxford University Press, Walton Street, Oxford OX2 6DP

London Glasgow New York Toronto
Delhi Bombay Calcutta Madras Karachi
Kuala Lumpur Singapore Hong Kong Tokyo
Nairobi Dar es Salaam Cape Town
Melbourne Auckland

and associated companies in
Beirut Berlin Ibadan Mexico City Nicosia

Oxford is a trade mark of Oxford University Press

First published 1983 as an Oxford University Press paperback
Previous publication of the first half of this book as part of
Soviet Foreign Policy 1962–1973
is acknowledged on page vii
Reprinted 1984

British Library Cataloguing in Publication Data

Edmonds, Robin
Soviet foreign policy—the Brezhnev years.—
(Chronology of international events 1956–82)
1. Soviet Union—Foreign relations—1953–1974
2. Soviet Union—Foreign relations—1975–
I. Title   II. Series
327.47   DK274
ISBN 0-19-285125-X Pbk

Library of Congress Cataloging in Publication Data

Edmonds, Robin
Soviet foreign policy—the Brezhnev years.
Bibliography: p. Includes index.
1. Soviet Union—Foreign relations—1953–1975.
2. Soviet Union—Foreign relations—1975– .
3. Brezhnev, Leonid Ilich, 1906– . 4. Detente.
I. Title.
DK274.E3 1983   327.47   83-4225
ISBN 0-19-285125-X (pbk.)

Printed in Great Britain by
Richard Clay (The Chaucer Press) Ltd.
Bungay, Suffolk

For Enid

Preface

THIS book is indebted to many people: to Sir Duncan Wilson, Dr Stephen White, and my wife, all of whom read the whole typescript; to Dr Gregory Treverton, who read most of the second half; to Professor Alec Nove, Miss Edwina Moreton, and Mr Richard Samuel, who read individual chapters; to Mr Raymond Hyatt, for the maps; to Sir Edgar Williams for reading the proofs; to Mrs Jacqueline Simms (Oxford University Press) for invaluable editorial help; and to Miss Diane Loryman for both deciphering and typing my manuscript. I am deeply grateful to all of them. My especial thanks go to Dr White, who read my typescript in its initial draft form as well as in its final stage, and also greatly facilitated the task of verifying references in Soviet sources.

The views expressed in the book are my own. But I hope that those who have read all or part of the typescript will find, in the book, a reflection of their kind but unsparing criticisms. I am also grateful to the Chinese People's Institute of Foreign Affairs for inviting me to visit China. If this book shows a clearer understanding of China than its predecessor (*Soviet Foreign Policy 1962–1973*), this is in large measure the result of long talks in Peking and Shanghai on three visits during the past two years. Readers of both books will find that although the first half of the present book retains the narrative chapters of the earlier one, substantially in the form in which they first appeared, they have been given a fresh perspective and revised to take account of subsequent developments. All the rest—the Introduction, Chapters 14–25, and the Appendix—is new material. The chronological cut-off date is 31 December 1982.

Monte Veritá
Ascona

Contents

Maps

Selective Chronology of International Events

1956	February	XXth CPSU Congress: Khrushchev denounces Stalin
	October	Second Arab–Israeli War (the Suez invasion); Hungarian revolt; Polish 'October revolution'
1957	October	First sputnik; Sino-Soviet nuclear agreement
	November	Mao Zedong's speech in Moscow
1958		Year of the Chinese Great Leap Forward
1959	June	Sino-Soviet nuclear agreement rescinded by Soviet Government
	September	Khrushchev's visit to USA
	September–October	Khrushchev's visit to China
1960	May	U-2 incident; abortive summit meeting in Paris
	July	Recall of Soviet experts from China
1961	April	Invasion of Cuba: the Bay of Pigs fiasco
	June	Meeting of Kennedy and Khrushchev in Vienna; beginning of second Berlin crisis
1962	October	Cuban missile crisis; Sino-Indian War
1963	July	CPSU Open Letter on Sino-Soviet dispute
	August	Partial Nuclear Test Ban Treaty signed in Moscow
1964	August	Tonkin Gulf incident, followed by joint Congressional Resolution on Vietnam
	October	Fall of Khrushchev, replaced by collective Soviet leadership; explosion of first Chinese nuclear device
1965	February	Kosygin visits Hanoi; US bombing of North Vietnam begins
1966		Chinese Cultural Revolution begins
1967	June	Third Arab–Israeli War
	November	Security Council Resolution 242 on Arab–Israeli dispute
1968	January	Dubcek becomes First Secretary of Czechoslovak Communist Party

	July	Nuclear Non-Proliferation Treaty signed; end of Chinese Cultural Revolution
	August	Invasion of Czechoslovakia
1969		Year of Soviet–US numerical strategic nuclear parity
	March	Sino-Soviet border clash
	July	First withdrawal of US troops from Vietnam
	September	Meeting of Soviet and Chinese Prime Ministers in Peking (Beijing)
	November	Soviet and US SALT delegations meet in Helsinki •
	December	Soviet–German talks begin in Moscow; Berlin talks proposed by Three Allied Powers; first moves towards multilateral European negotiations
1970	January	Soviet military intervention in Egypt
	March	Ratification of Non-Proliferation Treaty by Great Britain, US, and USSR •
	August	Signature of Soviet–German Moscow Treaty; Egyptian–Israeli cease-fire
	September	Allende elected President of Chile
1971	March–April	XXIVth CPSU Congress adopts Programme of Peace
	July	Announcement of US President's acceptance of invitation to visit China
	August	The dollar declared inconvertible into gold
	September	Quadripartite Agreement on Berlin signed
	October	Nixon invited to Moscow
	December	Indo–Pakistan War; Republic of China takes seat in UN
1972	February	Nixon's visit to China
	May	Nixon's visit to USSR; signature of first Soviet–US summit agreements; Quadripartite Berlin Agreement brought into force
	July	Soviet troops withdrawn from Egypt, at Egyptian request
	August	Last US combat troops withdrawn from Vietnam
	December	Basic Treaty between the two Germanies signed

1973	January	Britain, Denmark, and Ireland enter the European Economic Community; Vietnam cease-fire agreement signed in Paris
	April	CPSU Central Committee approves Brezhnev foreign policy and changes in Politburo
	May	Brezhnev visits Bonn
	June	Brezhnev visits US; Agreement on Prevention of Nuclear War signed
	September	*Coup d'état* in Chile; Geneva Conference on Security and Cooperation opens
	October	Fourth Arab–Israeli War; Vienna talks on mutual reduction of forces and armaments in Europe open
	December	World oil prices quadrupled
1974		Year of energy crisis
	February	Solzhenitsyn exiled
	April	Democracy restored in Portugal
	May	Indian explosion of a nuclear device
	June–July	Third Soviet–US summit meeting
	July–August	Cyprus crisis; Greek democracy restored
	August	Resignation of President Nixon, succeeded by Vice-President Ford
	November	Fourth Soviet–US summit meeting
1975	January	Soviet–US Trade Agreement cancelled
	April	Fall of Saigon
	June	Suez Canal reopened
	August	CSCE Final Act signed in Helsinki
	October	Cuban troops arrive in Angola
	November	Death of Franco
1976	January	Death of Zhou Enlai
	February–March	XXVth CPSU Congress
	February	MPLA victory in Angola
	June	Soweto riots
	September	Death of Mao Zedong
1977	July	Deng Xiaoping reinstated for second time
	August	XIth CCP Congress
	September	USSR and US agree to abide by SALT I after expiry

	November	Sadat visits Jerusalem; Soviet air-lift to Ethiopia
	December	Soviet SS-20s deployed
1978	August	Sino-Japanese peace treaty signed
	September	Camp David 'framework' agreements signed
	October	Karol Wojtyla elected Pope
	December	Vietnam invades Kampuchea; Soviet–Afghan friendship treaty signed
1979	January	Shah leaves Iran
	February– March	Chinese punitive invasion of Vietnam
	March	Egyptian–Israeli peace treaty signed
	June	SALT II treaty signed
	November	US Embassy in Teheran seized; 63 hostages taken
	December	Soviet invasion of Afghanistan; Zimbabwean settlement
1980	January	US Senate suspends SALT II debate
	August– September	Gdansk Agreement; *Solidarnosc* formed
	September	Iraq invades Iran
	December	Soviet–Syrian friendship treaty signed
1981	January	Reagan inaugurated as President of USA
	February– March	XXVIth CPSU Congress
	November	INF talks open in Geneva
	December	Martial Law imposed in Poland
1982	June	Israeli invasion of Lebanon; START talks open in Geneva
	August	XIIth CCP Congress
	October	Sino-Soviet talks resumed
	November	Death of Brezhnev, succeeded by Andropov
	December	Martial Law suspended in Poland

Abbreviations

ABM	Anti-ballistic missile
ALCM	Air-launched cruise missile
ASM	Air-to-surface missile
ASW	Anti-submarine warfare
CCP	Chinese Communist Party
CENTO	Central Treaty Organization
COMECON	Council for Mutual Economic Cooperation
CPSU	Communist Party of the Soviet Union
CSCE	European Conference on Security and Cooperation (the ordering of initials derives from the French *Conférence de sécurité et coopération européenne*)
DDR/GDR	East Germany (German Democratic Republic)
EEC	European Economic Community
FBS	Forward based system
FRG	West Germany (Federal Republic of Germany)
GATT	General Agreement on Trade and Tariffs
GLCM	Ground-launched cruise missile
GNP	Gross National Product
ICBM	Intercontinental ballistic missile
IISS	International Institute for Strategic Studies
IMF	International Monetary Fund
INF	Intermediate range nuclear forces
IRBM	Intermediate range ballistic missile
KGB	(Soviet) Committee for State Security
MAD	Mutually assured destruction
MARV	Manoeuvrable re-entry vehicle
MBFR	Mutual and Balanced Force Reductions (the title finally agreed was Mutual Force Reductions and Associated Measures)
MFN	Most favoured nation
MIRV	Multiple independently targetable re-entry vehicle
MPLA	Movimento Popular para a Libertacao de Angola
MRBM	Medium range ballistic missile
MRV	Multiple re-entry vehicle

NATO	North Atlantic Trade Organization
NLF	National Liberation Front
OECD	Organization for Economic Cooperation and Development
PLO	Palestine Liberation Organization
PZPR	Polish United Workers Party
RIIA	Royal Institute of International Affairs
SALT	Strategic Arms Limitation Talks
START	Strategic Arms Reduction Talks
SAM	Surface-to-air missile
SLBM	Submarine launched ballistic missile
SSBM	Ballistic missile submarine, nuclear
UNCTAD	United Nations Commission on Trade and Development

Note: Billion is used here as meaning a thousand million (1,000,000,000).

Introduction

IN June 1973—at the midpoint of his long ascendancy—Leonid Brezhnev sought to define the special responsibilities that super-power conferred on the Soviet Union and the United States. Backed by a fresh mandate for his foreign policy from the Central Committee of the Communist Party of the Soviet Union (CPSU), he offered his definition in language that was a far cry from the slogans of the cold war and for which the Leninist principle of peaceful coexistence offered no real precedent.[1] How this evolution of Soviet foreign policy came about is the subject of a book that I wrote at the time,* taking as its terminal points the Soviet–US confrontations in the Cuban missile crisis and in the Fourth Arab–Israeli War. Its first chapter, like the first chapter of the present book, described the paradoxes of Soviet super-power. The force of these paradoxes has not been diminished by the unfolding of history during the nine years that have gone by since then. The present book attempts a synthesis of the events of these nine years with those of the earlier eleven, in a single assessment of the development of Soviet foreign policy over the period 1962–82.

The new chapters take as their point of departure my 1973 forecast, which—as it has turned out—covered almost exactly the timespan of the later Brezhnev years.[2] They go on to study the way in which the course of international events during these years has affected Soviet foreign policy and their impact on the super-power relationship. The final chapters look forward to the foreign policy options that may be open to the Soviet leadership that succeeded Brezhnev's in November 1982, and seek to draw some conclusions for Western policy. Unlike 1973, I have described the events of the past nine years on a selective basis, without seeking to cover all aspects of Soviet foreign policy or every event of international significance that has affected the Soviet Union during this period. The decision to concentrate on what has, in my view, mattered most in these years, has been deliberate. But I am aware that in the process developments in

* *Soviet Foreign Policy 1962–1973: the Paradox of Super-power*

important geographical areas (such as Latin America) and functional areas (such as COMECON) have had to be omitted, as have developments in the Soviet dissident movement. They would have been included but for the constraints of time and space.

With rare exceptions the events of the later Brezhnev years make a dismal story. Each of the super-powers bears its share of responsibility for the gradual erosion of the super-power relationship. Although their relationship still seemed to have more positive than negative potential half-way through the 1970s, it has since been reduced to the bare minimum by the combined effects of the 'variables' in my forecast of nine years ago—technological temptation, political targets of opportunity, the pace of change in Eastern Europe; and, in addition, by the ebb and flow of American domestic politics. On the other hand, both the 'parameters' which I identified then—the first economic and the second nuclear—remain valid for the Soviet Union; and the second cannot be ignored by either super-power (or for that matter by the Europeans). The imperatives of agricultural productivity, energy development, and the whole problem of industrial management outside the privileged defence sector are even more compelling now for the Soviet Union than they were in the early 1970s. (The dimensions of the Soviet agricultural crisis were publicly acknowledged by Brezhnev himself in November 1981;[3] and they were given the widest possible publicity in the Soviet Union through the announcement of the Food Programme of May 1982.) As for the strategic nuclear parameter, today it is strikingly like the prospect that Kissinger forecast in the course of his press conference in Moscow in July 1974:

If we have not reached an agreement well before 1977, then I believe you will see an explosion of technology and an explosion of numbers at the end of which we will be lucky if we have the present stability, in which it will be impossible to describe what strategic superiority means. And one of the questions which we have to ask ourselves as a country is: what in the name of God is strategic superiority? What do you do with it? We will be living in a world which will be extraordinarily complex, in which opportunities for nuclear warfare exist that were unimaginable fifteen years ago at the beginning of the nuclear age . . . .[4]

There are no simple answers to Kissinger's questions, particularly the first. He suggested the outline of an answer himself, when—in the course of his address to the Senate Foreign Affairs Committee four months later—he described the prospect of one of the two super-powers gaining a decisive military advantage as politically intolerable for the other. Looking back, however, across the period of nearly forty years that has elapsed since the only atomic attack in history, it is a fact that all major wars since 1945 have been fought with conventional weapons. And it is maintained by some that at the moment of the most acute Soviet–US confrontation in 1962, although the Soviet strategic nuclear arsenal was much smaller than that of the United States (intercontinentally,[5] not much more than a powerful *force de frappe*), it was already large enough to have inflicted an unacceptable number of American casualties; and that the Cuban missile crisis was in the end resolved by the superiority, not of American strategic power, but of American conventionally armed forces in the Caribbean. In my view, the text of Khrushchev's messages to Kennedy leaves little doubt that, as the crisis developed, he became acutely aware of the danger that it would lead to a nuclear world war; moreover, he never attempted to use Soviet conventional superiority in and around Berlin as a bargaining counter during the Cuban crisis.*

However that may be, there is also the view of those who doubt whether any sane man would ever press the button unleashing a first-strike nuclear attack, knowing what the consequences would be, for the population of just one of his country's major cities,[6] of even a single megaton explosion forming part of a second-strike, retaliatory attack launched by the other super-power, still less the full consequences of an all-out second strike. Conversely, who would ever press the button for a second-strike attack, for the purposes of what would amount to a 'posthumous revenge'? But the terrible question remains: what is sanity in international relations? Both deterrence and security are largely states of mind; governments are controlled not by precise machines, but by fallible[7] men; and the governments of super-powers are no

---

* The point about Berlin, though in reverse, struck the then British Prime Minister when compiling his impressions of the Cuban crisis on 4 November 1962: see Harold Macmillan, *At the End of the Day*, Macmillan, London, 1973, p. 218, 'What Are the Strategic Lessons?'

exception. Thus it may be scientifically demonstrable that the destructive capacity of modern megaton warheads must reach a point of 'overkill' where it no longer makes sense for one super-power to seek to increase its own destructive capacity, either quantitatively or qualitatively, regardless of whether the other super-power does so; and that if none the less its capacity is so increased, the super-power will then be faced with Kissinger's third problem—what to do with it. Yet no computer will ever be devised whose calculations the leaders of any government will trust enough for it to determine for them exactly where this point lies. Therefore, so long as nuclear weapons exist, the government of a super-power must be haunted not only by the risk of sheer miscalculation in the heat of a crisis, to which each super-power is equally exposed, but also by the fear that the counsels of sanity may not prevail, and that its potential adversary will somehow or other contrive to steal a nuclear march. With states, as with individuals, to be aware of the truth is usually tolerable; what is dangerous is to act on fantasies conjured up by fear of the unknown; *omne ignotum pro magnifico*.

It was this fear that, in the rest of the 1970s, fuelled the 'explosion of technology and of numbers' on both the Soviet and the American side, about which Kissinger warned in 1974. In the event, the second strategic arms limitation agreement between the two super-powers—so far from being reached 'well before 1977'—was not signed until mid-1979; it remains unratified to this day—December 1982; and the latest development at the time of writing is the US Administration's proposal to base the MX missile system in a mode which, in the Soviet view, would constitute a violation of both SALT I and SALT II. Meanwhile, to take only one example, six years after Kissinger's outburst in Moscow the number of nuclear warheads in the Soviet strategic arsenal had more than doubled—to about 7,000—and the number of US nuclear warheads was nearing 10,000.[8]

That there was a change for the worse in the international climate in the second half of the 1970s is now recognized by official Soviet sources, although they lay the blame for this deterioration on the 'imperialist counter-attack'.[9] What no Soviet spokesman is prepared to admit is that during this period the Soviet power of menace also increased and that it is now too great for the comfort of most members of the international community. The phrase 'power of menace' was coined by Curzon nearly a century ago, to describe Russian policy in Central Asia.[10] Today the unremitting pace of Soviet weapons programmes, conventional as well as nuclear, has made it look disturbingly like Soviet policy throughout the world. Since the weaknesses of the Soviet economy oblige Soviet foreign policy-makers to rely heavily on military power (and also on arms transfers), rather than on the other instruments of modern diplomacy, the Soviet Union's opponents and critics are able to argue that, although the country is a super-power, it still has only one effective card to play—that of military power—in the Great Game.

This brings us to the central paradox of Soviet super-power. In spite of all Soviet rhetoric about the paramount needs of Soviet defence and the immense resources devoted to the defence sector, and in spite of the great changes in the conduct of Soviet foreign policy over which Brezhnev presided in the early 1970s, at the moment of his death the Soviet Union was no more secure, in reality, than it was eighteen years earlier—and moreover with six more divisions now deployed outside Soviet frontiers.[11] On the other hand, the impression that the Soviet authorities sought to convey throughout the Brezhnev years was that of immutability. This is not simply a reflection of the fact that Brezhnev was born in 1906 and was General Secretary of the CPSU from 1964–82. An aged Chinese leadership has demonstrated how much can be changed and how radically. In order to realize the degree of Soviet impermeability under Brezhnev's leadership one has only to pick up two copies of *Pravda* dated several years apart and observe how little had changed, or how little change was officially admitted.[12] The front page of the edition of *Pravda* that announced Brezhnev's death was a replica of the one published after the death of Stalin in 1953—almost as though the Soviet Union were outside the march of time.

Without anticipating the conclusions to be reached at the end of this book (or underestimating the resistance to change built into the Soviet system), I do not believe that history can ever be set in concrete. In the longer term, as Engels observed, 'a people which oppresses another cannot emancipate itself. The power which it uses to suppress the other finally turns against itself'.[13]

And in the medium term even the Soviet system is capable of change. Although the Russian character is fundamentally sceptical, creative energy remains an essential part of the Russian character as well, even if Soviet society allows it little opportunity at the moment. There are some shafts of light which may brighten an international landscape that has darkened over the past nine years. If they do appear, the West must be ready to respond to them creatively. Meanwhile the 1980s is a decade equally dangerous for all of us: West, East, China, and the countries of the developing world.

1. Paradox

WE must begin two years before Brezhnev became General
Secretary of the CPSU—in 1962, when the Soviet Union and the
United States suddenly found themselves on the brink of
thermonuclear war. Had this war been fought, such historians as
survived the holocaust would have recorded as its immediate
cause each side's interpretation of the other's intentions regarding a Caribbean island whose radical *caudillo* had made a solemn
profession of Marxist-Leninist faith in a televised broadcast to his
people on 1 December 1961. (Lenin would hardly have recognized Fidel Castro as a disciple, although he might well have seen
him, in traditional Russian terms, as a left-wing Social Revolutionary.) The more perceptive among these historians, mindful of
the belief of one of the two principal actors in the drama enacted
during this seminal crisis, that the mysterious 'essence of ultimate
decision remains impenetrable to the observer—often, indeed to
the decider himself . . . ',[1] would have added that the real reasons
for the conflict lay much deeper, in the relationship between the
two countries as it had developed since the end of the Second
World War, during which they had been the senior partners in
the Grand Alliance. The date on which the cold war was declared
and Europe was split in two is debatable: perhaps 2 July 1947,
when Molotov broke off negotiations in Paris, announcing that
the Soviet Union would not take part in the Marshall Plan for the
European Recovery Programme.[2] But there can be no question
when the cold war came closest to becoming literally a hot war:
22 October 1962, the day on which the presence of Soviet ballistic
missiles in Cuba was revealed to the world, and the six days that
followed until Nikita Khrushchev announced his decision to
withdraw them.

A decade later, although the Soviet Union and the United
States each remained at the head of the opposing alliances, both
of them regarded the cold war as over. Again, there is no exact
date for its conclusion, but as good as any is 22 June 1973, when
the Soviet–US Agreement on the Prevention of Nuclear War[3] was
signed by Brezhnev and Nixon in Washington, then being visited

by the General Secretary of the CPSU for the first time since the brief armistice in the cold war marked by Khrushchev's visit in 1959. And again, this transformation of the Soviet–US relationship did not come out of the blue, but took several years to develop. That their relationship underwent a change is beyond dispute. But the question remains, what exactly is it that changed and why? Is it Soviet as well as US foreign policy that altered; or is it only US foreign policy, reacting to what Soviet observers of the international scene regard as a change in the 'correlation of forces' in favour of the Soviet Union? The Marxist concept of this correlation is of something inherently unstable, which it is the task of the statesman to turn to his country's advantage, with the aid of the forces of history—an important difference from the traditional Western concept of the balance of power, designed to preserve international stability.

Defenders of the second view can point to the absence of any change in the doctrine of Soviet foreign policy as it has been formulated ever since 1956. (The one exception—the expansion of the concept of peaceful coexistence—will be examined in a later chapter.) The official History of Soviet Foreign Policy describes the policy's four basic tasks as:

1. To secure, together with the other socialist countries, favourable conditions for the building of socialism and communism;

2. To strengthen the unity and solidarity of the socialist countries, their friendship and brotherhood;

3. To support the national-liberation movement and to effect all-round cooperation with the young, developing countries;

4. Consistently to uphold the principle of peaceful coexistence of states with different social systems, to offer decisive resistance to the aggressive forces of imperialism, and to save mankind from a new world war.[4]

This formulation follows word for word the resolution on foreign policy approved by the XXIIIrd Congress of the CPSU in March 1966, which was repeated in turn by Brezhnev in his opening speech at the XXIVth Congress five years later.[5] To this formulation must be added two important riders. One is Lenin's statement that 'the deepest roots both of the international and of the external policy of our state are determined by the economic interests . . . of the ruling classes of our state':[6] the policy pursued

by the Soviet Government abroad is a reflection and an extension
of its policy at home. The other rider is a belief, also propounded
in the Official History,[7] that the danger of war, including the
danger of a Third World War, will continue as long as
imperialism exists: peaceful coexistence is therefore a form of the
Marxist class struggle. This belief was implicit in an article on
strategic arms limitation published in *Pravda* on the eve of
Brezhnev's visit to the United States, which reminded readers of his
statement made six months earlier at the celebration of the fiftieth
anniversary of the Soviet Union:

The . . . class struggle of the two systems . . . in the sphere of economics,
politics and, it goes without saying, ideology, will be continued . . . The
world outlook and the aims of socialism are opposed and irreconcilable.
But we shall ensure that this inevitable struggle is transferred to a
channel which does not threaten wars, dangerous conflicts, and an
uncontrolled arms race.[8]

True, there was a change in the conduct of foreign policy in 1964,
when the collective leadership took over from Khrushchev. But,
at any rate at the outset, the way in which they described the
difference between themselves and the man whom they had
removed from power was primarily one of style or posture: their
own approach they commended as that of prudent managers. As
Brezhnev put it in a definition of Soviet foreign policy in a speech
delivered to the Central Committee of the CPSU on 29
September 1965: 'we are striving to make our diplomacy active
and thrusting, while at the same time showing flexibility and
circumspection'.[9] Nevertheless, the doctrinal continuity of Soviet
foreign policy from 1956 onwards has been remarkable.

The West faces a bleak prospect if Soviet foreign policy really
has remained immutable, and if the only change is simply that
the rest of the world, notably the United States, has had to adjust
itself to an altered strategic power balance. This view is not
supported by the facts. The invasion of Czechoslovakia certainly
demonstrated the paramount importance to the Soviet leadership
of the first and second of the basic tasks of their foreign policy.
But the performance of the third task (support of the national-
liberation movements) has been erratic. And since 1972–3 the
Leninist[10] principle of peaceful coexistence has been given an

interpretation that goes far beyond anything ever suggested by Lenin, who described it to the VIIIth CPSU Congress as inconceivable over a long period of time. In fact, although Soviet foreign policy may have remained unaltered on paper for a quarter of a century, a gap has developed between its theory and its practice. For a Marxist, there can be no difference between theory and practice. In non-Marxist terms such a difference may be regarded as a conflict that cannot be tolerated indefinitely.

The strategic power balance between the Soviet Union and the United States is indeed very different from what it was twenty years ago. But in a world of two super-powers the international structure of power is exceedingly complex: a fact that Brezhnev himself seemed to be acknowledging in the last major speech of his life, which he delivered in October 1982.* The greatest achievement of the Soviet Union under Brezhnev's leadership was the attainment of strategic nuclear parity with the United States. Khrushchev's claim to this parity was proved hollow by the Cuban missile crisis. Today, the Soviet Union is universally acknowledged to be a super-power, militarily coequal with its old adversary in the cold war, the United States. The relationship between the two super-powers is both unique and ambivalent; and it has so far eluded attempts to define it in a single word or phrase. The word super-power is not part of the Soviet vocabulary; on the occasions when it is used, it appears in inverted commas; and Brezhnev brushed the term aside at his meeting with United States senators in June 1973.[11] The reason for this modesty is partly the pejorative significance that the word has acquired in the political vocabulary of the Chinese, who disclaim any intention of aspiring to super-power status themselves. Instead, the Soviet Union is described as one of the 'two nuclear giants' or, in the History of Soviet Foreign Policy, as 'one of the greatest world powers, without whose participation not a single international problem can be solved':[12] a definition which foreshadowed Brezhnev's statement, during his television broadcast in the United States in June 1973, that the economic and military power of the two countries invested them with a special responsibility for the preservation of universal peace and the prevention of war.[13]

* See Chapter 23.

It is instructive to compare Brezhnev's statement with the plea for collaboration between the super-powers made nearly thirty years earlier by William Fox, who first coined the term 'super-power' and attempted its first definition (a great power, whose armed force is so mobile that it can be deployed in any strategic theatre, as opposed to a great power whose interests and influence are confined to a single regional theatre).[14] This definition, made before Hiroshima and Nagasaki, holds good today, when the central strategic fact underlying the world power structure is the nuclear armoury of the super-powers. It is this armoury, combined with the expanded Soviet conventional military forces, both at sea and in the air, that entitles the Soviet Union to its global role. Yet in the process of achieving this goal, the Soviet Union, like the United States, became in many ways the prisoner of its power, which it must control, and of its responsibility, which it must seek to define. Today both the Soviet Union and the United States possess the capacity of assured destruction. In the 1960s American theorists defined this capacity as Mutually Assured Destruction (MAD). Soviet theorists never accepted the MAD doctrine;[15] and its conceptual weaknesses have since been the subject of much debate in the West. But both the Soviet Union and the United States now have at least one vital interest in common: not to destroy each other—an interest shared by most of the bystanders, who would be destroyed as well if the two super-powers were to come to thermonuclear blows. At first sight, the determination simply not to destroy may appear a negative concept. But it implies a determination to survive; and the logic of strategic nuclear power is so inexorable that sooner or later the relationship between the two super-powers was bound to become positive. Ten years ago this evolution did indeed begin between the Soviet Union and the United States, exemplified by their twenty bilateral agreements signed during 1972–3: a paradox which, before the nuclear age, would have been inconceivable for Lenin, which in its first years Stalin could not understand, and which Khrushchev only partly perceived.

By a further paradox, at the end of the 1960s, just as the Soviet leadership finally scaled the peak of super-power status that they had expended so much national effort to reach, they found themselves confronted with a dilemma at home, which was both economic and political. The Soviet economy had reached a point in its development where it could not meet both the demands of the defence sector and the aspirations of the consumer, except on one of two alternative conditions: either a root and branch reform of the Soviet system, or a massive importation of Western technology, capital, and in the end, management techniques. In accordance with the doctrine of the class struggle, while the former alternative was inconceivable, the latter was acceptable, as the lesser of two ideological evils, provided Western imports did not infect the Soviet Union with the germ of alien political ideas—a proviso that necessitated a sharp tightening of ideological discipline in the Soviet Union in the 1970s. On the other hand, voices of dissent were raised in the Soviet Union, proclaiming the eternal truth that material progress and the liberty of the human spirit are indivisible. Among these voices the most authoritative urged the West not to give the Soviet Union economic help unless intellectual freedom were assured within its boundaries, at the very moment when promises of such help were forthcoming from the Soviet Union's traditional enemies— Germany and Japan—and from its principal adversary in the cold war—the United States, with which Brezhnev was seeking a permanent relationship. These voices found a response in the West, both among those who believed that the Soviet Union should be helped only in return for political changes within that country, and among those who believed that such help would serve only to enable the Soviet Union to maintain and extend its military might. This response grew louder as the decade went forward, compounding the problem of Soviet national security, which—by a final paradox—was no more firmly assured at the end of the Brezhnev years than it had been at the outset.

To return to the 'mystery of ultimate decision'—any attempt to penetrate it should take account of de Tocqueville's observation:

men of letters who have written history without taking part in public affairs . . . are always inclined to find general causes . . . politicians who have concerned themselves with producing events without thinking about them . . . living in the midst of disconnected daily facts, are prone to imagine that everything is attributable to particular incidents, and that the wires that they pull are the same as those that move the world. It is to be presumed that both are equally deceived.[16]

Can the tools of modern political science help the historian, particularly in assessing what de Tocqueville called general causes? Unfortunately, not much.[17] Where events are concerned, the more that the modern historian can allow them to speak for themselves, the better. The model, which is partly medical, is illustrious. Thucydides' approach to history was influenced by medical theory; he was a contemporary of Hippocrates. Indeed, the essence of Thucydides' scientific approach is expressed in the words with which he prefaced his account of the plague of Athens:

others, whether doctors or laymen, may relate how each of them believes the plague first came about and what causes they consider adequate to explain its powerful effect on nature. But I shall describe what it was like as it happened, and the symptoms, knowledge of which will enable an observer to recognize it, should it ever break out again . . . [18]

Listening to the events of history—'as it happened'—is as difficult for the historian as listening to the patient is for the physician; the historian of a state inspired by a dialectical philosophy can best understand it if he observes closely what its rulers do; and if he observes a conflict between their thought and their actions, he must draw his own conclusions.[19] Where the Soviet Union is concerned, it has been well said that there are no degrees of knowledge, only degrees of ignorance. Our knowledge of the inner workings of the eighteen years of Brezhnev's leadership is still fragmentary. But there are by now enough substantial fragments of evidence to make possible the work of reconstructing, as a coherent whole, the foreign policy of the Soviet Union during this period and to assess Brezhnev's attempt to resolve the problems of Soviet super-power.

KHRUSHCHEV'S YEARS OF ADVENTURE

2. The Theory

SOVIET foreign policy during the Brezhnev years cannot be assessed without understanding the problems that Brezhnev and his colleagues inherited from the man whom they ousted in 1964.

There is a long tradition in Soviet politics (of which Stalin himself took full advantage) of stealing the Whigs' clothes while they are bathing. In March 1954, seven months after he had announced the Soviet thermonuclear bomb, Georgyi Malenkov warned the Soviet people that a new world war fought with contemporary weapons would mean the destruction of world civilization.[1] It is clear that had Malenkov remained in power, he would have pursued a foreign policy designed to allow the Soviet consumer, at long last, a fair share of his country's economic resources. Khrushchev ousted Malenkov with a return to the long-standing priority of heavy industry, on which the modernization of the Soviet Armed Forces depended; and he at once increased the defence budget. Yet by 1964 he had become an advocate of minimum nuclear deterrence, at loggerheads with both the 'steel-eaters' and the military, having taken the first steps towards an accommodation with the United States.

In the nine years of his erratic rule Khrushchev transformed Soviet foreign policy. During Stalin's last years, not only as a dictator of the Soviet Union but also as the acknowledged[2] leader of the Sino-Soviet bloc, even though he referred to the principle of peaceful coexistence (for example, in the *Economic Problems of Socialism*, the year before his death), the image of the Soviet Union's relationship with the non-communist world which he projected was that of a besieged camp, with Europe as its citadel. Khrushchev staked out a new political claim for the Soviet Union (no longer seen as besieged by the West, but the latter's challenger throughout the world), while at the same time seeking an understanding with the United States, based on the premise that the Soviet Union was already its equal, with the prospect of superiority, economic and military in sight.

This new policy had to be based on an ideological reformulation, which was approved by the XXth Party Congress, held in February 1956. At this historic meeting, in parallel with his destruction of the Stalinist idol, Khrushchev introduced three major changes, two of which are reflected in the third and fourth basic tasks of Soviet foreign policy. First, he laid a fresh emphasis on the principle of peaceful coexistence between communist and non-communist countries. This was no longer seen as a temporary phenomenon. Although imperialism was perceived as being as aggressive as ever, the socialist commonwealth was now held to be strong enough to make war avoidable. This change, coupled with his second innovation—that a country's transition to socialism could be carried out by peaceful means—paved the way for Khrushchev's visit to the United States in 1959 (the 'spirit of Camp David') and the non-summit in Paris the following year. Thirdly, he propounded a new approach to the Third World. For Stalin, a country such as India was governed by bourgeois, who as such deserved no support from the communist states. Khrushchev, on the contrary, saw Soviet championship of countries that had recently won their independence from the colonial powers, or were seeking independence, as part of the Soviet Union's new global role. These countries, and the United Nations—where they were soon to form the majority—were perceived in a new light. The visits which Khrushchev and Bulganin made in 1955 to India, Burma, and Afghanistan marked the beginning both of the Soviet foreign aid programme and of the Soviet Union's close relationship with India, while the arms deal with Egypt in the same year was the first to be concluded as part of a new policy of military aid to non-communist countries. It has been estimated that by the time of Khrushchev's fall, about 3 billion dollars worth of arms had been supplied to thirteen such countries in the preceding decade, amounting to nearly half the total of all Soviet economic aid to underdeveloped countries in the same period.[3]

Although the doctrines of peaceful coexistence and of peaceful transition to socialism, against the background of the 'thaw' within the Soviet Union, made Khrushchev appear at first sight easier for the West to deal with than Stalin had been, his new policy towards the Third World brought his country to the brink of nuclear war. For Khrushchev's foreign policy to succeed, two projections into the future—one economic and the other technological—had to be fulfilled. According to the first, announced by Khrushchev at the XXIInd Party Congress in October 1961, not only would the Soviet Union enter the phase of communism by 1980; in twenty years it would overtake the per capita standard of living of any capitalist country, and specifically reach 80 per cent above the 1960 American standard of living.[4] (By the time Khrushchev died, Japan was already in sight of overhauling his country as the world's second greatest industrial power.) The second projection arose from the successful launching of the first sputnik in September 1957. Whether Khrushchev really believed that the initial Soviet success in rocket technology would enable him to deploy intercontinental ballistic missiles (ICBMs) swiftly enough to achieve strategic nuclear parity with the United States is a matter for speculation.

It has been argued[5] that the successive Soviet boasts made between 1957 and 1962 should be regarded as bluff: these ranged from Tass's statement in August 1957 that it was 'now possible to send missiles to any part of the world', through Khrushchev's own claim, made to the Supreme Soviet in January 1960, that the Soviet Union by then had enough nuclear weapons and rockets to wipe out any country or countries that attacked the Soviet Union or other socialist states, to Malinovsky's statement in January 1962, that approximate nuclear parity existed between the Soviet Union and the United States.[6] It is questionable whether the public debate on the 'missile gap'[7] that these boasts provoked in the United States really affected the pace of the six strategic nuclear Research and Development programmes already being carried out by the three US armed services in the fifties. The momentum of these immense, crash programmes was by that time so great that by 1962 the result would probably have been the same in any case: a large number of American ICBMs and *Polaris* submarines confronting a much inferior Soviet strategic nuclear force. Be that as it may, the possibility that the Soviet

Union was indeed carrying out an effective crash programme of first generation ICBMs (in reality their design was one of extreme awkwardness) succeeded only in spurring on the Administration to greater efforts with their ICBMs and their *Polaris* submarines. In 1960 the first *Atlas* ballistic missile units became operational and the first *Titan* less than two years later, followed by the first *Minuteman* missiles towards the end of 1962; and the first *Polaris* missiles were deployed at sea in November 1960.[8] These American successes were such that in the autumn of 1962 Khrushchev resorted to a gambler's throw.

Khrushchev's changes in the doctrine of Soviet foreign policy, coupled with his claim for Soviet ballistic missile technology, contributed to the great schism in the communist world, which became public the year before his fall. Although both sides regard 1957 as the origin of the Sino-Soviet dispute, it is hard to see how the Soviet Union and China could have remained allies for long, given the growing divergence in their policies. Nevertheless, Khrushchev's impetuous nature, his conduct of the dispute by public abuse, and his attempt to have Chinese doctrines condemned by the majority of the international communist movement may well have loomed large in the minds of his colleagues when they finally decided to remove him from power.

Lenin's remark that 'abuse in politics often covers up the utter lack of ideological content, the helplessness, and the impotence of the abuser'[9] recalls the great schism between the Western and Eastern branches of Christianity. Unlike the Christian schism, which appears to have had remarkably little theological content, the Sino-Soviet dispute has from the outset been a conflict of ideas, not simply of national interests stemming from a secular difference of cultural tradition. The Chinese view of the dispute at the time was clearly expounded in *The Polemic of the General Line on the International Communist Movement*. The Soviet view of its ideological framework may be summarized as follows.[10] Having accepted, at the XXth Congress, the CPSU's line on de-Stalinization, peaceful coexistence, and the peaceful transition to socialism, the Chinese afterwards opposed it. The Chinese, on the other hand, maintained that they had disagreed about the XXth Congress from the outset. Basing themselves on the Maoist concept of contradictions within socialist society, they argued that revisionism, not dogmatism,[11] was the greater threat to the unity of the Sino-Soviet bloc, identifying the former first with Yugoslavia, and from 1963 onwards, with the Soviet Union itself. In their view therefore the CPSU had forfeited the position of head of the international communist movement. The CPSU responded by attacking the CCP as the exponent of dogmatism, and claimed that the class struggle had been virtually completed in the Soviet Union, where some relaxation was permissible. The Chinese alleged that bourgeois elements within the Soviet Union were increasing; and they regarded the picture of collectivist affluence painted by the XXIInd Congress as imitating the United States. For the Chinese, the commune experiment, together with the Great Leap Forward, showed them as pioneers, outstripping the Russians, on the path to pure communism; for the Russians, it discredited communism because it required a control over individual liberty even stricter than that which they themselves were in the process of discarding. The Russians maintained that the decisive event in world politics was the establishment of the world communist system, whose combined strength would expand communism by peaceful means. The Chinese replied that the imperialists would yield to force, if pressed, and that the tide was already running in favour of the communist movement.

Historically, the first duty of a Chinese Emperor was always the defence of the Empire. It was open to the Chinese Communists to choose to remain under the Soviet nuclear umbrella, which would have implied both an agreed policy over a wide range and a continuing trust in Soviet willingness to treat a threat to China as a threat to the Soviet Union. But their price for accepting this protection, and therefore opting out of the nuclear club themselves, was a more forward Soviet foreign policy than even the globalist Khrushchev could dare to contemplate. The fundamental differences between the Soviet and Chinese views of the nuclear issue were made plain by Mao Zedong in the speech which he delivered at the meeting of communist parties held in Moscow in November 1957 to celebrate the fortieth anniversary of the Russian Revolution. The full text has never been published, but it was on that occasion that Mao described the East wind as prevailing over the West, repeated his assessment of the United States as a paper tiger, and spoke of the millions of socialists who would survive a nuclear holocaust, which would leave imperialism razed to the ground.* At that moment Khrushchev was struggling to restore the unity of the world communist movement, in the wake of the Hungarian and Polish revolts of the preceding year. Perhaps therefore it was by way of compromise that he then granted Mao an agreement on new technology for national defence, which according to the Chinese version included the provision of a sample atomic bomb and the know-how for its manufacture.

The exact extent of defence cooperation between the two countries is uncertain.[12] In any event, according to the Chinese, 'the leadership of the CPSU put forward unreasonable demands designed to put China under Soviet control. These unreasonable demands were rightly and firmly rejected by the Chinese Government.' The collision over defence came to a head in 1958, simultaneously with the quarrel about internal policy; the Chinese Great Leap Forward, openly denounced by Khrushchev, reached its peak in the autumn. Thus the Sino-Soviet bloc, whose titanic potential mesmerized the West, really lasted little more than eight years, from the Sino-Soviet Treaty of 1950 until 1958, the year in which the two major communist powers set out on their separate ways. As additional grievances in that year, the Chinese could also point to the inadequacy of Soviet support during the Matsu–Quemoy crisis, and to the solution of the Jordan–Lebanon crisis. They saw the latter as an example of collusion between the governments of the Soviet Union and the United States, since Khrushchev's proposal was for a summit meeting of the Powers, which was to include India, but exclude China. In January 1959, Khrushchev proposed an atom-free zone in the Far East and the whole Pacific Ocean, which Zhou Enlai at first endorsed; but later he added the condition that this should

* This historic speech, which must have chilled the blood of Mao's Soviet listeners, was summarized in the course of *Pravda*'s major survey of Chinese foreign policy on 26 August 1973 as a 'declaration that, for the sake of the achievement of a specific political goal, it is possible to sacrifice half mankind'. It is reconstructed, from published extracts, in ch. VIII of John Gittings' *Survey of the Sino-Soviet Dispute 1963–67*, Oxford University Press, 1968. Quotations for these years of the Sino-Soviet dispute are drawn from this comprehensive collection of polemical documents unless otherwise stated.

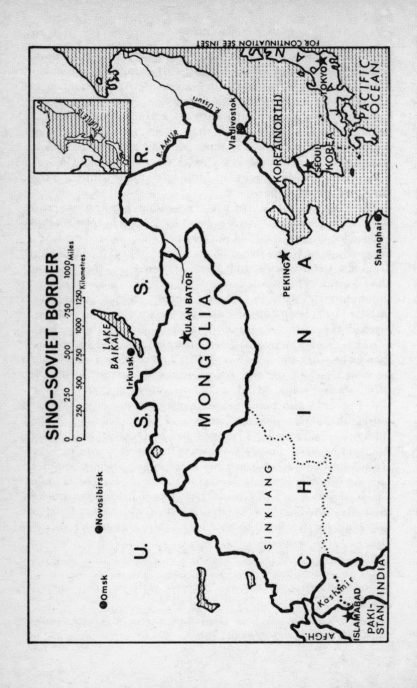

apply to all countries bordering the Pacific. In June 1959 (coinciding with Khrushchev's visit to the United States) the Soviet Government revoked the 1957 atomic agreement and, according to the Chinese, refused to supply the sample. In August, the Chinese Defence Minister was dismissed. A year later Soviet specialists of all kinds working in China were recalled.

Within the world communist movement, the first break between the Soviet Union and China took place in June 1960 at the Romanian Communist Party Congress, where Khrushchev (fresh from the failure of the Paris summit meeting) clashed with the Chinese delegate. The watershed was reached at the meeting of eighty-one communist parties held in Moscow in December 1960, where in another confrontation Albania supported China up to the hilt, while the Indonesian, North Korean, and North Vietnamese delegates remained neutral, although inclined towards the Chinese. In October 1961, at the XXIInd Congress of the CPSU, to which Albania had not been invited, Khrushchev attacked Albania—and implicitly China—for opposing the line agreed at the XXth Congress. Zhou Enlai protested, walked out, laid a wreath on the tomb of Stalin (whose body was removed a few days later from the Lenin Mausoleum), and then left Moscow. Only two-thirds of the parties represented at the Congress endorsed the attack on Albania; all the Asians remained silent. In the following year, when by a remarkable (but genuine) coincidence the Sino-Indian border war broke out two days before the Cuban missile crisis began, the two communist governments for a few days lent each other moral support. But by 5 November 1962 the Chinese had begun to criticize the Soviet withdrawal of missiles from Cuba, and the Russians had reverted to their earlier attitude of neutrality towards the Sino-Indian dispute, urging the need for a negotiated settlement and continuing to provide military aid to India. Following the events in Moscow a year earlier, it was only a short step for the Sino-Soviet dispute to become both direct and overt, as it did in 1963, and for China to claim leadership of the world communist movement.

Seen from Moscow, the last straw came in March 1963, when—as if the ideological and defence aspects of the Sino-Soviet dispute were not enough—a third dimension was added to it by the publication of the Chinese territorial claims against the Soviet Union.[13] The Chinese Government then declared that the nineteenth-century treaties of Aigun, Peking, and Ili were 'unequal', in the sense that the Tsarist Government of those days, as part of its expansionist policy in Asia, had taken advantage of Chinese weakness (as did other European Powers). The treaties were described in a *People's Daily* editorial of 8 March as raising outstanding issues; these should be settled peacefully through negotiations; until the time for such negotiations was ripe, the Chinese Government was prepared to maintain the status quo. From subsequent statements by both sides, it appeared that the Chinese wished to renegotiate the entire Sino-Soviet frontier— some 4,000 miles—although they were willing to accept the existing treaties as a basis for negotiations, provided that the Russians accepted their 'inequality'. For their part, the Russians denied the concept of inequality—a Russian Tsar was no worse than a Chinese Emperor—and were prepared only to make certain sections of the frontier more precise (much of it has never been delimited).

Under the terms of the Aigun and Peking treaties, the Russian Empire incorporated within its boundaries all the territory north of the Amur river and east of the Ussuri river, which was previously under Chinese suzerainty and today constitutes the Soviet Maritime Province in the Far East. The Ili treaty ceded part of Chinese Xinjiang (then Turkestan) to Russia, where it now forms part of the Kazakhstan Soviet Republic in Central Asia. But the 1,540,000 square kilometres of Chinese territory annexed by the Tsarist Government were not all that was called in question by the Chinese Government a century later. The Sino-Soviet Treaty of 1950 (also perhaps unequal, but in a different sense) had confirmed the independence of Outer Mongolia. Four years later Mao Zedong reopened this question with Khrushchev. That he had done so was revealed by Mao in July 1964, when he was reported by the Japanese press as having taken the opportunity of the visit of a Japanese Socialist Party delegation to back the Japanese claim for the return of the Kurile Islands, and even to criticize other Soviet post-war territorial acquisitions from Romania, Poland, and Finland.

No Soviet Government could fail to take seriously the claims of March 1963 (let alone the rest). The Soviet Union is the biggest landowner in Asia; and east of the Urals most of its thinly spread population is not Slav. The Soviet press gave publicity to the Chinese territorial claims, including the question of the status of Mongolia. A year later *Pravda* published a mammoth report by Mikhail Suslov to a plenary meeting of the CPSU Central Committee on 'The Struggle of the Communist Party of the Soviet Union for the Unity of the International Communist Movement'. Dated 14 February 1964, its publication was delayed for nearly two months while the Romanian Communist Party attempted mediation (one of the first signs of Romania's independent foreign policy). The report was the bitterest and most comprehensive attack yet made by the Russians against the Chinese, whose deviation was described as *petit bourgeois*, nationalistic, and neo-Trotskyite, hard on the heels of a personal attack in the Chinese press on Khrushchev as the arch-revisionist. It was rumoured in Moscow that Suslov's report was not his own work; that whole passages were written by a member of Khrushchev's personal staff; and that Suslov agreed to accept authorship on condition that the report would not be published.[14] If true, this would explain why he was credited in October 1964 with organizing the removal of Khrushchev, who by that time had lost his colleagues' confidence in his conduct of Soviet policy both at home and abroad.

3. The Cuban Missile Crisis

DURING his years of secret ideological combat with the Chinese, Khrushchev stood in urgent need of a diplomatic victory over the West to prove his point. He tried in Europe, over Berlin; in Africa, over Egypt and the Congo; and finally on the Americans' own doorstep, in the Caribbean. The Berlin crisis lasted off and on for nearly four years from November 1958, when Khrushchev suddenly declared that the Soviet Government no longer recognized its obligations under the Potsdam Agreement, in particular those affecting Berlin. It had only one consequence of far-reaching importance: the erection of the Berlin Wall in August 1961. The Egyptian arms deal, together with the subsequent financing of the Aswan Dam, was a success. But in the Congo, after it became independent in 1960, the Soviet Union backed two successive losers—Lumumba and Gizenga. Khrushchev may have calculated that even though he lost in the Congo itself, this was compensated for by the influence that the Soviet Union began to win in Africa as a whole (hence the university in Moscow named after Lumumba). But the Congo affair led him into a quarrel with the United Nations Secretary-General, Hammarskjöld, whom Khrushchev accused of arbitrary and lawless behaviour. On 23 September 1960 Khrushchev addressed personally the special emergency General Assembly, calling on Hammarskjöld to resign and proposing instead his troika arrangement, whereby the office of Secretary-General was to be converted into a commission of three men, one representing the Western bloc, one the Soviet bloc, and one the neutrals. This proposal made little headway. Having declared in the following February that it would no longer recognize Hammarskjöld as an official of the United Nations, the Soviet Government was spared further embarrassment by his death in an air crash seven months later. Khrushchev's performance at the General Assembly was memorable for his shoe-banging during Macmillan's speech, an incident which did not put the British Prime Minister off his stride but was no doubt chalked up by Khrushchev's opponents at home as *nekul'turnyi* behaviour, unbecoming to a Soviet statesman.*

There is by now little doubt what happened during the fourteen days of the Cuban missile crisis, which lasted from 14 to 28 October 1962. Nor is there any lack of evidence about the American handling of the crisis or about American motives. But the precise nature of Soviet motives both before and during the crisis is a matter for speculation and is likely to remain so until much more Soviet and Cuban evidence is made public.

Of these fourteen days, three really matter. On 14 October, incontrovertible photographic proof of the presence of Soviet

---

* According to a well-placed eye-witness, Khrushchev had both his shoes on at the time. *Nekul'turnyi*, literally 'uncultured', is the Soviet word for 'uncouth', 'boorish', 'ill-mannered'.

nuclear missiles in Cuba was submitted to the US President. On 22 October, after eight days of agonized debate with his closest advisers, Kennedy announced the presence of the missiles in an address to the American nation, and he imposed a naval quarantine (a word that he had personally substituted for the original 'blockade') of all offensive military equipment under shipment to Cuba. Kennedy described the quarantine as an initial step and declared that any nuclear missile launched from Cuba against any nation in the Western hemisphere would be regarded as an attack by the Soviet Union on the United States, requiring a full retaliatory response upon the Soviet Union. Finally, on 28 October, after an exchange of ten personal messages between Kennedy and Khrushchev (in two of which—those of 26 and 27 October—Khrushchev suggested the outlines of a compromise), Khrushchev announced publicly that a new order had been issued 'to dismantle the weapons, which you describe as offensive, and to crate and return them to the Soviet Union', and expressed his respect and trust for Kennedy's statement, in a message sent on the previous day, that 'no attack would be made on Cuba and that no invasion would take place—not only on the part of the United States, but also on the part of the other countries of the Western hemisphere'.

That Khrushchev backed down in the face of American determination is not surprising. What is uncertain is why he decided to install nuclear missiles in Cuba at all. At first the Soviet attitude towards the Cuban Revolution had been cautious. But from 17 April 1961 onwards—when the CIA-sponsored landing of Cuban exiles at the Bay of Pigs was repulsed—events moved swiftly. In June a Soviet–Cuban communiqué acknowledged Cuba's free choice of 'the road of socialist development'; in July Castro announced the formation of a new political party, whose creed was unmistakably proclaimed when five months later he declared 'I am a Marxist-Leninist, and I shall be a Marxist-Leninist until the last day of my life';[1] and thereafter the Soviet Government, whatever its earlier doubts about the orthodoxy of Cuban communism, had no choice but to admit Cuba to the socialist bloc, a decision which was made formally apparent at the May Day celebrations in Moscow. (One Albania was enough.) An exposed member of the socialist bloc, even though not a member of the Warsaw Pact, was bound to look to Moscow to ensure its physical survival. Moscow could not therefore afford to ignore any danger, however remote, to Cuba at a moment when the lunatic fringe in the United States was clamouring for a second attack on Cuba of a different kind from the Bay of Pigs fiasco. Yet it is a fact of history that Kennedy had no intention whatever of repeating the mistake of 1961; and Khrushchev himself in his 'Friday Letter' to Kennedy of 26 October 1962* recorded that he had regarded with respect the explanation for the Bay of Pigs affair which Kennedy had offered him at their meeting in Vienna shortly afterwards (namely, that the invasion had been a mistake). Yet the same letter stated emphatically that it was only the constant threat of armed aggression which hung over Cuba that prompted the despatch of Soviet nuclear missiles to the island. Did Khrushchev believe in this threat? We cannot altogether exclude the possibility that the Soviet Government was misinformed.[2] Today such a misreading of American presidential intentions would scarcely be possible. In 1962 perhaps it was—just. But even if it was, it remains as obvious today as it must have been then that if the Soviet aim was only to deter an American attack on Cuba, it could have been achieved simply by stationing on the island 20,000 Soviet troops, equipped not with nuclear but with conventional weapons: a close symmetry with the Western presence in Berlin.[3]

The risks that Khrushchev ran were so high in 1962 that the only explanation which does justice to his undoubted intelligence, and also squares with Castro's own evidence, is that he decided that the risks were worth running because the prize was far greater than the security of Cuba, important though this had become to Soviet national interests. This prize was nothing less than to establish a strategic balance with the United States,

---

* The full text in translation of this famous letter, together with the other nine exchanged during the Cuban missile crisis, was at last published in November 1973, in the *State Department Bulletin*, vol. 69, no. 1795, pp. 643–5. The style leaves no possible doubt of its authorship. It differs in significant respects from previous attempts to reconstruct it, e.g. Allison, op. cit., pp. 221–3. Allison's book, although published before the full text of all the letters was available, remains the most complete exposition of the facts of the crisis as known from American sources; and unless otherwise stated, facts mentioned in the present section of this chapter are derived from it.

which would make possible an accommodation between the
Soviet Union and the United States across the board, leading not
only to a settlement of the Berlin problem but also to the
prevention of either West Germany or China from acquiring
nuclear weapons—a diplomatic triumph of such brilliance that
no one in the Soviet Union would ever have dared to challenge
Khrushchev's personal leadership again.[4] The other possible
explanations are: first, bad professional advice from the Soviet
military; second, the possibility that Khrushchev's assessment of
Kennedy's character, formed at the time of the Bay of Pigs and at
their meeting in Vienna the previous year, was wrong; third, a
false deduction by Khrushchev from the Suez crisis six years
earlier that atomic blackmail always paid; and fourth, that by the
time Kennedy issued his first, unmistakable warning, in early
September, Khrushchev decided that it was too late to put the
Cuban missile operation into reverse, and that he might as well
be hung for a sheep as for a lamb.

For the first of these four explanations there is no evidence: if
anything, it points the other way, in that Marshal K. S.
Moskalenko, a Deputy Defence Minister, was relieved of his
command of the Strategic Missile Forces in April 1962, about the
time when contingency planning of the Cuban operation was
presumably in its initial stage.[5] The reason for Moskalenko's
removal is unknown, but it does not require much imagination to
guess the likely reaction of the commander of this Soviet force
when asked to commit part of it to a strategic theatre where,
without almost inconceivable luck, it risked either destruction or
capture by the American forces only ninety miles away. As for the
second explanation, Khrushchev may well have hoped to frighten
Kennedy, whom he perhaps regarded as a brash young man, and
to establish a personal ascendancy over him at Vienna. Yet the
American accounts of this difficult meeting given by three
American eye-witnesses record only plain speaking, with no
ground given on either side.[6] One records[7] that the President's
greatest concern before his meeting with Khrushchev was that it
might create another spirit of Camp David; and Kennedy's
parting words to Khrushchev were not those of a broken
man—'it's going to be a cold winter'[8] (he was referring to
Khrushchev's ultimatum about West Berlin). What did happen,[9]

was that Kennedy's private briefings of the press were 'so grim, while Khrushchev in public appeared so cheerful, that a legend soon arose that Vienna had been a traumatic, shattering experience, that Khrushchev had bullied and browbeaten the President, and that Kennedy was depressed and disheartened'. But this was a legend, and although Khrushchev may have helped to create it, it was not something in which he himself had any reason to believe. Finally, Khrushchev could hardly have convinced himself that it was his own atom-rattling, rather than the United States Government's sustained pressure, that obliged the British and French Governments to halt their Suez operation in November 1956, or that he lacked the authority to take voluntarily in September 1962 a decision that he was compelled to take six weeks later. This is surely a case of the simplest explanation being the best: Khrushchev was a man who played for the highest possible stakes; and on this occasion he miscalculated the odds.

For Khrushchev's Cuban plan to succeed, the United States had to be confronted, without warning, by the presence of a Soviet nuclear force in Cuba—already operational and manned by some 20,000 Soviet troops, in sites protected by surface-to-air missiles—consisting of twenty-four medium range and twelve intermediate range ballistic missile launchers, together with some forty Ilyushin-28 jet bombers capable of carrying nuclear weapons. The range of the former launchers was 1,000 and that of the latter 2,000 nautical miles. The exact number of IRBM launchers planned seems uncertain; none arrived, although their sites were constructed. Certainly, had the plan succeeded, it would have given the Soviet Union extra strategic deterrence on the cheap, by comparison with the cost of bringing Soviet intercontinental and submarine-launched ballistic missiles up to the American level; and the number of minutes' warning of oncoming missiles received by the Americans would have been greatly reduced. But even so, this would still not have given the Soviet Union anything resembling superiority. At the time of the crisis not only did the United States have about 144 missiles launched from *Polaris* submarines, as well as 294 ICBMs,[10] but the Caribbean was an area in which the United States possessed complete superiority in conventional weapons—at sea, in the air,

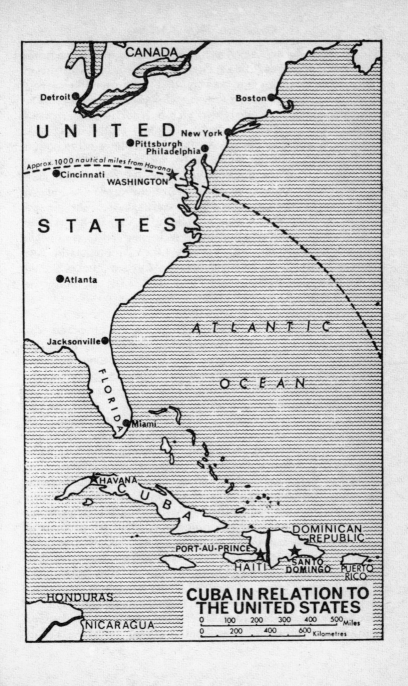

CANADA

Detroit

Boston

U N I T E D

New York

Pittsburgh
Philadelphia

Approx. 1000 nautical miles from Havana

Cincinnati

WASHINGTON

S T A T E S

Atlanta

A T L A N T I C

Jacksonville

O C E A N

FLORIDA

Miami

HAVANA

C U B A

DOMINICAN
REPUBLIC

PORT-AU-PRINCE

HAITI

SANTO
DOMINGO

PUERTO
RICO

HONDURAS

NICARAGUA

**CUBA IN RELATION TO
THE UNITED STATES**

0   100   200   300   400   500 Miles

0   200   400   600 Kilometres

and on land (during the crisis, a force of some 200,000 men was assembled in Florida). It can only be assumed that Khrushchev relied on everything going his way: that Cuba would be covered by ten-tenths cloud during the critical phase, that if the missiles were discovered, Kennedy (in the heat of a Congressional election) would dither, and that once he had decided on a course of action, it would be opposed by the United States' allies both in the Organization of American States and in NATO. Not one of these conditions was fulfilled—quite the reverse in each case. Granted what must have been known in Moscow about the performance of the U-2 reconnaissance aircraft, from the one shot down over the Soviet Union in 1960, it is hard to see how the arrival of the missiles could have been expected to escape the notice of these aircraft, which overflew the island regularly, once American suspicions had been aroused. Moreover, the risks of the Soviet operation were increased still further by the number of mistakes made in its execution—for example, no attempt was made to camouflage the missile sites.[11]

Nor was there any lack of formal warning from the American side. On 4 September the White House issued a statement that the gravest issues would arise if offensive ground-to-ground missiles were installed in Cuba. On 12 September, four days after the first ship carrying Soviet missiles had docked in Cuba, *Pravda* published a governmental statement denying the need for the Soviet Union to 'set up in any other country—Cuba, for instance—the weapons it has for repelling aggression, for a retaliatory blow' and asserting that the power of Soviet nuclear weapons and missiles was such that there was no need to find sites for them beyond the boundaries of the Soviet Union. On the following day Kennedy himself repeated the warning of 4 September. Yet, according to all American sources, Khrushchev proceeded to give Kennedy the lie direct about the presence of missiles in Cuba: speaking himself to the US Ambassador on 16 October—the day on which the photographic evidence of their presence was first submitted to the President—and via Gromyko to the President two days later. Whatever was said or left unsaid on these two occasions, as late as 25 October, *Izvestiya* observed that it was unnecessary to recall that both the Soviet Union and Cuba had recently emphasized that no offensive weapons and no long-range nuclear missiles were deployed on the island; and the next day two *Pravda* correspondents in Massachusetts described the allegation about the sudden appearance of Soviet nuclear long-range rockets in Cuba as a fantasy that did not inspire confidence among well-informed Americans.

From a crisis which, according to all the rules, should have ruined him, Khrushchev extricated himself with skill, by portraying himself as the world's peacemaker. In this he was helped by Kennedy, whose commitment not to invade Cuba cost him nothing, although it was sound as a means of saving Khrushchev's face. But it was paper-thin for the Chinese, who later accused the Soviet leadership of the double error of 'adventurism' and 'capitulationism' and enquired whether what had been done in the name of defending the Cuban Revolution was not in reality political gambling.[12] How do Soviet writers see their country's part in the crisis? Although there is nothing on the Soviet side of the Cuban equation remotely resembling Western analyses[13] in depth of the factors that made up its American side, what Soviet evidence there is should not be ignored. On one point all Soviet sources are unanimous: it was 'a damned nice thing'.[14] Making no precise mention of the missiles, which are referred to only as 'a series of new measures intended to strengthen Cuba's capacity for defence', the History of Soviet Foreign Policy describes the crisis as 'the most acute, in all the post-war years, which put mankind face to face with the threat of world-wide thermonuclear catastrophe'. There can be no quarrel with this verdict, which reflects the thought that (as the personal messages to Kennedy make clear) was in the forefront of Khrushchev's mind during the latter days of the crisis, which must have been as hard to manage in Moscow as it was in Washington. Western historians have tended to forget that during this crisis, Khrushchev had to contend not only with Kennedy's messages but also with Castro's. According to Khrushchev's subsequent report to the Supreme Soviet,[15] it was on the morning of 27 October that the Soviet Government became convinced, among other things, by telegrams from Havana 'displaying extreme alarm, which was well founded', that Cuba would be invaded within two or three days.*

* This assessment was, as we know from American sources, correct.

The nearest approach to a Soviet explanation of why Khrushchev led with his chin consists of two articles published in 1971,[16]
by Anatolyi Gromyko, son of the Soviet Foreign Minister, on the
Caribbean crisis ('or, as they still sometimes call it in the West,
especially in the USA, the "Cuban Missile Crisis" '). The articles
draw mostly on American sources, but the first is notable for a
lengthy account of the author's father's interview with Kennedy
on 18 October, which in general counters the accusation that the
Soviet Foreign Minister misled the President and in particular
criticizes Robert Kennedy's account[17] of the interview as
tendentious. The titles of the articles are themselves instructive:
the first is 'The Instigation of the Caribbean Crisis by the
Government of the USA' and the second is 'The Diplomatic
Efforts of the USSR to Solve the Crisis'.

It is central to the argument of these articles that in 1962 it was
the aim of the US Government's Cuban policy to prepare secretly
a fresh attack against the island. The U-2 flights (which more
than any other single factor wrecked Khrushchev's plan) are
therefore portrayed as offensive, not defensive, in intention. But
the accuracy of the deductions drawn in Washington from the
critical U-2 flight of 14 October is in no way disputed:
'medium-range rockets' were indeed delivered to Cuba, for
defensive purposes. American sources are quoted as proving that
the presence of Soviet missiles in Cuba did not alter the strategic
balance of power between the USSR and the USA, which the
writer describes as based primarily on intercontinental strategic
rockets. As Robert McNamara, then Defence Secretary, remarked during the crisis, 'it makes no great difference whether
you are killed by a missile from the Soviet Union or from Cuba'.
The conclusion is drawn that the Administration was governed
more by political than by military considerations.

In his interview with the President on 18 October the Soviet
Foreign Minister is said to have informed Kennedy unequivo-
cally that since the governments of the USSR and Cuba feared a
military attack on Cuba, the Soviet Union could not remain
inactive, but that Soviet help to Cuba 'contributed only to its
defensive capacity and to the strengthening of its economy';
Soviet specialists' training of Cubans in the handling of weapons
intended for the defence of their country was a threat to no one. It

is granted that the President read out to Gromyko, at the end of their talk, the text of his declaration of 4 September; but since Kennedy did not once raise directly the question of the presence in Cuba of Soviet missiles, he could not be given an answer. The tables are then turned, by accusing the President of deluding the Soviet side about his intentions, and this leads to the conclusion that it is enough to ask why the diplomatic representatives of the USSR were obliged to inform the United States Government in advance of these or other defensive measures, taken for the protection of a friendly state, while the USA never supplied the Soviet Union with information about the supply of arms to its own allies. The contention that if only Kennedy had put a straight question about the missiles to Gromyko, he would have got a straight answer, is not as odd as it sounds: the interpretation of 'interesting silences'* forms an integral part of Soviet diplomatic style.

The second theme that runs through both these articles is that if only the President had sought an 'elucidation of the situation' through diplomatic channels before embarking on a course as dangerous as a naval blockade—let alone an attack on Cuba recommended by the hawks among his advisers—the crisis would never have arisen. The only credit given to Kennedy is that he stood his ground against right-wing pressure. It is the Soviet Government that, according to the second article, played the decisive part in ensuring that events were brought under control. Khrushchev is nowhere mentioned by name, but his letter of 26 October is credited with suggesting the compromise formula which settled the crisis—correctly, although the recently published text makes it clear that the letter did not propose the compromise in precise terms, which were spelled out more clearly in Khrushchev's 'Saturday' letter of 27 October, this time linked with the suggested deal over American bases in Turkey.† Robert Kennedy is also correctly accused of omitting from his account the Soviet warning which accompanied this suggestion, namely

---

* Jane Austen, *Emma*, ch. XV, in which Mr Elton says to Miss Woodhouse: 'Allow me to interpret this interesting silence. It confesses that you have long understood me.'

† The second letter, though it caused confusion and dismay in Washington, did not, in my view, formally contradict the first, nor is there any marked difference in tone between the two.

that if the naval quarantine was intended as the first step towards war, then the Soviet Union would have no alternative but to accept the challenge.[18] This posture is twice described in the article as one of firmness coupled with flexibility, a phrase also used in the History of Soviet Foreign Policy. But the most important message that these two articles were intended to convey was this: in 1962 there would have been no crisis at all if at an early enough stage the US Government had been willing to treat the Soviet Government as its equal and to settle the problem bilaterally at the highest level. What they could not say was that in 1962 the Soviet Union was still far from achieving parity with the United States.

The temporary détente

Khrushchev survived this error of Himalayan proportions for two years. The remainder of his time in office was a period of relative relaxation of tension between the Soviet Union and the West. Khrushchev allowed the Berlin crisis to fade away. In June 1963, in a major speech addressed to the American University, Kennedy called the cold war in question; the Soviet press published the text in full. Within a year following the crisis, the hot line was set up between Moscow and Washington, designed to eliminate the time factor in crisis management that had complicated the messages exchanged in October 1962; Great Britain, the Soviet Union, and the United States signed the partial Nuclear Test Ban Treaty in Moscow; at the United Nations it was agreed not to put into outer space 'any objects carrying nuclear weapons or any other kinds of weapons of mass destruction'. (This was to be embodied in treaty form in January 1967.) Other signs of the times were the dropping of the troika idea; the cessation of Soviet jamming of Western broadcasts; and the Soviet–American pledge to reduce the production of fission-able material for nuclear weapons. Why did Khrushchev not go further along the road towards a Nuclear Non-Proliferation Treaty, the conclusion of which would surely have been as much a national interest for the Soviet Union then as it was five years later? Perhaps he was held back by internal opposition; or by Chinese criticism; or both.[19] The eruption of the territorial aspects of the Sino-Soviet dispute in March 1963 was bad enough, but the Nuclear Test Ban Treaty coincided with the final parting of the ways between the Soviet Union and China in July of that year. The three-power negotiations in Moscow before the signing of this document, rightly regarded at the time as a landmark in post-war history, opened simultaneously with an eleventh-hour attempt by the Russians and the Chinese to settle their differences through bilateral talks, also held in Moscow. The Soviet Central Committee's 'Open letter to Party organizations and all communists of all the Soviet Union' published in *Pravda* on 14 July—the day before the Test Ban talks opened— provided the Soviet public with their first full account of their country's quarrel with China. Nearly 20,000 words in length, it included the vivid phrase: 'the nuclear bomb does not adhere to the class principle—it destroys everybody who falls within range of its devastating force'.[20] The Sino-Soviet talks were adjourned *sine die* on 20 July, just before the Test Ban Treaty was signed.

Meanwhile, having failed to attain parity with the United States on the cheap, Khrushchev fell back on the Malenkov concept of minimum nuclear deterrence. True, he had steadily increased the deployment, mostly in the western USSR, of a force of medium and intermediate range ballistic missile launchers targeted on Western Europe, which by 1964 levelled off at around 700. These served the purpose of a deterrent to Western European countries, but not the United States. Intercontinentally, the Soviet Union remained greatly inferior to the United States: in 1964, an estimated 200 Soviet ICBMs against 834 American, and 120 Soviet submarine-launched ballistic missiles against 416 American equivalents.[21] There is also abundant evidence[22] that by October 1964 Khrushchev intended to increase the production of consumer goods by cutting the defence budget, mainly at the expense of conventional ground forces; the Ground Forces Command was suspended as a separate entity shortly before his fall.[23]

The fall of Khrushchev

Things did not go well for Khrushchev at home after the Cuban crisis. True, in November 1962 he secured the Central Committee's approval of a reform of Party apparatus, which was then divided into agricultural and industrial specialists. But in 1963 the harvest was poor and the rate of growth of Soviet national income was down. Khrushchev's de-Stalinization policy ran into the sand (but not before Alexander Solzhenitsyn's *A Day in the Life of Ivan Denisovich* was published, in November 1962). Perhaps the last straw for his colleagues was the knowledge that he was contemplating a sweeping reform of the agricultural system, which would have been submitted to the Central Committee in November 1964. Khrushchev's handling of the Party could have been sufficient reason in itself for his removal,[24] but the evidence points to a combination of factors. Certainly one of them was that Khrushchev was contemplating a fresh European initiative, this time directly with the new Federal German Chancellor (Erhard, who had succeeded Adenauer in October 1963), at a moment when the ink was scarcely dry on the signature of a new treaty of friendship concluded between the Soviet Union and the German Democratic Republic on 12 June 1964. The terms of this treaty cannot have satisfied Ulbricht—in particular, it explicitly left unaffected rights conferred on the Four Powers by their agreements on Germany, including the Potsdam Agreement— and it coincided with a series of signs that something was in the wind between Moscow and Bonn. These culminated in the visit of a party of three Soviet journalists to the Federal German Republic in July and August. This visit looked innocent enough. But the fact that the Volga Germans[25] were rehabilitated in August can hardly have been a coincidence; and it seems virtually certain that the senior member of the trio, Alexei Adzubei, Khrushchev's son-in-law (whom he had made editor of *Izvestiya*), was sent by Khrushchev to pave the way for a visit that he himself would pay to Bonn, probably in December. Had the visit taken place, it would have been historic: the first time, nearly twenty years after the German surrender, that the ruler of the Soviet Union had visited the Federal Republic. That Khrushchev should have entrusted his son-in-law with such an important mission was resented; it seems likely that he laid himself open to the suspicion that he was planning some deal with the West Germans over the heads of the East Germans (now no longer living in a slum, but on the way to performing their own economic miracle) and of the Poles; and two of his own colleagues, Brezhnev and Suslov, made speeches on the eve of Khrushchev's fall reassuring the East Germans, on the occasion of the fifteenth anniversary of the German Democratic Republic in early October.

As has been suggested earlier, the Soviet Politburo may well have felt that however intractable the Chinese might be, a change of Soviet leadership might increase the chances of at least a marginal improvement. Relations between the two communist parties had reached their nadir. Khrushchev was committed to holding a preparatory meeting in Moscow in December of the twenty-six members of the 1960 conference drafting committee; but it is unlikely that they would have given the CPSU unqualified support against the Chinese Communist Party. In their letter to the CPSU of 28 July 1964, the Chinese warned that 'the day of your so-called meeting will be the day you step into the grave'. By a superb coincidence, the Chinese exploded their first nuclear device on the day that Khrushchev fell—14 October. He died in 1971, unforgiven and unhonoured by the Soviet state.

4. Defence Policy

THE triumvirate which succeeded Khrushchev hastened to make it clear that the decisions of the XXth Congress, taken under his leadership, held good so far as doctrine was concerned: their validity was reaffirmed both in the CPSU Central Committee's communiqué announcing Khrushchev's resignation and in Brezhnev's speech delivered at the celebrations of the October Revolution. True, whereas the concept of peaceful coexistence between states with different social systems had, under Khrushchev, been described as the general line of the foreign policy of the Soviet state, in the formulation approved at the first party congresses presided over by his successors it was demoted to fourth place. But so long as American forces were fighting in Vietnam, the new leadership could scarcely have avoided this change of emphasis. Their indictment of Khrushchev was indirect: *Pravda* of 17 October 1964 described the Leninist Party as the enemy of subjectivism and drifting in communist construction; and as foreign to hare-brained scheming, immature conclusions, hasty and unrealistic decisions and actions, boasting, and idle talk. At a pinch, this could be construed as the indictment of an old man in a hurry at home, rather than in his foreign policy; and indeed radical changes on the home front were soon effected. The new leaders also lost no time in reassuring the military that the Party had the interests of the armed forces at heart;[1] and it is significant that the epithet 'hare-brained' recurred in the military newspaper *Krasnaya Zvezda* four months later, when Zakharov, reappointed Chief of Staff, wrote: 'with the appearance of nuclear weapons, cybernetics, electronics, and computer technology, a subjective approach to military problems, hare-brained schemes, and superficiality can cost very dear and cause irreparable harm.'[2]

The broad aims of Soviet foreign policy remained a global role for the Soviet Union and an accommodation with the United States. Both were to be pursued with prudence; there were to be no more games of bluff. At the same time, a further attempt would be made to restore order in the world communist movement. Finally—and this affected foreign policy as much as it did policy at home—the new leadership was collective. The importance that the new leadership attached to the principle of collective leadership, and their criticisms of Khrushchev's personal failings, emerged clearly from the leading article in *Pravda* of 17 October, which was intended as the keynote of the new regime. It is inconceivable that the great issues which the triumvirate had to face did not give rise to sharp differences of opinion; but so far as we know at present, these never attained the dimensions of a true struggle for power. None of Khrushchev's colleagues was dismissed with him. Brezhnev soon[3] emerged as *primus inter pares*—at the latest, by March 1966, when he resumed the old title of General Secretary of the CPSU at the XXIIIrd Congress. But it remains unlikely that a single member of the Soviet élite will be allowed to assume all the offices held by Khrushchev. Khrushchev was not only head of both Party and Government; he also held the post of Supreme Commander-in-Chief (a view supported by the last paragraph of Grechko's article on Khrushchev's seventieth birthday in *Izvestiya* of 17 April 1964). In any case, he was *ex officio* chairman of a body variously referred to as the War (or Defence) Committee and the Higher Military Council.[4]

In 1964 what the Soviet Union needed was a period of consolidation. This process was to be presided over by three men—Leonid Brezhnev, General Secretary of the CPSU, Alexei Kosygin, Prime Minister, and Nikolai Podgorny, who succeeded Mikoyan as Head of State in December 1965. Their intentions were harder to interpret at first, since they were not well-known to Western observers, who were to miss the outbursts that had often illuminated the policies of Khrushchev.

The Khrushchevian concept of minimum nuclear deterrence was set aside. It is a matter of debate whether the new leadership deliberately decided to achieve strategic parity with the United States; or whether they aimed at strategic superiority; or whether they embarked on the defence build-up over the next five years without any single clearly defined aim. Whichever is correct, it is also true that the Research and Development work on the weapons systems deployed by the end of the decade had already been begun under Khrushchev: the SS-9 ICBM did not spring out of the ground like the Theban warriors. In this sense it is arguable that Soviet defence policy developed continuously throughout the sixties. But there is a vast financial and economic difference between allowing resources to be committed to the Research and Development of a major weapons system and taking the final decision to produce and deploy it on a large scale. The factor common to all three of these objectives[5] is that the missile gap, which had grown even wider—to the advantage of the United States—since 1962, should be closed as quickly as possible. The underlying concept is summed up in a remark allegedly made after the Cuban missile crisis by a senior Soviet diplomat to an American interlocutor: 'you will never do that to us again!' At the same time the Soviet armed forces were now to be trained and equipped alike for general nuclear war, conventional operations, and operations in which nuclear weapons would be used on a limited scale. The management of defence industries, one of the victims of Khrushchev's policy of decentralization, was brought back to the centre.

Khrushchev's scale of deterrence was minimal only by Soviet standards: that is to say, a defence posture of strategic nuclear inferiority which would still have assured the Soviet Union posthumous revenge in a second-strike, retaliatory attack that would have inflicted immense damage on the United States. His successors were content neither with this, admittedly high, status of inferiority, nor with the single, nuclear option on which Khrushchevian defence policy was based. After 1965 the Soviet military budget rose annually, reaching a figure of 17.9 billion roubles in 1969, while the figure for scientific research doubled in the same period. In a series of papers presented to the Joint Economic Committee of the United States Congress in September 1970, it was even argued that by the end of the Soviet Five-Year Plan in that year the Soviet armed forces might be getting as much as 40 per cent more hardware than the United States armed forces, which would have meant that Soviet defence and space expenditure had increased more than fivefold between

1958 and 1968.⁶ Any calculation of the proportion of the Soviet budget devoted to defence depends on how much defence expenditure is concealed in other sections of the budget: in particular, the cost of nuclear warheads, Research and Development on advanced weapons systems, and the military elements of the space programme. *Military Balance 1969/70* suggested that, on a conservative estimate, Soviet declared defence appropriations of 17,700 million roubles for 1969, if calculated on the basis of the real resources mobilized by the Soviet Union in equivalent American prices, were the equivalent of 42 billion dollars, and that the total defence expenditure was the equivalent of 53 billion dollars. (Based on a GNP over twice the size of that of the Soviet Union, United States defence estimates for 1969/70 were 78,475,000,000 dollars, of which an estimated 25–30 billions were attributable to the Vietnam War.) Brezhnev's allusions to defence expenditure, made at the XXIVth Party Congress and in a speech in June 1971, suggested that this is a delicate subject within the Soviet Union. Of one thing there can be little doubt: the size of the resources committed to the defence sector in the second half of the 1960s contributed to the Soviet economic dilemma at the end of the decade.⁷

As well as the massive deployment of offensive strategic nuclear weapons, a start was made with the deployment of an anti-ballistic missile system round Moscow in 1966. But the Strategic Missile Forces—the élite of the Soviet armed forces, numbering some 350,000 men—were not the only recipients of funds designed for expansion. The substantial Soviet Mediterranean Squadron, which made its first appearance in 1963, became an accepted feature of the strategic naval scene. The Indian Ocean was first visited in 1968 by a cruiser and a destroyer from the Soviet Pacific Fleet; today the Soviet naval presence there is permanent. The Soviet naval infantry arm (disbanded after the Second World War) was revived shortly before Khrushchev's fall; its strength was doubled between 1966 and 1969; and from 1967 onwards there was increasing emphasis on amphibious operations. The new Soviet Navy's role was no longer confined to defence of the Soviet Union's coasts, but became long range, as was to be demonstrated in 1970 by the *Okean* manoeuvres, in which over 250 Soviet ships took part, in every ocean (and some rivers) of the world. The new navy's main weakness was its lack of air support, although in 1973 this gap was partly filled by the first Soviet aircraft carrier. Finally, the size of the Soviet fishing fleet, the largest and most modern in the world, is also a factor to be reckoned with, given the electronic intelligence duties of its vessels. At the same time the Soviet Air Force was expanded and modernized, with the aim of establishing air superiority over the battlefield, and its capacity to intervene was also greatly increased.

The collective leadership broadly continued Khrushchev's policy of re-equipping and modernizing the forces of the Soviet Union's allies in the Warsaw Pact, with the main emphasis on conventional warfare, although tactical nuclear missile launchers were also supplied (the nuclear warheads remaining in Soviet hands). The lion's share of new equipment went to the northern tier countries—Poland, Czechoslovakia, and East Germany—in whose territory most of the joint Warsaw Pact manoeuvres were held, these becoming much more frequent than under Khrushchev. Because of this policy, these three countries provided a large addition to Soviet military strength in Central Europe. The value of the Czechoslovak contribution became doubtful after 1968. But neither this setback, nor quarrels with the Romanians about burden-sharing and nuclear planning (both familiar concepts in the West), deterred the Russians from making full use of the Pact for both political and military purposes. The frequent meetings of the Pact's Political Consultative Committee (consisting of Communist Party First Secretaries, Heads of Governments, and Foreign and Defence Ministers of the member countries) became an important means of coordinating policy, for example, on the question of the European Conference; and in 1969 the command structure of the Pact was reformed. Whereas before the Eastern Europeans had little or no say, the new structure bore at least some resemblance to an integrated command, even though Soviet influence remained paramount.[8]

Finally, the Soviet Government introduced a major reform in 1967, when conscripted military service was cut to two years. This was followed in 1968 by compensating regulations which made participation in pre-conscription training obligatory. The 1967 law also established sixty as the compulsory retiring age for all senior officers below the rank of marshal. The second half of the 1960s was the period in which the Soviet officer corps was reformed and rejuvenated. (This process had been begun by Khrushchev, as part of his successive reductions of Soviet military manpower from the peak of 5.7 millions reached in 1955; in 1958–60, 250,000 officers were demobilized, and in 1960, 454 new generals were appointed.) What was most striking about this reform was the priority given to engineer officers, who by 1969 accounted for 80 per cent of the officer corps of the Strategic Missile Forces.[9] The influence of these military technocrats in Soviet society must be considerable, though this does not imply a conflict of interest between the military and the Party. In 1966, 93 per cent of all officers were members either of the Party or of the Komsomol. And Brezhnev's attendance at the final parade of the *Dvina* manoeuvres in 1970 (a year in which fifty-eight marshals, generals, and admirals were elected to the Supreme Soviet) marked the close relationship between the military and the Party—and particularly himself.

To sum up, the political consequence of this relationship, underpinned by the Soviet leadership's allocation of national resources to the armed forces, both nuclear and conventional, was that in the next decade Brezhnev was able to embark, with full military backing, on a Soviet-American dialogue of a different kind from that which had been attempted by Khrushchev: a dialogue between super-powers.

5. Asia

The Vietnam War

IT is the official Soviet view that the two principal causes of the worsening of Soviet–American relations in the second half of the 1960s were the Vietnam War and United States support of Israel. To these an objective historian must add the invasion of Czechoslovakia, although East–West relations did not take long to absorb this shock. But if the Americans had not become engaged in Vietnam on the vast scale which followed the Tonkin

Gulf incident of August 1964, would the Soviet leaders have been ready for a full dialogue with them sooner than they were, that is to say, before they could conduct it as equal partners? It seems doubtful.[1]

The American involvement in Vietnam was a windfall for the Soviet Union, for a number of reasons: whereas Soviet support for North Vietnam was not expensive, the war took up a large slice of the United States defence budget (over 100 billion dollars in the years 1965–72); it increasingly antagonized world opinion against the United States Government; as Vietnam absorbed American attention more and more, the Administration found it increasingly difficult to give the problems of the rest of the world all the attention that they deserved; and finally it split American society and brought down President Johnson. Even so, the war in Indo-China must have given the Soviet leadership some anxious moments, for they could not tell for certain—any more than any other government—how far the war would develop; it complicated their quarrel with the Chinese still further; and the Soviet military may have envied their American opposite numbers their ability to test modern weapons systems in battle conditions (the Soviet armed forces, though highly trained, had barely heard a shot fired in anger since the Japanese Armistice, whereas the American armed forces saw active service almost continuously from 1941 until their final withdrawal from the war in Indo-China).

Following Khrushchev's agreement with Kennedy on the neutralization of Laos at their meeting in Vienna, the Soviet Government proposed in July 1964 that the Geneva Conference on Laos should be reconvened (a proposal to which the United States was known to be hostile), and gave warning that the Soviet Government might be compelled to withdraw from its position as co-Chairman of the Conference. Khrushchev may well have wished to disengage from Indo-China altogether. Certainly, the first Soviet reaction to the incident of August 1964 and to the Joint Congressional Resolution* which followed it was to support the American proposal, rejected by the North Vietnamese, to take the matter to the Security Council. The Chinese protested

* This Resolution approved Johnson's 'determination to take all necessary measures' in Vietnam.

both against the incident and the proposal. One of the first decisions of the new Soviet leadership was to reverse Khrushchev's decision. In November the Soviet Government pledged its support for the North Vietnamese Government if North Vietnam was attacked by the Americans. No doubt they had several motives for this: conceivably, the hope that the United States Government might think again; certainly, the hope of winning back the support of the North Vietnamese and the North Koreans from the Chinese; and probably, the belief that failure to come out in support of Hanoi would be used against them by the Chinese, who had sent a senior delegation to the celebrations of the October Revolution in Moscow, while both sides had suspended polemics. Even so, when Kosygin visited Hanoi the following February (and also North Korea, calling twice at Peking, where he talked with the Chinese leaders), he not only supported the convening of a new Geneva Conference on Indo-China, but also, according to the Chinese, conveyed to the North Vietnamese an American warning to stop supporting the National Liberation Front (NLF) in South Vietnam and to put an end to attacks on cities there. In the event, while the Soviet Prime Minister was in Hanoi, American bombers raided North Vietnamese targets, in retaliation for an attack by South Vietnamese NLF forces on their base at Pleiku in South Vietnam. The United States Government declined to consider negotiations. In April 1965 the First Secretary of the Central Committee of the North Vietnamese Communist Party visited Moscow at the head of a delegation; agreement was reached on the aid which the Soviet Union would give North Vietnam; and the NLF was allowed to establish a mission in Moscow. For the rest of the decade the Soviet role in Vietnam was no less important in the context of the Sino-Soviet dispute than in that of Soviet–American relations.

The Sino-Soviet dispute

The lull in polemics between the CPSU and the CCP did not last long. There was no meeting of minds between the new Soviet leadership and the Chinese delegation when they talked in Moscow in November 1964, and the year that followed exacerbated the dispute still further. The meeting of the drafting committee, which Khrushchev had intended to take place in December 1964, was held the following March. Only eighteen out of the twenty-six communist parties were represented, and the communiqué was equivocal, agreeing only that a new international conference should be held at a suitable time, after thorough preparation in which all fraternal parties should take part. But it did call for united action in support of the Vietnamese people. Coming just before the arrival of the Vietnamese delegation, this was a gain for the Russians, who from now on used the Vietnamese issue as a stick for beating the Chinese. Their accusations made at the time are repeated in the History of Soviet Foreign Policy: over several years the Chinese 'created obstacles to the transportation of arms and supplies across Chinese territory' and held up deliveries for a long time. How serious these obstacles were is hard to say; some could have been caused simply by the chaos of the Chinese Cultural Revolution, which in 1968 was such that in the border province of Guangxi the Red Guards stormed the North Vietnamese consulate at Nanning and assaulted its staff, on 2 June.[2] But the Chinese were on weak ground in rebutting Soviet charges on this score, although they accused the new Soviet leadership as hotly as they had Khrushchev, not only of revisionism, but also of Soviet–American collaboration for the domination of the world, which in Chinese eyes made the Soviet call for united action over Vietnam fraudulent. (Not that the Chinese did not give the North Vietnamese military aid themselves—they did, although Soviet military aid, estimated at 1,660 million dollars in 1965–71, was nearly three times as great as the Chinese during the same period.)[3]

During the Indo-Pakistan war of August/September 1965, the Chinese accused the Russians of supporting the Indian 'reactionaries'. The success of the Tashkent meeting in January 1966, when the Indian and Pakistani leaders met the Soviet Prime Minister in the role of mediator, must have been galling to the Chinese, since it showed the Soviet Union as an Asian Great Power exercising its influence for peace. The Russians also scored over the Chinese in the affair of the Second Afro-Asian Conference, from which the Chinese sought to exclude them. It should h ˈe been held in Algiers in June 1965, but in the end it never took place. By that time the opening shots of the Cultural Revolution were being fired. This movement, literally translated 'a full-scale revolution to establish a working-class culture', was to put the Chinese Government in baulk internationally in 1966. Not surprisingly, the Chinese sent no delegation to the XXIIIrd CPSU Congress in March of that year. But the eighty-odd parties who were represented included those of North Vietnam and North Korea. In January 1967 Red Guards blockaded the Soviet Embassy in Peking; in February, the families of Soviet Staff were evacuated; and the Chinese withdrew their students from the Soviet Union after riots in Red Square.

Whereas the Soviet Government gave full support to the North Vietnamese proposal of January 1967—that talks with the Americans could begin if the latter unconditionally stopped bombing and other acts of war against North Vietnam—the Chinese eventually condemned it as a Soviet–American conspiracy to compel the Vietnamese to give in, and accused the Russians of seeking to put the North Vietnamese and themselves at loggerheads. By now the Soviet leaders were 'the biggest group of renegades and scabs in history' for the Chinese, for whom Mao Zedong was Lenin's genuine successor. The Russians, as well as ridiculing the Cultural Revolution and the adulation of Mao, sought to draw a distinction between the Maoist group on the one hand and the CCP and the Chinese people on the other. Moreover they accused the Chinese of a tacit agreement with the Americans over Vietnam. This was partly based on Chinese statements that they would not intervene militarily in Vietnam unless themselves attacked by the United States, but may also have been connected with the Chinese formula for a North Vietnamese victory; a protracted people's war (such as they themselves had successfully fought for so many years), to be won primarily through self-reliant effort, rather than with the aid of sophisticated Soviet military equipment—a formula which, in Soviet eyes, could be interpreted as meaning that the Chinese would be content for the war to last indefinitely.

Thus there was too much at stake for a Sino-Soviet *rapprochement* to be possible: the leadership of the world communist movement and competition for influence throughout the Third

World, to which the Chinese offered the Maoist slogan that the
'world city' must fall to the assault of the 'world village'. In Asia
the only major communist parties to remain pro-Soviet, other
than the Mongolian Party, were those of India and Ceylon.
Elsewhere the Chinese had only modest success. Rival communist parties were set up in the 1960s in several countries with
Chinese support; pro-Chinese groups appeared in Europe, where
both ruling (Romania partially excepted) and non-ruling parties
were broadly pro-Soviet; but in Latin America, where the
existence of guerrilla movements and the Che Guevara mystique
might have been expected to offer exploitable opportunities, such
pro-Chinese groups as were formed remained minuscule. (Castro, who by the middle of the decade[4] had adopted a position
somewhere between the Chinese and the Russians, was a
complicating factor.) In the Middle East the Chinese continued
to accuse the Russians of cooperation with the Americans. They
officially recognized the Palestinian *fedayeen* by signing an
agreement with the PLO as early as 1965, promising diplomatic,
military, and economic support. (The Soviet attitude was
ambivalent until 1974, when the Soviet Government finally gave
official recognition to the PLO.) And they worked hard further
south: in Africa their most spectacular achievement was the offer,
which was accepted by the governments of Tanzania and
Zambia, of 400 million dollars for the construction of the
Tanzania–Zambia railway—more than the Russians had given
for the Aswan Dam.

Behind all this lay the Soviet Government's conclusion,
reached towards the end of 1965, that it was to its advantage to
sign a Nuclear Non-Proliferation Treaty, which the Chinese
regarded just as they had the Test Ban Treaty: an obstacle
deliberately set in the way of the nuclear capability that they were
slowly developing. Given the state of Sino-Soviet relations in the
1960s, it would have been surprising if there had been no
incidents along the 4,000 mile frontier. 60,000 Chinese Moslem
inhabitants of Xinjiang are believed to have been given asylum
by the Soviet Union in 1962, for example; and the climax was
reached in March 1969, when a major engagement was fought on
Damansky Island,[5] the first among a series of incidents between
March and August of that year. More Soviet troops were moved

eastwards (they had been stationed in Mongolia since 1967); a new Central Asian Military District was established, with responsibility for the Xinjiang border; and a missile specialist, General V. F. Tolubko, was appointed in August to command the Far East Military District. On 16 September Victor Louis, the Soviet journalist who had scooped the fall of Khrushchev, wrote an article in the *Evening News* about the danger of war, which included the following passage:

The Soviet Union is adhering to the doctrine that socialist countries have the right to interfere in each other's affairs in their own interests or those of others who are threatened. The fact that China is many times larger than Czechoslovakia and might offer active resistance is, according to Marxist theoreticians, no reason for not applying this doctrine.

In that month two Chinese nuclear tests took place in Xinjiang. Although the Chinese had not yet developed modern delivery systems for nuclear weapons, they were within sight of launching their first earth satellite (in April 1970). China was just reaching the most vulnerable point in the development of strategic nuclear power: the moment when its nuclear force was beginning to pose a threat but was not yet certain of being able to survive a first-strike attack. By the autumn there were rumours of a Soviet pre-emptive strike against China. They were no more than rumours; for if such an extreme course was ever considered in Moscow, by that time the strike would have had not merely to destroy the Chinese nuclear installations, both in Xinjiang and in eastern China, but also several thousand Chinese nuclear scientists as well. Undeterred, or perhaps even spurred on, by Soviet psychological warfare, the Chinese Government warned the population of the danger of a Soviet attack, and shelters were dug in the cities.

As had happened a decade earlier, this conflict coincided with ideological dissension. At the IXth CCP Congress, held in April 1969, the Chinese leadership formally elevated Maoism to a position of equality with Marxism-Leninism, denouncing the revisionism of the Soviet leadership, who became in Chinese terms 'social imperialists'. Yet in September the Soviet and Chinese Prime Ministers met in Peking, as Kosygin was on his way back from a visit to Hanoi. They agreed that, however acute their ideological rivalry, a working relationship between the two governments should be restored (both missions had been reduced to the level of Chargés d'Affaires, and the Chinese Embassy in Moscow had left its broken windows unrepaired as a reminder of the past). Ambassadors were exchanged in 1970, the year in which Chinese diplomacy[6] was released from the paralysis imposed by the Cultural Revolution. But talks on the frontier question, over a period of ten years, achieved no perceptible results. Even though the Soviet and Chinese governments were again on speaking terms, they remained as far apart as ever on questions of substance.

Conference of the world communist parties

In June 1969 the Soviet leadership did succeed in holding this long deferred conference. As it turned out, the delegates met with the invasion of Czechoslovakia as much in mind as the Sino-Soviet dispute (but for the invasion, the conference would have been held six months earlier). Seventy-five parties took part. Of the fourteen ruling parties, five boycotted the conference—China, Albania, North Korea, North Vietnam, and Yugoslavia—and Cuba sent only an observer. There were no representatives from Japan, Indonesia, or any East Asian or South-East Asian party. Exceptionally, *Pravda* published summaries of speeches even when critical of Soviet policies. These included a statement by Enrico Berlinguer, Secretary-General of the Italian Communist Party, sympathizing with the Czechoslovak experiment and condemning the invasion of 1968, and one by Nicolae Ceausescu describing China as the great socialist state and declaring that no force in the world could conquer a nation which was fully determined to defend courageously its freedom and national independence.[7] A group of parties submitted a draft declaration, which was chiefly the work of the Russians, the Hungarians, and the French. Over 400 amendments were submitted, of which a hundred found their way in one form or another into the compromise text, an anodyne document which some parties refused to sign (the Romanians did sign it). Even though the conference achieved little, the fact that it was held at all was a Soviet achievement.[8] Nevertheless, by the end of the decade, the

Soviet leadership had proved no more successful than Khrush-chev in restoring the unity of the world communist movement.

6. The Third World

Policy towards the underdeveloped countries

UNDER Khrushchev, the stilted jargon of the third of the basic tasks of Soviet foreign policy (to support national liberation movements and to cooperate in every way with underdeveloped countries) expressed an ambitious new approach towards former colonies comparable in scope with Canning's calling in the New World to redress the balance of the Old.

Khrushchev's new policy complicated relations between the CPSU and the local communist parties, even in Cuba.[1] In the Middle East, the communist parties of one country after another split under the strain of Soviet support for the government that was suppressing them (a strain that was aggravated by the Sino-Soviet dispute). True, this dichotomy between Soviet national interest and that of a local communist party was not a new phenomenon: one of the earliest examples was the suppression of the Turkish Communist Party by Atatürk, who was cultivated by the Soviet Government soon after the Revolution. But it was sharpened under Khrushchev. Moreover, his policy toward the Third World met with some grievous disappointments, such as the fall of Lumumba, Nkrumah, Kassem, Ben Bella, and Sukarno. Of these, by far the worst blow to the international communist cause was the last. Although Sukarno was not formally deposed as President until two and a half years after the fall of Khrushchev, in the fighting that followed the abortive *coup d'état* of September 1965 at least 100,000 members of the Indonesian Communist Party were slaughtered, and an equal number of the Party's sympathizers. Politically, this blow was as hard to bear in Peking as it was in Moscow. But financially, it was the Soviet Government that suffered. Not only was the new Indonesian regime left a handsome legacy of Soviet military hardware, including tanks and warships, but the Soviet Union was left with an unpaid Indonesian debt of over 1,000 million dollars, 791 million of which was for military equipment; and in 1970 the debt rescheduling agreement finally reached between the Soviet and Indonesian governments provided for the period of repayment to be extended until the end of the century.[2]

In the early 1960s the approved model for a developing country was defined as an independent state of national democracy, which, based on a strong peasant-proletarian alliance with *petit bourgeois* support, could prepare the way for 'non-capitalist' development. Such a regime must be anti-imperialist, friendly towards the Soviet Union, and ready both to execute radical social and economic reforms and to give local communist parties full freedom of political action. But by 1964 Nasser, who did not treat Egyptian communists kindly, had been made a Hero of the Soviet Union. The role of local communist parties was now defined as that of friend and assistant of the national democrats: cold comfort for the parties concerned and grist to the Chinese mill. By the end of the decade, developing countries were broadly divided into three categories: those which had adopted the path of 'non-capitalist', or 'progressive social', development; those trying to strengthen their national independence and to create a modern economy with the broad participation of the national bourgeoisie; and those accepting a semi-colonial way of life and acting as the accomplices of imperialist exploiters. And in 1971 it was recognized by a Soviet theorist that in many, if not in most, of the developing Asian and African countries, no forces except the national democrats were capable of 'a nation-wide struggle for the attainment of the aims of the present stage of revolution'.[3] National democrats might well be army officers, as in Peru, whose military regime received Soviet support after the *coup* of October 1968. In short, the Khrushchevian belief that 'within the briefest period of time the overwhelming majority of former colonies would allegedly take, if not the socialist, then at least the non-capitalist, road of development' was acknowledged as an 'illusion'.[4]

Under the new Soviet leadership, economic policy towards the Third World became selective and pragmatic. The terms of Soviet aid are less generous than those of either the Chinese or the International Development Association: a Soviet loan, granted in inconvertible roubles, is usually repayable over ten to fifteen years, with interest at 2½–3 per cent. Any comparison of the Soviet aid programme with that of the United States or of any major Western country is difficult, because Soviet aid figures are not published; according to the OECD's 1972 *Review of Development Cooperation*, three-quarters of the Soviet aid flow went to communist countries; and confusion frequently arises between amounts of Soviet aid offered and Soviet aid actually delivered. On a rough estimate, Soviet bloc and Chinese aid delivered to non-communist developing countries totalled about 600 million dollars in 1972, half of which came from the Soviet Union. But the rising flow of debt repayments from the developing countries to the latter probably reduced the net Soviet aid flow to the Third World from a high point of 300 million dollars, at the time of Khrushchev's fall, to less than 100 million dollars in 1972—a year in which one of the four major recipients of Soviet aid, economic and military, India, paid to the Soviet Union 35 million dollars more than the value of Soviet deliveries, even though India had been provided by the Soviet Union with a multi-million dollar turn-key project—the Bhilai steelworks, which was on a scale comparable to that of the Aswan High Dam in Egypt. At the Second United Nations Conference on Trade and Development, held in Delhi in 1968, the representatives of the Soviet Union and its allies abstained from voting on the resolution committing developed countries to adopt one per cent of gross national product as the target for their annual transfer of resources to the developing countries.

American intervention in Vietnam made that country a special case for the Soviet Union, justifying almost any level of expenditure. Of all the aid programmes ever undertaken by the Soviet Government, the one that must have troubled the cost-effectiveness experts in the Kremlin most is the aid, direct and indirect, extended to Cuba. Whichever government originally suggested the installing of Soviet missiles in Cuba in 1962, it is certain that the negotiations for their removal were carried on over Castro's head; it is therefore not surprising that for the rest of the decade he remained a difficult ally for the Soviet Union. The difficulties were both economic and political. In the early years after the Cuban Revolution, its leaders looked to a combination of rapid industrialization and the establishment of giant state farms, run by officials responsible to highly centralized direction from Havana, as the key to economic progress, with unfortunate results,[5] which were accentuated by Che Guevara's belief that Cuba had already entered the final Marxist phase of pure communism. Under the terms of the original trade agreement negotiated by Mikoyan during his visit to Havana in February 1960, the Soviet Government had agreed to buy nearly 5 million tons of Cuban sugar over the next five years, and offered a credit of 100 million dollars in aid. At the end of 1963, in conditions bordering on economic chaos, Castro decided to abandon his original plan of economic autarky and to make agriculture the basis of Cuban economic development for the rest of the decade, sugar being given top priority. The Soviet Government was therefore obliged increasingly to underwrite the Cuban economy, mainly by taking annually rising quantities of Cuban sugar at prices higher than those on the world market. By 1973 it was estimated that in all, Cuba was costing the Soviet Union 1,500,000 dollars a day and that repayment of the Cuban debt would last into the twenty-first century.

During the 1960s the basic political[6] difference between the Soviet Union and Cuba centred on the fact that Castro—who had come to power in Havana straight from his guerrilla base in the Sierra Maestra—continued to advocate the *via armada* (as opposed to the *via pacifica*) as the model for Latin American communist parties. At its XXIIIrd Congress the CPSU even found itself under Cuban fire for not doing more to help North Vietnam. For the Soviet Union, the Cuban alliance was an irritant in cultivating relationships with other Latin American countries. But Castro's qualified support of the invasion of Czechoslovakia (which, in a speech on 28 August 1968, he described as a bitter necessity)[7] marked the beginning of the closer alignment between the policies of the two countries that followed in the 1970s.

After what happened in October 1962, and with the Chinese as watchful rivals in Havana, Soviet historians would no doubt argue that no Soviet Government could have acted towards Cuba in any other way during the rest of the decade. Yet, if at some future conference Soviet and American historians were invited to rewrite, with the advantage of hindsight, a fresh scenario for

US–Cuban and Soviet–Cuban relations during the 1960s, it is hard to believe that they could not devise better policies than those actually pursued by their governments towards Cuba, and that they could not suggest ways in which both could have contributed to the development of a small island inhabited by a gifted people.

The Middle East

If the Cuban aid programme was in financial terms the most costly legacy of Khrushchev's policy towards the Third World, in political and strategic terms by far the most important was the Soviet commitment to the Middle East, which in the 1970s was to replace South-East Asia as the most explosive source of conflict in the world. Today this commitment has two aspects: one strategic and the other politico-economic. The former antedates Khrushchev, and for that matter the Russian Revolution itself. The traditional thrust of Tsarist diplomacy towards the Straits and southward from Central Asia was resumed by Stalin immediately after the Second World War (Stalin's request for a base in the Straits, the territorial claims made against Turkey, formally dropped only after Stalin's death in 1953, and the Azerbaijan episode of 1945–6). A glance at the map is enough to show that strategically the Middle East is for Russia—whether Tsarist or Soviet—what the Caribbean is for the United States: its backyard. After the failure of this forward policy towards Turkey and Iran in 1946, Stalin withdrew to his European fortress. Under Khrushchev, the strategic aspect of Soviet policy towards the Middle East received a fresh emphasis, beginning with the Egyptian arms deal. (Formally the arms then supplied to Egypt were Czechoslovak, but the deal must have received the approval of the Soviet Government, which by 1958 had assumed the main responsibility for equipping the Egyptian armed forces.) Soviet financing of the Aswan Dam and Soviet purchase of Egyptian cotton at premium prices in the mid-1950s added a new dimension to Soviet foreign policy: politico-economic rivalry in the Middle East with the Western countries whose exclusive preserve it had been ever since the break-up of the Ottoman Empire nearly forty years earlier. Among these countries Britain

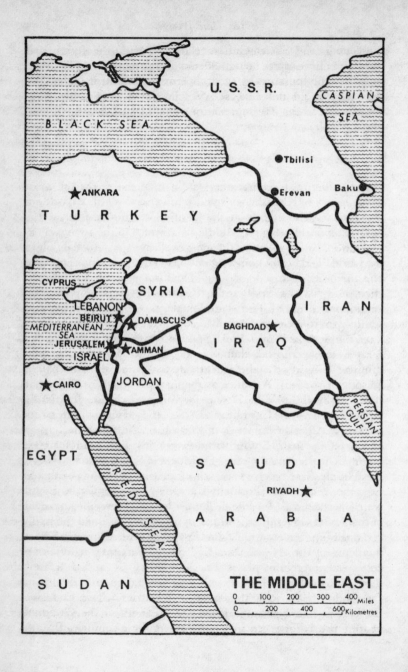

remained the predominant power in the Middle East until the collapse of the Anglo-French Suez expedition in 1956. The steady erosion of British power in the area left a vacuum which the United States found it hard to fill, because of its commitment to Israel, and which it would have been hard for the Soviet Union not to fill, even though it had been one of the State of Israel's original sponsors in 1948. As the Soviet Union gradually filled this vacuum, so too it assumed the role of the champion of the Arab cause against Israel, in the process acquiring a position in the Middle East which recalls that of Tsarist Russia in the Balkans.

The Middle East may indeed be described, in politico-strategic terms, as the Balkans of the late twentieth century. Thus, in pursuing its new policy in the Middle East, the Soviet Union has had to contend with the volatility fo Arab politics, as well as with the problem of underpinning this policy with respectable ideological justification. In the northern tier, Soviet national interests—in particular mistrust of the CENTO[8] Alliance—obliged the Soviet Union to mend its fences with Turkey and Iran. This *rapprochement* was cemented under the collective leadership by official visits paid by Kosygin to Teheran in 1968 and to Ankara in 1966. (The Soviet–Iranian agreement of January 1966, whereby Iran undertook to deliver natural gas to the Soviet Union for twelve years, in return for industrial projects in Iran carried out by the latter, also marked a turning point in Soviet oil policy.) The Soviet leadership began by attempting to define some of the Arab states as 'progressive social'—for example, the Ba'ath regimes in Iraq and Syria. But in the Middle East, as elsewhere, this attempt ended with the acknowledgement of reality quoted in the previous section of this chapter; and the touchstone of Soviet policy in Arab eyes became more and more the Soviet leadership's policy towards the dispute between the Arab states and Israel.

The Arab–Israeli dispute

This dispute erupted again in June 1967. Soviet motives for stoking the fire that led to the Six Day War are obscure. On 21

April 1967, presumably under Arab pressure, the Soviet Government addressed a note of protest to Israel against the air raid which—as a reprisal—the Israeli Air Force had carried out on Damascus a fortnight earlier (previously the Soviet press had spoken only of border clashes). At the end of April Kosygin had talks in Moscow with a visiting Egyptian delegation, led by Anwar Sadat. According to a speech made by Nasser after his defeat, the delegation was told, presumably by the Soviet Prime Minister, that Israel was concentrating troops with the premeditated intent of attacking Syria. When Nasser closed the Straits of Tiran in May, the Soviet Government did not condone his action; but the Soviet press gave no hint of disapproval; on the contrary, *Pravda* of 26 May stated that the gulf waters could not be regarded as Israeli waters under any United Nations decision, three days after the Soviet Government had declared that aggressors in the Middle East would face not only the united strength of the Arab countries, but also a firm riposte from the Soviet Union. On this evidence, either the Soviet leadership completely miscalculated the military situation on the ground, or 'no one calculated at all'; in any event, having urged restraint on both sides, Brezhnev, Kosygin, and the Defence Minister left Moscow, to spend the critical days from 31 May to 4 June inspecting the Soviet fleet at Murmansk and Archangel.[9]

Whatever the explanation for Soviet behaviour before the Six Day War, there is no doubt about the energy with which the Soviet Government reacted to it. The Soviet Prime Minister used the hot line to the US President more than once. After the cease-fire, a summit meeting of communist states was held in Europe. Soviet leaders visited their Middle Eastern friends; Soviet warships were sent to Alexandria and Port Said; the vast Egyptian losses of equipment were swiftly made good; and although the Algerian President publicly blamed the Russians* for the humiliating Arab defeat—which left Israeli forces occupying the Sinai peninsula, the west bank of Jordan, and the Golan heights in Syria—the Soviet position in the Arab world and the eastern Mediterranean was soon restored. In November 1967 the Soviet Union intervened militarily in the Yemeni civil

---

* The Russians themselves blamed both the superiority of Israeli equipment and Nasser's betrayal by the military bourgeoisie.

war, from which Egyptian troops were at last pulling out, and in the following year an agreement on military and technical assistance was signed with the new South Yemen Government, which was established after the British withdrawal from Aden. In the Cyprus crisis of November 1967, the Soviet Government succeeded in maintaining an even-handed posture towards both the Turkish and the Cyprus governments, while blaming the West for allegedly pursuing policies in Cyprus which brought two NATO allies—Turkey and Greece—to the brink of war.

Meanwhile, in the aftermath of the Six Day War, Kosygin led the Soviet delegation to the United Nations. (While he was in the United States he met President Johnson at Glasboro, without result). On the Arab-Israeli dispute the Security Council finally adopted a compromise resolution on 22 November, for which the British delegation was entitled to the credit. This resolution was an ingenious attempt to square the circle. The preamble to the resolution having emphasized, among other things, 'the inadmissibility of the acquisition of territory by war and the need to work for a just and lasting peace, in which every state in the area can live in security', the resolution itself consisted of three points. The first of these was:

the establishment of a just and lasting peace in the Middle East, which should include the application of both the following principles:

(i) Withdrawal of Israeli armed forces from territories occupied in the recent conflict;

(ii) Termination of claims or states of belligerency, and respect for the acknowledgement of the sovereignty, territorial integrity and political independence of every state in the area and their right to live in peace within secure and recognized boundaries free from acts or threats of force.

The resolution's second point affirmed the necessity for:

(a) guaranteeing freedom of navigation through international waterways in the area;

(b) achieving a just settlement of the refugee problem;

(c) guaranteeing the territorial inviolability and political independence of every state in the area, through measures including the establishment of demilitarized zones.

Thirdly, the Security Council requested the Secretary-General of the United Nations to designate a Special Representative to go to the Middle East, in order to help to achieve a peaceful and accepted settlement in accordance with the provisions and principles of the resolution.

To this day, this resolution, which the Security Council was to reaffirm in 1969 and in 1973, remains at the centre of the dispute. Whether it would have been passed unanimously if there were a definite article in the Russian language is an interesting speculation: the Soviet Union supported its Arab clients in interpreting the word 'territories' in 1(i) of the resolution as meaning all 'the territories',[10] whereas it was a cardinal point of the Israeli case that there were certain territories which they could never reasonably be expected to return to Arab hands, such as the Golan Heights, Sharm-el-Sheikh, and Jerusalem itself. U Thant's Special Representative, Gunnar Jarring, then Swedish Ambassador in Moscow, made repeated efforts over the years that followed to fulfil the mission entrusted to him. The main rocks that he hit were: on the Israeli side, their unwillingness not only to return all that they had conquered but also to negotiate other than directly with the Arab governments concerned; and on the Arab side, a matching reluctance to negotiate before a complete Israeli withdrawal, as well as the special problem of Jerusalem and the future of the Arab refugees, their numbers swollen by the outcome of the 1967 war.[11]

The year 1969 opened with a Soviet initiative: on 2 January the Soviet Government suggested the outline of a settlement to the British, French, and United States governments. This led in the course of the year to discussions between the Representatives of the Four Powers in New York and to a Soviet–American bilateral dialogue, in which the two governments, as well as negotiating with each other, were also acting as lawyers for their respective clients in the Middle East. On the ground matters grew steadily worse. By April the United Nations Secretary-General reported that open warfare was being waged: the War of Attrition, as it came to be called. Against a background of Arab guerrilla operations conducted in the territories occupied by Israel, in Israel itself, and in many other countries, the Egyptian Army used its superiority in artillery to conduct a shelling duel across the Suez Canal, while the Israeli Air Force, using the Phantom aircraft supplied by the United States, attacked targets nearer and nearer Cairo. These attacks were to lead the Soviet Union, early in 1970, to embark on a massive, direct involvement in Egypt: the first of several Soviet military interventions in the developing world in the new decade.

7. Europe

New ideas

UNDER Stalin, Europe was central to Soviet foreign policy. Under Khrushchev, in spite of his adventures in the Third World, it remained so. The heart of the matter was Germany. In 1958 the Soviet Government put forward a draft Treaty of Friendship and Cooperation of European States; and in 1960 the Warsaw Pact governments made, not for the first time, a proposal for a non-aggression pact between the NATO and the Warsaw Pact groups of states. Both these proposals would have involved recognition of the German Democratic Republic by the West, and hence the jettisoning of the Hallstein doctrine, which ostracized the GDR. In the 1960s new ideas were beginning to be discussed, both in Western and in Eastern Europe.

In Eastern Europe, the new look began in Romania, from which Soviet troops had been withdrawn in 1958, in the aftermath of the convulsions that had wracked Eastern Europe after the XXth Congress of the CPSU two years before. The Romanian attempt to mediate between the Russians and the Chinese in 1964 was part of a broad decision to pursue an independent foreign policy, based on what the Romanian leadership perceived as their country's national interests, while at the same time allowing no relaxation of party-imposed discipline at home. They began in the field of foreign trade, claiming the right to trade with whom they pleased, and rejected the Soviet proposal put forward in COMECON in 1962, for the division of labour between members of that organization in accordance with the directives of a central planning organ.[1] The new Romanian constitution of 1965 included a provision intended to prevent Romania from becoming involved in war except by its own decision. In May 1966 Ceausescu, who had become leader of the Romanian Communist Party the year before, delivered a speech[2] in which he publicly attacked the concept of military blocs and touched a raw Soviet nerve by referring to the lost provinces of Bessarabia and Northern Bukovina (acquired by the Soviet Union as a fruit of the Nazi–Soviet Pact of 1939). Romania was the first Eastern European country, other than the Soviet Union itself, to enter into diplomatic relations with the Federal Republic of Germany; and the Soviet Union had to acquiesce in Romania's maintaining relations with Israel after the 1967 war—and ultimately in her resumption of relations with China, where Ceausescu was to receive a lavish welcome in 1971.

'Polycentrism' (as it was described in the Italian Communist leader Togliatti's memorandum, published in *Pravda* after his death in September 1964) was matched in the West by de Gaulle's concept of Europe from the Atlantic to the Urals. According to Soviet theory, relations between communist countries are unique, because they involve not only their governments but also their whole peoples, led by their respective Communist parties.[3] The international obligations of the working class did not permit of any divergence of interest between one communist country and another. Nevertheless, the Soviet leadership decided to put up with the Romanians, and to foster a special Franco-Soviet relationship, because with it went the idea of Europe for the Europeans—not to mention the gap in the NATO order of battle left by the French forces, which de Gaulle withdrew from integrated international command before his visit to Moscow in 1966.

Most important of all, *Ostpolitik* was being rethought in West Germany itself. On 26 January 1965, the *Frankfurter Allgemeine Zeitung* published a memorandum on this subject written by Willy Brandt the previous August. This memorandum took as its premise that it was a Western interest to support the independence of East European nations and their efforts to use their field of manoeuvre. Such a policy should concentrate on economic and cultural measures (linked with 'humanitarian regulations'), respecting each East European state as an equal partner, and taking into account its military and ideological links. Brandt foresaw, though he described the time as not yet ripe for it, a major increase in East–West trade, for which the Western countries would have to be prepared to grant substantial economic and financial support, and the development of joint projects on a European scale. The memorandum stopped short of recommending any change in the policy of refusing to recognize the Soviet Zone of Germany as an independent state, but contemplated greater economic and cultural contact between it and the Federal Republic, and expressed the hope that increased contact between the West and other Eastern European countries would affect the Soviet Zone as well. And towards the end, the memorandum recalled Brandt's remark in a speech made in New York in May 1964, that it was time to acknowledge the fact that Europe does not end at the Iron Curtain.

Six weeks before Brandt's article was published, the Polish Foreign Minister briefly remarked, at the United Nations General Assembly, that the time was ripe for convening a conference of all European states, to examine the problem of European security as a whole. (Rapacki expressly added that both the Soviet Union and the United States should take part.) On 20 January 1965 the political Consultative Committee of the Warsaw Pact countries endorsed the Polish initiative, proposing a conference of European states (with no mention of the United States or Canada) to discuss measures for collective security in Europe,[4] and followed this up at Bucharest, in July 1966, with a long 'Declaration on Strengthening Peace and Security in Europe'.[5] This foresaw an all-European declaration providing for pledges on the part of signatory states to be guided in their relations with one another by the interests of peace, to settle disputed questions only by peaceful means, to hold consultations and exchange information on questions of mutual interest, and to assist in the comprehensive development of economic, scientific-technical, and cultural ties with one another: a proposal repeated in the Karlovy Vary statement of European communist parties of 26 April 1967, according to which European security[6] depended on:

respecting the realities of post-war Europe . . . the inviolability of the existing frontiers in Europe, especially the Oder–Neisse frontier and the frontier between the two German states . . . the existence of two sovereign German states with equal rights . . . denying the Federal

German Republic access to nuclear weapons in any form either European or Atlantic[7] . . . recognizing the Munich Pact as invalid from the very moment of its conclusion.

The Karlovy Vary statement was important not only because it made it clear that the idea of a European conference was already linked in the minds of its proposers with the German question, but also because it followed the announcement in the Bundestag, in December 1966, of the new *Ostpolitik* proposals of the Grand Coalition Government of Christian Democrats and Social Democrats, in which Brandt held the post of Foreign Minister. Although these proposals stopped well short of recognizing the German Democratic Republic, with whom a policy of 'regulated coexistence' was envisaged, they marked the beginning of the end of the Hallstein doctrine of 1955, whereby the Federal German Government had refused to recognize any government—with the single exception of the Soviet Union—which recognized the German Democratic Republic. Romania, which boycotted the Karlovy Vary conference, established diplomatic relations with the Federal Republic on this basis without delay. The East Germans and the Poles denounced the new policy as German revanchism in a new guise. After a period of apparent hesitation, the Soviet Union joined the Germans and the Poles. As though to emphasize the unity of the Eastern European bloc, in the course of 1967 all its members, except Romania, signed bilateral treaties of mutual assistance with the German Democratic Republic, and the Soviet Union began to bring its bilateral treaties with each member country up to date. But in the second half of 1967 and the first half of 1968 the Soviet Government did not feel inhibited from engaging in bilateral talks with the Federal German Government on the possibility of an agreement renouncing the use of force—with no result, although the talks proved to be the forerunner of the Soviet–German negotiations of 1970.

No direct response was made by the Western Alliance until the very end of 1969. But after the ministerial meeting held in Brussels in December 1967 the communiqué had annexed to it the Harmel Report on the future tasks of the Alliance.[8] The essence of this report was the concept that military security and a policy of *détente* were not contradictory, but complementary. The report spoke of 'realistic measures designed to further a *détente* in

East–West relations', not as the final goal, but as 'part of a long-term process to promote better relations and to foster a European settlement'. Its final paragraph contained the first mention of balanced force reductions. Six months later—the French abstaining—NATO Ministers meeting at Reykjavik formally put forward a proposal for such reductions in Europe, and invited the Warsaw Pact countries to 'join in this search for progress towards peace'. But in August 1968 the dialogue was brusquely interrupted, when the forces of the Soviet Union, together with some units supplied by its Warsaw Pact allies (excluding Romania)—some half million men in all—invaded Czechoslovakia.

Czechoslovakia

Ironically, it was Czechoslovakia, where Stalin's gigantic statue had been left standing in Prague long after Khrushchev had denounced him at the XXth CPSU Congress, that produced the first serious threat to Soviet authority in Eastern Europe since the Hungarian Revolution, and, in the process, retarded the Soviet grand design for Europe by one year. The origins of the Czechoslovak upheaval were complex: political (general dissatisfaction with fifteen years of rule by Antonin Novotny, who during most of this period combined the offices of President and First Secretary of the Czechoslovak Communist Party); regional (the Slovaks demanded the same rights as the Czechs); and economic. E. G. Liberman's thesis on profitability had been published in *Pravda* in September 1962; it was not followed up until three years later, when the Soviet leadership introduced a limited measure of economic reform, which was attacked by the Chinese as a big step towards the restoration of capitalism and 'a new *kulak* economy'. The success of the German economic reforms has already been mentioned; the Hungarian reform began in 1968; the Czechoslovak reform, approved in 1965, began on 1 January 1967, but was diluted by the conservatism of party officials. On all these grounds Brezhnev, who visited Prague in December 1967, cannot have been greatly surprised when Novotny was obliged to resign as First Secretary of the Czechoslovak Communist Party in January 1968 (three months later he was succeeded as President

NORWAY
OSLO

SWEDEN
STOCKHOLM

FINLAND
HELSINKI

DENMARK
COPENHAGEN

U. S. S. R.
●Minsk

BERLIN
G.D.R.

POLAND
★WARSAW

Kiev●

F.R.G.

PRAGUE
CZECHOSLOVAKIA

VIENNA
AUSTRIA

BUDAPEST
HUNGARY

ROMANIA

BELGRADE
YUGOSLAVIA

BUCHAREST

ITALY
ROME

SOFIA
BULGARIA

ALBANIA
TIRANA

Istanbul

GREECE

TURKEY

TUNIS

ATHENS

TUNISIA

EASTERN EUROPE
0   100   200   300   400 Miles
0   200   400   600 Kilometres

by General Svoboda). His successor as First Secretary, Alexander Dubcek, the Moscow-trained First Secretary of the Slovak Communist Party, may well have seemed reliable enough at first. From start to finish he was at pains to stress his commitment to the communist cause; and hence to keep Czechoslovakia in COMECON and in the Warsaw Pact. Indeed he reversed the Romanian experiment: his 'socialism with a human face' was loyal to Moscow abroad and became increasingly heterodox at home.

There is no evidence that when Dubcek, who combined diffidence with obstinacy in a remarkable way, took over in Prague in January 1968, he had any intention of liberalizing the Czechoslovak political system as he did during the next seven months, although he must have approved of Ota Sik's economic reforms. He was borne along by the wave of popular expectations, rather like Wladyslaw Gomulka in Poland twelve years earlier, but—unlike Gomulka—he did not drive it back again. Events moved so rapidly that on 2 May *Rude Pravo* was able to write of the springlike blossoming of a new public life and of the breath of fresh air brought by democratic freedoms. It might have been nearer the truth at that moment to describe Dubcek as unwilling to rule the country by force and unqualified to rule it by democratic means. He therefore fell between two stools. For example, having discontinued press censorship in March, at the end of May the Ministry of Interior announced that the formation of new political parties—in particular, this applied to the resuscitation of the Social Democratic Party—would be considered illegal. Yet the Ministry allowed a preparatory committee of the 'club of engaged non-party members' to operate, recognized the statute of the society for human rights, and permitted the Communist Party-sponsored youth organization to divide into a number of independent groups. Soviet influence in the Ministry of Interior and in the Czechoslovak Army was curbed. Worst of all perhaps in Soviet eyes was the Czechoslovak Party's decision, taken in May, to hold a Congress on 9 September, which was expected to consist of delegates holding reformist views.

Soviet concern at this trend of events was expressed to Dubcek and his colleagues at their first confrontation with representatives of five Warsaw Pact powers (Romania alone being absent) at Dresden on 23 March. This concern was heightened by the Czechoslovak Central Committee's approval, on 5 April, of the liberal Action Programme. On 27 June seventy prominent Czechoslovaks published a manifesto calling for even more radical reform, *The Two Thousand Words*, which led *Pravda* on 11 July to draw an ominous comparison between Czechoslovakia in 1968 and Hungary in 1956.[9] The Warsaw Letter of 15 July,[10] addressed to the Czechoslovaks by their five Warsaw Pact allies (they themselves had refused to attend the meeting), laid particular emphasis on the Czechoslovak Party's loss of control of the mass media. Of their allies' chief anxieties, the first was political: the fear that the Czechoslovak Communist Party would sooner or later lose control of the levers of power. ('Undermining the leading role of the Communist Party leads to the liquidation of socialist democracy and of the socialist system . . . ') The second was military. ('The frontiers of the socialist world have moved to the centre of Europe, to the Elbe and the Sumav mountains.') The third was a bit of both: fear of West Germany, and the response among the ruling circles in Czechoslovakia which the Federal Republic's overtures were allegedly meeting. The Warsaw Letter was followed by a Soviet demand that the Czechoslovak Presidium should meet the Soviet Politburo, either in Moscow or in the Ukraine. The Czechoslovaks agreed to the meeting, but succeeded in persuading the Soviet Politburo, all but two of whose members attended, to hold the meeting in Czechoslovakia.

Czechoslovakia was invaded on the night of 20/21 August, in spite of the apparent agreement reached between the Soviet and Czechoslovak party leaderships at Cierna[11] and between the leaders of all six parties at Bratislava,[12] at the end of July and the beginning of August respectively. The Czechoslovaks seem to have left the former meeting convinced that the Soviet troops who were conducting manoeuvres in Czechoslovakia would leave their country; that the Warsaw Letter was abrogated; and that Czechoslovak sovereignty was assured. Equally the Soviet leadership appear to have believed that the Czechoslovak leaders were now committed to regaining control over the mass media. The wording of the Bratislava Declaration was woolly. In any event, the political factor must have loomed larger in Soviet eyes after 10 August, when proposals for revising the statutes of the Czechoslovak Communist Party were published, condoning what in orthodox eyes was the crime of fractionalism: the right of the minority to state its views in public after a majority decision had been passed. Other visitors to Czechoslovakia during August included Presidents Tito and Ceausescu, Janos Kadar, and Ulbricht. The popular welcome given to the two presidents must have infuriated the Russians; Kadar, anxious for the future of his own economic reform, may well have advised Dubcek to slacken the pace; Ulbricht can only have reported in black. Throughout the summer the Soviet leaders were under pressure from Ulbricht and Gomulka, the second of whom feared the effect of his own regime (weakened by disorders that had taken place in Poland in March) if the Dubcek experiment succeeded. It was also widely believed that the Soviet leaders, particularly Piotr Shelest, then First Secretary of the Ukrainian Communist Party, were anxious lest the Czechoslovak liberal infection should cross the border into the Ukraine. Thus, the Russians were influenced by a domino theory in Eastern Europe similar to the one that obsessed American thinking on South-East Asia.

Was it the political or the military factor that in the end prevailed within the Soviet Politburo? Bismarck is reputed to have said that the master of Bohemia is the master of Europe. At the time of Dubcek's visit to Moscow in May, *Le Monde* published a report (later denied), according to which the Soviet Army was ready to answer appeals from faithful Czechoslovak communists for help in safeguarding socialism;[13] and Kovalev's article published in *Pravda* of 26 September alluded to the possibility that NATO troops might approach Soviet borders and that 'the commonwealth of European socialist countries might be dismembered'. (The same article included a warning shot against Yugoslavia, pointing out that non-aligned socialist states owed their national independence to the power of the socialist commonwealth and primarily to that of the Soviet Union.)

In my view, the political factor carried the greater weight. But the question remains why the members of the Soviet Politburo, beset by both political and military anxieties, took so long to make up their minds to take what the official History of Soviet

Foreign Policy describes as an extraordinary but essential measure. (The role of the Central Committee seems to have been purely formal: it met on 20 August a few hours before the invasion began.) The delay in deciding on the invasion strongly suggests that there was a division of opinion within the Soviet leadership. No doubt all members of the Politburo must have hoped in the early months of the Dubcek regime that the combined pressure of five of Czechoslovakia's allies would eventually prevail without the need to resort to arms; and some of them may have gone on hoping against hope, as late as August. Those who believed in the *Westpolitik* of the Karlovy Vary meeting must have been prepared to go to considerable lengths to maintain the image of a Soviet Union dedicated to a peaceful Europe. On the other hand, with the Americans embroiled in a presidential electoral campaign as well as in Vietnam, and remembering the Western reaction to events in East Berlin in 1953 and Budapest in 1956, they can hardly have feared a Western response strong enough to outweigh the disadvantages of a Czechoslovakia ruled by reformists. As the summer went by, they could not have failed to note Western signals that any response would in no circumstances be military, but purely political. And politically, they had more reason to be concerned at the effect on the world communist movement, above all on China. It is also conceivable that the Soviet military, whose doctrine 'directs its primary attention towards the preparing of the nation and the armed forces for a world-wide thermonuclear war',[14] did not relish the prospect of the Soviet Army being employed in this uncongenial police role, more especially since the operation turned out to be based on the false premise that pro-Soviet members of the Presidium of the Czechoslovak Communist Party would at once come forward to take over from the leaders whom the invaders had imprisoned. It remains an interesting sidelight on the composition of the invasion force that it included units equipped with tactical nuclear weapons.[15]

The answer to the question why the Soviet leadership hesitated would throw a great deal of light not only on the whole Czechoslovak affair, but on the decision-making process in the Soviet Union and the relationship between the CPSU and the Soviet military. Once the decision to invade Czechoslovakia was taken, what it did demonstrate was both the paramount importance to the Soviet Union of maintaining its glacis in Eastern Europe and the frailty of the Eastern European communist regimes (Bulgaria being perhaps the only exception). As a military operation, the massive invasion of Czechoslovakia was effectively conducted. It is no reflection on the competence of the Soviet military planners to add that it could hardly have been otherwise, given that Warsaw Pact manoeuvres had been continuously in progress either in Czechoslovakia or on its borders since the beginning of June. But it was met with equally massive—though largely non-violent—opposition; Ludvik Svoboda refused to negotiate on the formation of a new government; and it became apparent that the invaders had no plan to cope with this contingency. Worse than that, they failed to gain control of either the mass media (which continued to operate, clandestinely) or the telecommunications network. The Soviet Union was therefore obliged to achieve its aims in Czechoslovakia according to a time-scale of months, instead of hours. This involved first releasing Dubcek, who had been abducted to the Soviet Union, together with other members of the Presidium, and then tolerating his remaining in office as First Secretary until the following April, when he was succeeded by Gustav Husak. But Dubcek had to accept, in October, a treaty sanctioning the stationing of Soviet troops on Czechoslovak territory (which not even Novotny had done), and he had to invalidate the XIVth Congress of the Czechoslovak Communist Party, which had met in a factory soon after the invasion. Slowly under Dubcek, and more effectively under Husak, Czechoslovak political life returned to normal. For his part, Dubcek refused to pronounce a self-criticism, and was stripped successively of his offices, including his short-lived mission to Turkey, and finally of his party membership.

Having done what was required of him (among other things, on 9 September 1969 the Czechoslovak Presidium rescinded its condemnation of the invasion a year before), Husak received the formal Soviet blessing during a visit to Moscow in October. That the Soviet leadership continued to feel uneasy about the intervention and the continuing presence of large Soviet forces in Czechoslovakia—eventually reduced to five divisions—is suggested by the fact that they sought to justify both by what has come to be known in the West as the Brezhnev doctrine. This was already implicit in the concluding paragraphs of the statement published in *Pravda* of 22 August, which declared flatly that counter-revolution could not be allowed 'to wrest Czechoslovakia from the family of socialist states', and described the defence of Czechoslovakia as an international socialist duty. It was also anticipated in the *Pravda* article of 26 September, which described socialism as indivisible and declared its defence to be the common cause of all communists. And although three years later—speaking at a banquet given in his honour by Tito in Belgrade on 22 September 1971—Brezhnev himself denied the existence of the 'so-called new doctrine of limited sovereignty',[16] he remains on the record as having told the Vth Polish Party Congress on 12 November 1968:

when internal and external forces, hostile to socialism, seek to reverse the development of any socialist country whatsoever in the direction of the restoration of the capitalist order, when a threat to the case of socialism arises in that country, a threat to the security of the socialist commonwealth as a whole—this already becomes not only a problem of the people of the country concerned, but also a common problem and the concern of all socialist countries.[17]

The immediate effect of the Soviet intervention was a general outcry of horror. Not all the Soviet Union's non-communist friends joined in, however. (Cairo radio took the Soviet side in its broadcasts; so did the Iraqi Government; and Mrs Gandhi, though expressing profound concern, blocked a parliamentary resolution condemning the invasion.) Perhaps the European non-ruling communist parties suffered most damage: only the Luxembourg and the Greek Cypriot communist parties supported the Soviet Union. Both the Romanians and the Yugoslavs publicly condemned the invasion of Czechoslovakia; the following February, when Tito met Ceausescu in Romania, their communiqué emphasized the importance of respect for the principles of the United Nations charter (an indirect attack on the Brezhnev doctrine). In March the Romanian Government adopted regulations making it impermissible for the troops of other Warsaw Pact countries to enter Romania (a country surrounded on all sides by Warsaw Pact countries, except for its common frontier with Yugoslavia) without Romanian consent, no doubt recalling the Warsaw Pact manoeuvres of the previous June in Czechoslovakia. The Yugoslav leadership, for whom the years 1962–8 had been a period of *rapprochement* with the Soviet Union, took the Czechoslovak lesson to heart. The concept of total national defence was now adopted, whereby in the event of war units of the regular army would fight in depth alongside the newly created territorial defence force, transforming the whole country into a military 'hedgehog' and thus compelling the invader to fight all the way.[18] For the Chinese the invasion of Czechoslovakia (like the talks on the Arab–Israeli dispute) was an example of Soviet–American collusion. Much more important, seen from Peking, the Brezhnev doctrine offered a potential precedent for a Soviet attack on China.

East–West relations were frozen. In the communiqué[19] issued after their meeting in Brussels four months after the invasion, NATO foreign ministers continued to denounce both the invasion and the Brezhnev doctrine. Yet in May 1969 they announced their intention to explore possibilities for negotiation with the Soviet Union and the other countries of Eastern Europe.[20] The reason for this, at first sight remarkable, switch was neither Western cynicism nor Eastern cunning. Rather, both sides were led by a complex of reasons into a new era of multilateral diplomacy.[21]

8. The Turning Point

By the middle of 1968 the momentum of nuclear logic carrying the Soviet Union and the United States towards each other had become so powerful that even the Czechoslovak tragedy could not arrest it for more than a brief interlude. The year 1969 was, both abroad and at home, a turning point for the Soviet Union.

On the eve of the invasion of Czechoslovakia—on 1 July 1968, five years after the signature of the Nuclear Test Ban Treaty—the three signatories of the earlier agreement, banning nuclear tests in the atmosphere, outer space, and under water, finally signed the Treaty on the Non-Proliferation of Nuclear Weapons. Under the terms of this treaty, each signatory possessing nuclear weapons undertook 'not to transfer to any recipient whatsoever nuclear weapons or other nuclear explosive devices or control over such weapons or explosive devices directly, or indirectly; and not in any way to assist, encourage, or induce any non-nuclear-weapons State to manufacture or otherwise acquire nuclear weapons or other nuclear explosive devices, or control over such weapons or explosive devices'. Each signatory not possessing nuclear weapons gave an undertaking complementary to that given by those possessing such weapons; and also undertook to accept certain safeguards designed to prevent diversion of nuclear energy from peaceful uses to nuclear weapons or other nuclear explosive devices. The treaty committed all parties to it 'to pursue negotiations in good faith on effective measures relating to cessation of the nuclear arms race at an early date and to nuclear disarmament, and on a treaty on general and complete disarmament, under strict and effective international control'. The treaty included a clause whereby it would not enter into force until forty-three signatories, including Great Britain, the Soviet Union, and the United States, had deposited their instruments of ratification (a point which was not reached until nearly two years later). A further clause laid down that five years after the treaty's entry into force the parties to the treaty would hold a conference in Geneva, in order to review its operation and to ensure that its purposes were being realized.[1]

Like its forerunner, this treaty was initially trilateral, in the sense that all three capitals—London, Moscow, and Washington—were designated for the depositing of instruments of ratification. But the second agreement was far more Soviet–American* than the first, because the protracted negotiations that led up to its signature were conducted in the forum of the Geneva Disarmament Conference, whose co-Chairmen were the Soviet Union and the United States, and because one of the conditions enabling the other, non-nuclear, governments to accede to the non-proliferation treaty was in effect a joint guarantee offered them by the Soviet and the US governments. This guarantee took the form of Security Council Resolution No. 255, under the terms of which the Governments of Britain, the United States, and the USSR declared on 17 June 1968 that aggression with nuclear weapons, or the threat of such aggression, against a non-nuclear-weapon state 'would create a qualitatively new situation in which the nuclear-weapon states which are Permanent Members of the United Nations Security Council would have to act immediately through the Security Council to take the measures necessary to counter such aggression or to remove the threat of aggression . . . ' They also affirmed their intention, in such a contingency, to 'seek immediate Security Council action' to assist any non-nuclear-weapon signatory 'that is a victim of an act of aggression or an object of a threat of aggression in which nuclear weapons are used'.

* The agreement was trilateral because France and China remained aloof, for the same reasons as in 1963. For the extent to which it was seen as bilateral in Washington as early as 1965, see William C. Foster (then Head of the State Department Disarmament Agency), 'New Directions in Arms Control and Disarmament', *Foreign Affairs*, 43, 1965, in which he suggested that a non-proliferation treaty would be worthwhile even if it meant some 'erosion of alliances resulting from the high degree of US–Soviet cooperation which will be required if a non-proliferation programme is to be successful'.

Eighteen months before this second major nuclear treaty was signed, President Johnson had proposed that the governments of the United States and the Soviet Union should engage in what became known as SALT—Strategic Arms Limitation Treaty—talks. There must have been divisions of opinion in Moscow about the wisdom of accepting this potentially far-reaching proposal, for it was not until June 1968 that the Soviet Foreign Minister formally did so, shortly before signing the Nuclear Non-Proliferation Treaty. One of the factors that no doubt weighed heavily in the Kremlin scales was the need to have rough numerical strategic parity at least in sight before accepting even the principle of such a negotiation. By 1969 the Soviet Union had at last achieved this goal. Although the United States remained well ahead in numbers of ballistic missile-launching submarines and strategic bombers, the Soviet Union had overtaken the United States in intercontinental ballistic missiles. The estimates of Soviet strengths for the end of the year were: 1,200 land-based ICBMs (including 270 massive SS-9s, with a yield of 20–25 megatons) against the United States' 1,054; 230 submarine-launched ballistic missiles against the United States' 656; and 150 strategic bombers against the United States' 540. The Soviet Union also had 67 anti-ballistic missile launchers round Moscow, while the United States had not so far deployed any.[2] On 20 January 1969—the day of Richard Nixon's inauguration as President of the United States—the Soviet Ministry of Foreign Affairs convened a special press conference in order to declare Soviet readiness to begin a serious exchange of views with the United States on the 'mutual limitation and subsequent reduction of strategic nuclear delivery vehicles, including defensive systems'. A week later Nixon referred in his first press conference to the concept of strategic sufficiency, thus in effect renouncing the American claim to strategic superiority over the Soviet Union; and he said that he was in favour of SALT.

By the time the delegations of the two super-powers finally began the SALT talks in Helsinki in November 1969, it was no longer simply a question of recognizing the fact that both sides now possessed a vast capacity of overkill. (In the course of his evidence given to the United States Senate Foreign Affairs Committee in 1969[3], Melvin Laird, then Defence Secretary, estimated that 200 nuclear warheads of one megaton each would be enough to destroy 55 per cent of the American population and that it would take 1,200 equivalent American warheads to destroy 45 per cent of the more scattered Soviet population.) 'Lead-time' made it essential to plan as much as ten years ahead. Among the developments were: first, new and more precise guidance systems, capable of greatly increasing missile accuracy; second, multiple re-entry warhead systems and—more important still—multiple, independently targetable re-entry vehicles (MIRV), each warhead being programmed for its specific target; and finally, anti-ballistic missile systems. On 14 March Nixon announced his decision to go ahead with the *Safeguard* anti-ballistic missile system, a decision which was confirmed in the Senate by a narrow vote in August. The SALT talks, which lasted until 23 December, were only preparatory. Nevertheless, they marked the opening of the first formally bilateral strategic negotiation between the two super-powers, each of whom had China's future potential in mind. As the Soviet Foreign Minister put it, in his report to the Supreme Soviet in July 1969, 'in questions of the maintenance of peace, the USSR and the USA can find a common language'.[4] Of a different order of import-ance, but none the less a sign of the times, was the Soviet–American agreement, in October, on a draft treaty banning the emplacement on the sea-bed of nuclear weapons, other weapons of mass destruction, or installations for the storing, testing, or using of such weapons.

By the end of the year the Soviet leadership must have had a further consideration in mind: in July the first American troops were withdrawn from Vietnam.* In November Nixon's broadcast about 'Vietnamization' made it clear that sooner or later, and if possible before the next presidential elections, he intended to pull out of Vietnam altogether. This was in line with the so-called Guam doctrine of stimulated self-help.[5] With the end of the United States' involvement in Indo-China at last in sight, and with no foreseeable conclusion to the Sino-Soviet dispute (which had erupted into armed conflict in March), it had become a major Soviet interest not only to engage the Americans in a direct dialogue but also to seek to bring about a European settlement.

* Twelve days before the first American astronauts landed on the moon.

Here fate intervened: after the West German elections in October the Christian Democrats found themselves in opposition for the first time. Brandt became Federal Chancellor, depending for his majority in the Bundestag on his party's new alliance with the Free Democratic Party Liberals, whose leader, Walter Scheel, became Foreign Minister. On 28 October, in his inaugural speech, the Chancellor announced his concept of two German states within one nation; a month later the Federal German Republic signed the Non-Proliferation Treaty; and on 8 December Soviet–German talks began in Moscow. In parallel, on 16 December the three Allied Powers renewed their proposal, first made to the Soviet Government in August, for talks on Berlin.

Meanwhile, the Warsaw Pact Political Consultative Committee had relaunched their proposal for an all-European conference at its meeting in Budapest in March, and seven months later in Prague they put forward two questions for the agenda: 'European security and the renunciation of the use of force or threats of force in relations between European states', and the expansion of 'trade, economic and scientific and technical ties'.[6] In May the Finnish Government had suggested Helsinki as the site of the conference, an offer which all the Warsaw Pact countries accepted. Finally, at Brussels in December 1969, NATO ministers made their first positive response to the prolonged barrage from Eastern Europe. It was guarded, mentioning careful advance preparation, prospects of concrete results, and the need for an assurance that such a meeting would not serve to ratify the existing division of Europe, and making it clear that progress in Soviet–German negotiations and in the Berlin negotiations would influence their future attitude to the proposal for a European Conference, 'in which, of course, the North American members of the alliance would participate'.[7]

These, then, were the beginnings—between the two super-powers, between the Soviet Union and West Germany, and between the two alliances—of the years of negotiation. Paradoxically, although the Soviet leadership entered this new era basking in American acknowledgement that their country had become a co-equal super-power, and confident that, at least for the time being, the Soviet presence in Eastern Europe had been made secure, they simultaneously faced a dilemma at home.

The change in the Soviet Union's international status was evident to any visitor to Moscow at the time. It was a city that had visibly arrived. In the year of Stalin's death, if the visitor could for a moment blot out from his mind both the dazzling cluster of monuments that form the Kremlin and the grotesque Stalinist skyscrapers, the greater part of Moscow looked like a provincial town, resembling a capital city far less than Leningrad, which still retained its elegance half a century after the transfer of the seat of government to Moscow. The boulevards were by Western standards almost empty of traffic; and what perhaps struck the visitor most of all was the queues of poorly-dressed Muscovites patiently waiting outside the shops. By contrast, the Moscow of 1970 was a bustling city. Still shabby and ill-lit at night—this, together with the large number of men walking about in uniform, recalled London towards the end of the Second World War—but none the less a great capital, it now accommodated the diplomatic missions of close on a hundred countries, compared with the handful represented in Moscow seventeen years earlier. (Most of the staff of these embassies lived in a diplomatic ghetto, their working hours spent in seeking Soviet attention and Soviet information, and their leisure in fulfilling the obligations of a social round whose formal character seemed to be accentuated, as through osmosis, by the hierarchical structure of the society by which they were surrounded.) An occasion which typified Moscow's transformation was the reopening of the magnificent Hall of St George, the largest room in the Kremlin, its white walls decorated in gold with the names of Tsarist regiments and knights of the Order of St George, the highest military distinction in Tsarist Russia. This gleaming chamber provided the setting for the first lavish evening reception offered by the Soviet leadership for several years, to which all the ambassadors were invited, in honour of the visit paid to Moscow by Svoboda and Husak in October 1969.

By 1970 the Khrushchevian concept of the taxi had yielded to that of the private car; there were now a million on Soviet roads, with the factory built by Fiat[8] due to produce 660,000 private cars annually after its completion. The suburbs of the city now consisted of mile after mile of new blocks of flats, housing a population that had almost doubled in two decades. In the Arbat, the old quarter in the centre of the city, there were new buildings which would not look out of place in a Western capital. This new construction had already alarmed the Soviet conservationists; still more dignified old buildings were threatened by future plans. Nevertheless, large sums were being spent on restoring old monuments, both secular and religious, in Moscow, as elsewhere in the Soviet Union. The city teemed with tourists, Soviet and foreign. True, there were still queues to be seen, but the woollen shawls, quilted jackets and felt boots of earlier years had almost disappeared. In short, the people of Moscow had 'never had it so good'. This was the centenary of Lenin's birth; and Moscow, even if no longer acknowledged by all Marxists as the Third Rome, had by universal consent become the centre of one of the world's two super-powers.

If this had been all that five years of power had given the Soviet leaders who succeeded Khrushchev, they would have had reason to congratulate themselves. The very fact that they felt able to enter into major negotiations proved the new confidence that they felt in themselves and in the immense military power that they had built up since October 1964. But this was not the whole story.

9. The State of the Union

THE dilemma faced by the Soviet leadership, at the very moment when they may have expected to enjoy the fruit of their labours in the field of foreign relations, was both economic and political. It has been analysed in depth in *Kniga o sotsialisticheskoi democratii* by Roy Medvedev.[1] For him, as for Andrei Sakharov, the two sets of problems, in the economic and in the political field, are interdependent. Sakharov's book *Progress, Coexistence and Intellectual Freedom* includes this passage:

We are now catching up with the United States only in some of the old, traditional industries, which are no longer as important as they used to be for the United States (for example, coal and steel). In some of the newer fields, for example, automation, computers, petro-chemicals, and especially in industrial research and development, we are not only lagging behind, but are also growing more slowly . . . [2]

Coming half a century after the October Revolution and seven years after Khrushchev's boast at the XXIInd Party Congress, this was a devastating indictment, even though what its author dared to write in 1968 was on the same lines as an article published in the Moscow *Journal of World Economics and International Relations* in January 1973, which listed the chemical industry, automobile construction, several branches of mechanical engineering, computer technology, gas processing, pulp and paper, and a range of branches of light industries among those sectors of modern industry in which Western development had reached a higher technical level. What had gone wrong with the Soviet economy? A great deal, as was reported to the CPSU Central Committee on 15 December 1969, and—in guarded terms—to the Soviet public by *Pravda*[3] a month later; so much so that the XXIVth Party Congress, which should have been held in 1970, and the publication of the new Five-Year Plan were both postponed.

In order to understand why it was that Soviet economic problems came to a head at the end of the 1960s, we must go back to Stalin's decision, forty years earlier, to abandon Lenin's moderate New Economic Policy and to launch the Soviet Union on its race to become a great industrial power, a ruthless transformation largely financed by the Soviet peasantry, whose land was forcibly collectivized in order to provide cheap food for the workers in the swiftly growing cities. This extraordinary feat, directed entirely from Moscow, from which every decision was handed down (*spuskat'*), lasted under Stalin's rule for a quarter of a century, through the purges, the Second World War, and the reconstruction of the country that followed, to be summed up afterwards by a distinguished Polish economist[4] as a *sui generis* war economy—surely one of the greatest understatements in history.

A year after the XXth CPSU Congress, Khrushchev attempted to put new life into the Soviet economy by decentralizing it. In consequence, all but two of the specifically industrial ministries were eliminated, and instead 105 regional economic councils were established (later reduced to 47). In September

1965 his successors abolished these councils and restored the ministries in Moscow, but with a difference—the Economic Reform.[5] The new Soviet leadership took a whole year to decide the terms of this reform, whose execution Kosygin described to the Central Committee as unthinkable without significant worker participation in management. In the event the scope of the reform was modest; its success was limited; and a most important measure—the formation of regional or all-union corporations, operating on the basis of autonomous profit-making—was not finally approved until April 1973.[6] By the end of the Five-Year Plan, not only had the notoriously inefficient and wasteful Soviet system of agriculture achieved a far smaller increase in production than had been hoped, because it had been starved of the capital investments and the quantity of machinery laid down in the plan (as Brezhnev reported to the Central Committee in July 1970), but many key Soviet industrial products had failed to achieve their planned targets, even though the industrial output plan as a whole was fulfilled.[7]

How was it that Soviet industry could produce hundreds of SS-9 intercontinental ballistic missiles and put the *lunakhod* vehicle on the moon, and yet find it difficult to cover the Soviet Union with a chain of modern hotels (as was done in the space of a few years in the impoverished Italian *Mezzogiorno*)? In its article reporting the Central Committee meeting of December 1969, *Pravda* admitted that the key problem was an increase in productivity; the quantitative approach to the Soviet economy was no longer good enough; new methods and new decisions were required. This was true. But there were many other things that *Pravda* did not, or could not, say. Among these, six may be singled out. The first was the growing technological gap between East and West, which Sakharov described in the passage quoted above, and which was to be publicly admitted later within the Soviet Union. The second was the managerial gap. The reasons for both these gaps are complex. They became evident at a time when the pace of change in industrial and in management techniques in the West was so great that it amounted to a second Industrial Revolution. One of the essentials of the technological revolution—the ability of an industrial society to diffuse new technology swiftly through all sectors of its economy—is discouraged by the very nature of the Soviet system, partly for reasons of security. As for management, to the sheer size of the Moscow bureaucracy must be added what has been described by the Soviet critic as the greatest single obstacle: the absence not only in the political system, but also in the economy, of an effective mechanism for renewing management.[8] Third, in a non-market economy, a qualitative as opposed to a quantitative approach depends on its planners' ability to identify success indicators that will encourage a prompt response to demand: this is something that Soviet planners have found hard, even though the economic reform of 1965 modified the cult of gross output—the essence of Stalinist economics.[9] Fourth, the Soviet economy no longer had at its disposal the reserves of labour which—through a concentration of effort on key sectors of the economy—helped it to win its greatest successes in the past. (In the construction industry in September 1972, Kosygin revealed that the volume of investments immobilized in uncompleted projects had almost trebled in four years, to reach a total of 61.4 billion roubles.)[10] Fifth, the aspirations of the Soviet consumer were at last beginning to make themselves felt: for example, the meat shortage—the consequence of the deficiencies of Soviet livestock production—could in 1970 no longer be ignored. Finally, whatever the statistical doubts mentioned in an earlier chapter, it must be concluded that part of the strain imposed on the entire Soviet economy by the end of the 1960s was caused by the over-commitment of resources to its defence sector.

At the same time there was a profound political malaise in the Soviet Union. Just when their country's military power had grown to a size which, for example, enabled them to carry out the military intervention in Egypt in 1970, the Soviet leaders seemed to see themselves as the embattled defenders of Marxist-Leninist orthodoxy in the Kremlin, assailed alike by any new idea put forward within the boundaries of the Soviet Union, by the schismatic Chinese, by the reformist Czechoslovaks, and by the New Left in the West. The Soviet Communist Party showed no sign whatsoever of sympathy with the perpetrators of the Parisian *chie-en-lit*[11] of 1968. Marcuse was described as an ideologist of *petit-bourgeois* rebels and an old fool. At first sight it may seem strange to find the General Secretary of the CPSU devoting a whole paragraph of his report at the XXIVth Party Congress to an attack on a group of Marxist 'renegades' so disparate as Roger Garaudy, Ernst Fischer, the Italian 'Manifesto Group', and Teodoro Petkoff (formerly a member of the Venezuelan Communist Party), until one recalls that the heretic appears to the faithful to pose a greater threat than the infidel.[12] As if to break the monotony, the Soviet leadership decided to make a major event of Lenin's centenary year. Few of the thousands of words written and spoken about this extraordinary man in 1970 would have given him pleasure—certainly not *Pravda*'s misquotation of a passage from one of his works, which did not escape Chinese ridicule.

New ideas within the Soviet Union covered a wide spectrum. The connecting link was the conviction that scientific and industrial progress was inseparable from intellectual freedom. Sakharov emerged as the leader and co-founder of the first, unofficial, civil rights movement[13] in the Soviet Union. A group was formed of individuals resolved to see that the rights conferred on the citizen by the Soviet Constitution were observed to the letter. What these dissidents regarded as illegal acts began to be publicized in 1968 in the *Samizdat* news-sheet *Khronika Tekushchych Sobytii*—passed from hand to hand (like Akhmatova's lyric poems during the war)—and from 1970 in the *Ukrainian Herald*. Copies of these news-sheets regularly reached the West. The dissident movement[14] arose in protest against constraints which have been interpreted by some observers as neo-Stalinism. If by neo-Stalinism is meant the arrest of liberalizing tendencies, coupled with the fact that, after his total eclipse under Khrushchev, Stalin was partly rehabilitated in official statements (Soviet war films, for example, depicted him as a wise and benign leader), there is no need to quarrel with this assessment. But there can be no question of a return to historical Stalinism, if for no other reason than that this involved the physical destruction of the CPSU, including most of the senior members of the Soviet officer corps.*

---

* 'History never repeats itself—historians repeat themselves.' But if any analogy is to be drawn, the atmosphere of the reign of Tsar Alexander III (1881–94) offers a closer parallel than that of the Great Terror. For the important distinction between neo-Stalinists and moderate conservatives in the CPSU, see Medvedev, op. cit., pp. 55 ff.

Under the collective leadership, the literary freedom allowed under Khrushchev had been steadily eroded. True, Tvardovsky did what he could, so long as he was editor, to defend the literary journal *Novyi Mir* as a bastion of liberalism. Dimitri Shostakovich was allowed to compose as he wished: the performances of his tragic Fourteenth Symphony cannot have pleased the censors. And, after several years' delay, Moscow audiences were allowed to see Andrei Tarkovsky's politically ambivalent and intensely religious film *Andrei Rublev*. But what the regime found intolerable was the growing habit of publication in the West of works[15] banned in the Soviet Union. Thus, in February 1966 Andrei Sinyavsky and Yuli Daniel were sentenced to seven and five years' forced labour respectively for having published abroad, under pseudonyms, allegedly anti-Soviet writings; two years later Alexander Ginsberg and three others were convicted on charges based, *inter alia*, on their having compiled a White Book on the Sinyavsky–Daniel case; and in 1969 Solzhenitsyn, the heir to the great tradition of the Russian novel, all but one of whose major works have been published abroad, was expelled from the Writers' Union. In the same year Piotr Grigorenko, a dissident General who had espoused the cause of the Crimean Tartars (deported from their homes during the war by Stalin's order), was committed to a mental home—a way of dealing with political opposition which has since been repeated with other dissidents.[16]

The Soviet leadership could not accept the link between the solution of their country's economic problems and that of its political problems, in the sense advocated by men like Sakharov and Medvedev. To have done so would have led them down the path of pluralism, which the Czechoslovak reformers had followed and to which they themselves were adamantly opposed. But they were seized of the necessity to seek to meet the needs of the Soviet consumer and to close the economic gaps between East and West—technological and managerial. Their solution was a compromise: at home, an intensification of ideological discipline; abroad, an intimate economic cooperation with the Soviet Union's cold war adversary, the United States, and with its former enemies, Germany and Japan, which would, they hoped, make ultimately possible the development of the vast resources of Siberia, such as the Tyumen' oil-field and the copper deposits of

Udokan. A start in the direction of economic cooperation had already been made by one of the most forward-looking departments of the Soviet bureaucracy, the State Committee for Science and Technology, a new agency established under the collective leadership. It was this committee which was primarily interested in the conclusion of inter-governmental agreements for the exchange of scientific and technological know-how (a word now transliterated into cyrillics to form part of the Soviet vocabulary). The French Government led the way in 1965, followed by the Italian Government in 1966, and the British Government in 1970; by then Britain, France, and Italy all had considerable numbers of men helping to establish industrial plants in the Soviet Union, the biggest of which was the giant Fiat factory already mentioned. But at a time when Western firms were not yet allowed to open permanent offices for their representatives in Moscow, this was only a beginning.

The compromise solution was presented to the XXIVth Congress of the CPSU on 30 March 1971, by which time the Soviet leadership was also influenced by the events leading to the fall of Gomulka three months earlier. The supreme aim of the Party's economic policy was described to this Congress as the raising of the Soviet standard of living, the planned increase in real income per head of the population being almost one third. For the first time priority for consumer goods was written into the Five-Year Plan, although this did not mean that concern for heavy industry was being slackened (the planned increase was 42–46 per cent). Kosygin made it clear that 80–85 per cent of the entire planned increase in material income during the period of the plan would have to be derived from increased productivity. And Brezhnev added two interesting footnotes: the first at the Congress, when he stated that 42 per cent of the defence industry's output was used for civilian purposes, and the second in the course of an electoral speech delivered in a Moscow constituency on 11 June, when he said that socialism was powerful enough to secure both reliable defence and the development of the economy, although the Soviet economy would have advanced much more quickly, had it not been for large defence expenditures.[17]

In the field of foreign policy, the basic tasks were reiterated in

Brezhnev's report to the Congress, when he spoke of 'the great alliance of the three basic revolutionary forces of our day—socialism, the international workers' movement, and the peoples' national-liberation struggle'.[18] As is expected of a communist party leader on such an occasion, he described the general crisis of capitalism as deepening. (He was right: the dollar crisis finally erupted the following August, bringing the Bretton Woods international monetary system to an end.) The conduct of affairs with the United States was, he said, complicated by the 'frequent zigzags of American foreign policy', which he attributed to internal political manoeuvres. Nevertheless, he left the door ajar. Soviet policy towards the United States was based on the premise that an improvement in relations between the two countries was possible: 'our line of principle in our relations with capitalist countries, including the USA, is consistently and fully to realize in practice the principles of peaceful coexistence . . . '

The CCP's ideological-political platform on the fundamental questions of international relations and the world communist movement was condemned as incompatible with Leninism. The talks about the Sino-Soviet frontier questions were going slowly; if they were to be concluded successfully, a constructive attitude was required from both sides. The Chinese 'slanderous inventions' about Soviet policy, instilled into the Chinese people from Peking, were rejected. Nevertheless, he said, the CPSU and the Soviet Government were profoundly convinced that an improvement in relations between the Soviet Union and the Chinese People's Republic would correspond to the long-term interest of both countries; they were therefore ready to cooperate across the board not only in order to normalize relations, but also to restore good-neighbourliness and friendship; and they were certain that in the final reckoning this would be attained.

A last word had to be said about Czechoslovakia. The network of Soviet bilateral treaties with its Eastern European allies, taken together with the latter's treaties with each other, was described by Brezhnev as a comprehensive system of mutual commitments of a new, socialist type. Czechoslovakia had received international assistance in defending socialism against the forces of imperialism and counter-revolution in the exceptional circumstances of 1968, for reasons of 'class duty, loyalty to socialist—

internationalism, concern for the interests of our states and for the fate of socialism and peace in Europe'.

International communist attendance at the Congress must have satisfied the CPSU. Most Asian communist parties were represented; the North Vietnamese delegation repeated their 1966 practice of stopping in Peking on the way to Moscow, but they praised the CPSU, with only a passing reference to China. This time the Cuban delegate, President Dorticòs, described his country's friendship with the Soviet Union as indestructible and he thanked the Soviet Government for its aid to Cuba.

The policy approved by the XXIVth Congress was presented by the leadership to the Soviet people and to the world as a Programme of Peace. This programme took on a new dimension in the next three years, when Soviet foreign policy underwent changes that proved to be as important as those of 1956. It is arguable that these changes would have taken place in any case. But they were, at the least, accelerated when, a few weeks after the Congress had ended, the Soviet leadership suddenly found themselves outflanked by the Metternichian diplomacy of Henry Kissinger.

10. The Year 1970

Europe

So far the evolution of Soviet foreign policy has been treated thematically, each chapter covering a span of several years. The next four chapters will record, baldly, and with the minimum of comment, the conduct of Soviet foreign policy during the period 1970–3, in roughly chronological order, reproducing some of the kaleidoscopic effect that the swift unfolding of the events of these remarkable years presented to the leadership in the Kremlin.

In Europe, the critical date—from which everything that has followed in Europe stems—was 12 August 1970. Exactly thirty-one years to the day after the signature of the Soviet–Nazi Non-Aggression Pact,[1] the Soviet Union and the Federal Republic of Germany concluded the Treaty of Moscow. The preamble and the five articles that make up this brief document[2] formed the basis of what today amounts to a *de facto* European peace settlement. It was welcomed by most Europeans, Western as well as Eastern, although in the Federal Republic the Opposition remained unconvinced of the wisdom of the whole concept of Brandt's *Ostpolitik* and therefore opposed the treaty with all the means at their disposal. (The Bundestag did not ratify it until nearly two years later.) At first reading, this treaty may appear to be no more than the mutual renunciation of force and the recognition of existing frontiers in Europe, including those between the two Germanies and the western frontiers of Poland. Indeed, on his return to Bonn after signing the treaty, the Federal Chancellor claimed in a television statement that with this treaty nothing had been lost which had not been gambled away long before. This remark, however, referred to the German loss of what are known as the Western Territories of Poland: a loss rendered virtually irrevocable by the fourth paragraph of Article 3 of the treaty, under whose terms the German signatories 'regard' the Oder–Neisse line as 'inviolable now and in the future'. But the wording of the treaty is subtle. At least in the Federal Government's view, the specific reference in the preamble to the Adenauer–Bulganin Agreement of 1956 and the implied reference in Article 4 to the Paris Agreements of 1954, coupled with the opening words of Article 3, provided sufficient legal backing to preserve the right of the ultimate reunification of Germany in the text of the treaty, in spite of the commitment to regard the frontier between the two German Republics as inviolable. And to make doubly sure, Scheel simultaneously wrote a letter to Gromyko, published five days later, stating that the treaty did not stand in contradiction to the political aim of the Federal German Republic; this remained a peaceful European settlement in which the German people would regain its unity through self-determination.

The Federal German side made it clear to the Soviet side that their ratification of the treaty was conditional on a satisfactory conclusion of the Four-Power talks on Berlin, which had opened in March, and that the question of Allied rights and responsibilities with regard to Germany as a whole and to Berlin was not affected by the treaty. This second statement—together with Gromyko's oral acknowledgement of it—was recorded in an exchange of notes between the Government of the Federal Republic and the British, French, and US governments. The treaty was also regarded by both sides as part of a package of other related agreements, the first of which was the Treaty of Warsaw,[3] signed between the Federal Republic and Poland in December. And both sides saw it as the prelude to a large expansion of trade; in the preceding February the two governments had already concluded an agreement whereby West Germany was to supply the Soviet Union with large-diameter pipe in return for future delivery, by pipeline, of large quantities of natural gas: an important precedent for the future.

The Moscow Treaty, the cornerstone of Brandt's *Ostpolitik*, was for the Soviet Union a radical turning-point not only in its relationship with the Federal German Republic, but also in the post-war history of Europe.[4] Two years after accusing the Czechoslovaks of yielding to the blandishments of German revanchists, why did the Soviet Union itself enter a close bilateral relationship with the Federal Republic—and this (suspected at the time and evident in April 1971, when Ulbricht was succeeded by Erich Honecker) in the teeth of the opposition of the redoubtable East German communist leader, one of the few survivors of the old guard who had known both Lenin and Stalin personally? It is significant that two meetings of the Warsaw Pact Political Consultative Committee were held, one in Moscow a week after the signature of the Moscow Treaty and the other in Berlin on 2 December, both of which set the seal of all the Eastern European governments' approval on the treaty. The turn of the decade may have seemed to the Soviet leadership to have constituted one of Hegel's unique moments in history: Brandt's electoral victory in 1969; his government's signature of the Nuclear Non-Proliferation Treaty;[5] and Soviet recognition of their country's urgent need of German capital and technology. A *rapprochement* with the West Germans may well have been considered a different matter in the Kremlin provided that it was made clear to the world that the way to it lay through Moscow, not through the capitals of the Soviet Union's Eastern European allies. And it was not at all untypical of Soviet diplomacy that the news of the *rapprochement* was broken to the Soviet public with little advance preparation, nearly eight months after talks had begun in Moscow with the Federal Chancellor's personal representative, Egon Bahr, and three years after the beginning of the earlier round of talks between the two governments. Yet the fact remains that it was one of the most dramatic changes in post-war history, which cannot have been decided on by the Soviet leadership without much debate. Even now it is still too early to answer the Leninist question *kto kogo?*[6] The nearest historical parallel is the seventeenth-century Treaty of Westphalia; and it is to be hoped that the compromise enshrined in the Moscow Treaty of 1970 will be found by later historians to mark the beginning of the end of the twentieth-century European civil wars.

In the summer of 1970 the proposal for a European Conference took what proved to be a decisive step forward, when the two alliances reached the point of exchanging memoranda on a possible agenda. In the communiqué issued after their meeting in Rome in May, the NATO Foreign Ministers suggested that (subject to progress in the talks already being conducted, especially on Germany and Berlin) the subjects to be explored should include: 'the principles which should govern relations between states, including the renunciation of force' and 'the development of international relations with a view to contributing to the freer movement of people, ideas, and information and to developing cooperation in the cultural, economic, technical, and scientific fields as well as in the field of human environment'. In a separate declaration (from which the French abstained, as at Reykjavik) NATO ministers laid down certain principles for their proposed negotiations on mutual balanced force reductions. The NATO proposals, which were communicated to the Warsaw Pact governments by the Italian Government, in its capacity as host at the Rome meeting, met with a rapid response. In a memorandum approved in Budapest on 21–22 June, the Warsaw Pact foreign ministers suggested three questions for the agenda of a very early meeting: 'the safeguarding of European security and renunciation of the use of force or the threat of the use of force in inter-state relations in Europe; expansion on an equal basis of trade, economic, scientific, technical, and cultural ties, directed towards the development of political cooperation between the European states; and creation at the all-European conference of a body for questions of security and cooperation in Europe'. Although they continued to refer to the conference as all-European, they envisaged for the first time participation by the United States and Canada, as well as by both Germanies; and they also made another concession: the 'question of reducing foreign armed forces on the territory of European states . . . could be discussed in a body whose creation is proposed at the all-European conference, or in another form acceptable to the interested states'.[7]

These quotations make the difference in the objectives of the two alliances evident. What the NATO countries had in mind was the Brezhnev doctrine and an opening-up of Eastern Europe, including the Soviet Union, to Western ideas. The first objective was made still more explicit in the final communiqué of the Brussels ministerial meeting of December 1970, which listed three principles[8] which must in their view be respected as the basis for any genuine and lasting improvement in East–West relations in Europe. They were also well aware of the growing pressure in the US congress, stemming from Senator Mansfield's resolution, first moved in 1966, for a reduction of the 300,000 American troops deployed in the European theatre.

The Warsaw Pact countries' original objectives in calling for a conference in the sixties are clear enough. They are listed in the History of Soviet Foreign Policy as: first, recognition of frontiers, including the Oder–Neisse line and the frontier between the two Germanies; second, recognition of the German Democratic Republic as a sovereign state; and third, denial of all nuclear armament whatever to the Federal Republic of Germany.[9] Each of these aims had either already been attained, or was on the point of being attained, by the time of the Budapest meeting. Why then did the Soviet Government in particular continue to press for the holding of a European conference, as it did again in Berlin in the following December, after both Moscow and the Warsaw Treaties had been signed, when it must have realized that once a conference was convened, it could not expect to avoid discussion of subjects which were sensitive for the Soviet Union? The least convincing explanation is that the idea of a conference had achieved such momentum through the years, thanks largely to Soviet effort, that the Soviet Government could no longer reverse it, especially as some of its allies wanted the conference to further their own national interests. Soviet diplomacy was fully capable of having made such an abrupt change of course, even later than 1970, if the Soviet leadership had judged this to be in the national interest. If so, we are left with two explanations, which do not exclude each other. Soviet diplomacy is not only flexible; it is also formal. However an agreement involving the Soviet Union may be arrived at, it must be recorded in black and white at the end of the day. The Soviet leadership may therefore have wanted some kind of overarching agreement, witnessed by the signatures of all Europe, as well as by Western Europe's trans-Atlantic allies, which would directly or indirectly constitute general approval of the *de facto* settlement of post-war Europe. They may also have been searching for some kind of all-European framework, jointly guaranteed by both the Soviet and the United States governments, within which they and their Eastern European allies would be able to contain the enlarged Western European Community, a factor that must have begun to loom large in the planning of Soviet foreign policy at the very latest after Edward Heath's agreement with Pompidou during his visit to Paris in May 1971. Some colour is lent to this interpretation of Soviet motives by the proposal made in the communiqué[10] issued on 19 April 1974 in Warsaw by the Warsaw Pact ministers, calling for the establishment of 'a permanent security council for Europe aimed at building new relations between all states'.

It has been argued by some that the main Soviet object in holding a conference in the 1970s was part of a wider plan to remove the United States forces from Europe, and to secure for the Soviet Union due recognition as the most powerful country in Europe; once the American forces were out of the way, the rest of Europe would, in effect be 'Finlandized'. It is questionable whether an immediate withdrawal of all US forces from Europe would have been in the Soviet interest. In any case, the term 'Finlandization' does less than justice to the Finns, the one people of the former Russian Empire who have succeeded in remaining outside the borders of the Soviet Union ever since 1917. The 1948 Soviet–Finnish Treaty (renewed for another twenty years in 1970) is unique, as are Soviet–Finnish relations. It obliges Finland to defend its own territory in the event of an attack against the Soviet Union being directed across it: an echo of 1941.

In the course of 1970 the Soviet Union also completed its network of bilateral treaties with its allies by signing new treaties of friendship with Czechoslovakia and Romania, in May and July respectively. Whereas the latter was worded to take account of Romanian susceptibilities, the former reflected the Brezhnev doctrine. Its preamble described the 'support, strengthening, and protection of the socialist achievements of the people' as 'the common international duty of socialist countries'; under Article V of the treaty the parties undertook to take the necessary measures to this end; and in the words of the History of Soviet Foreign Policy,[11] the treaty reaffirmed the principles of the Bratislava Declaration of 3 August 1968, regarding the collective defence of socialism in any country of the socialist common-wealth. But at the very end of a year which must otherwise have given the Soviet leadership much satisfaction, this common-wealth was shaken once again, in Poland, where the government was overthrown—in the streets—for the second time in fourteen years.

In 1956, 'bread and freedom' was the demonstrators' slogan in Poznań. This time the issues at stake were chiefly economic—the mismanagement of the economy by the Gomulka regime, culminating in increases in price of essential food items, tactlessly introduced just before Christmas. The battles between strikers and police, reinforced by the army, that followed in the Baltic cities were so severe, (a total of 45 dead and over 1,000 injured was officially admitted),[12] that Gomulka was obliged to resign after over fourteen years as Party Secretary. He was swiftly succeeded by Edward Gierek, who rescinded his predecessor's economic measures, made concessions to the workers, and—so it was rumoured—received Soviet economic aid to help him meet his country's difficulties. Like Gomulka in 1956, Gierek both admitted the errors committed by the previous Party leadership and made it clear that there was no question of Poland seeking to break loose from the Soviet alliance. And unlike Dubcek, he not only succeeded in restoring a measure of popular confidence for the time being, but also reassured the Soviet Union that the rule of the Party would be upheld in Poland. Nevertheless, the Soviet leadership, however relieved they may have felt at the outcome of the Polish crisis, must have asked themselves how they would have reacted had it developed according to the Czechoslovak model. Poland lies athwart the lines of communication between the Soviet Union and its forces in East Germany. Another invasion, little more than two years after the invasion of Czechoslovakia, and only a few days after the conclusion of the Treaty of Warsaw with the Federal Republic of Germany, would have presented an appalling dilemma, which was to become actual ten years later.

Relations between the super-powers

Relations between the Soviet Union and the United States at the beginning of the decade could already be described as edging towards the 'middle ground of peaceful, if somewhat distant, coexistence . . . lying somewhere between the intimacy we cannot have . . . and the war there is no reason for us to fight'.[13] That this is how things seemed in the Kremlin is suggested by an article which appeared in the journal of the Soviet–USA Institute,[14] written by Lyudmila Gvishiani, a historian and daughter of the Soviet Prime Minister. The article consisted of an account of Bullitt's ill-fated mission to the Soviet Union in 1919, and quoted George Kennan's favourable verdict in his memoirs (that the peace proposals put to Bullitt by Lenin offered an opportunity that should not have been let slip by the Allied Powers). The chief interest of the article, however, lay in its opening and concluding paragraphs. The former described the principle of peaceful coexistence of states with different social systems as one of the basic principles of the Leninist foreign policy of the Soviet State, and went on to say that the 'realistic approach' of the Soviet Government and of Lenin personally appeared with the greatest clarity in the history of Soviet–American relations in March 1919. The article ended:

Lenin demonstrated the possibility of reaching agreement with capitalist countries, and first and foremost with the United States. To dogmatists the decisions of Vladimir Ilyich Lenin in the sphere of foreign policy might appear too bold, or, as G. V. Chicherin wrote, 'for all of us the sudden change from the early opinions of an underground revolutionary party to the political realism of a government in power was extremely difficult'.[15]

In the light of subsequent developments it is perhaps not fanciful to regard this as a prescription, inspired at high level, for a new Soviet–American relationship, on a basis of equality, half a century after Lenin's death. But who were the dogmatists—the Chinese, or opponents within the CPSU Politburo of such a relationship, or both? This the author did not explain.

Meanwhile both sides continued their SALT talks—in Vienna from mid-April to mid-July and again in Helsinki from 2 November to 18 December, after which they were adjourned until the following March. The Nuclear Non-Proliferation Treaty was brought into force in March 1970, when Great Britain, the Soviet Union, and the United States simultaneously deposited their ratifications. Over Indo-China, there could be no meeting of minds, particularly after the American–South Vietnamese 'incursion' into Cambodia in April–June (a similar operation was conducted in Laos in 1971). This followed the deposition *in absentia* of Prince Sihanouk, the Cambodian Head of State. It was the Chinese Government which acted as his host and sponsor in March, and in the following month joined with him in convening a summit conference of Indo-Chinese peoples. By comparison, Kosygin's denunciation of the incursion—although carried on television, the first such appearance by a Soviet Prime Minister within the Soviet Union—seemed a mild reaction; and the Soviet Union retained diplomatic relations with the new Cambodian Government for the next three and a half years.

In Latin America, both Chile and Cuba might have caused trouble between the two super-powers had the Soviet–US relationship still been as it was eight years before: Chile, when its electorate voted the Marxist leader of the Chilean Socialist Party, Salvador Allende, into power in September, and Cuba, when (following a visit by the Soviet Defence Minister to Havana) a Soviet submarine tender was anchored at Cienfuegos, accompanied by special barges for the storage of effluent from submarine reactors. As it was, the Soviet Government made no attempt to make Chile into a second Cuba, although it welcomed the new Chilean Government's nationalization measures and the swift re-establishment of Chilean diplomatic realations with Cuba; and the following May a modest Soviet–Chilean credit and technical assistance agreement was signed in Moscow,[16] which was visited by a Chilean trade delegation. The Soviet Government denied that it was building a base for ballistic-missile submarines in Cuba: an assurance that the US government appeared disposed to accept.

By far the most difficult area was the Middle East, which in 1970 replaced South-East Asia as the principal source of conflict in the world, despite the fact that the American involvement in Indo-China was to drag on for another three years. Here, while officially adversaries, the Soviet Union and the United States cooperated in practice, both in multilateral (together with the British and the French) and in bilateral talks, and notably by persuading Egypt and Israel to accept a cease-fire in August. In January, the Israeli Air Force's deep raids came within five miles of Cairo. Nasser could not be expected to survive a challenge on this scale. Following a hurried visit which he paid to the Soviet Union on 22 January, the Soviet Government took a major decision: to deploy in Egypt a force of about the same size as that despatched to Cuba in 1962—150 Mig-21J aircraft and over 300 mobile and modern SAM-3 (surface to air) missiles.[17] This force, together with six Soviet-controlled airfields, was led by a Soviet air defence commander, General V. V. Okunev, from his headquarters in Cairo.

The Soviet Government took pains to assure the other governments concerned that the role of this force, which was sent to Egypt by air, was purely defensive and that the Soviet objective in the Arab–Israeli dispute remained a political settlement. Unlike 1962, on this occasion Moscow's assurances were accepted, as was the fact that the Soviet Defence Ministry could hardly forego side-benefits for Soviet national interests conferred by the operation that they had mounted: extra naval facilities at Mersa Matruh and an increased ability to keep watch on the US Sixth Fleet and allied navies in the Mediterranean from the air. The operation was successful, at a cost of the lives of four Soviet pilots shot down on 30 July. After mid-April Israeli deep raids virtually ceased; and the air defence of Cairo, the Nile valley, and the Delta was thus assured. The Israeli Air Force, which had hitherto enjoyed undisputed command of the air, now began to suffer losses, and by taking advantage of the cease-fire in August, the Russians were finally able to establish a complete air defence both of the Suez Canal itself and of a narrow stretch of Israeli-occupied Sinai immediately to the east of it.

Meanwhile both advocates were exercising pressure on their clients, the United States Government by refusing, in March, to supply Israel with more Phantom aircraft, and the Soviet Government by applying pressure on Nasser in July, during another visit to the Soviet Union, to accept the American proposal for a cease-fire on the Canal and a military stand-still fifty kilometres either side of it. Unfortunately, the negotiations through Jarring, the UN mediator, that should have followed the cease-fire (which came into effect on 7 August), never got off the ground, because the Israeli Government withdrew from them in protest against the Soviet–Egyptian violations of the stand-still agreement. Had the Soviet Government resisted the temptation to move the SAMs forward to the Suez Canal in August, Jarring might have been able to make progress. As it was, an opportunity was missed, given the conciliatory statements made by both Golda Meir and Nasser before the cease-fire began. (Six months later, Soviet forces were withdrawn from the Canal, leaving the SAM-3 sites substantially in Egyptian hands.) However, during the Jordanian civil war in the following month, both Nasser and the Soviet Government exercised a moderating influence, the former on the Palestinians and the latter on the Syrian Government, which was persuaded to withdraw the armoured force that had crossed the Jordanian frontier.[18] An anxious moment passed; this final exertion may well have hastened Nasser's death; but the cease-fire between Egypt and Israel, originally intended to last ninety days, held good. Nasser was succeeded as President of Egypt by Sadat, who in the course of the next three years was to set his country on a new course and, in the process, to bring the super-powers—for a few hours—closer to a nuclear confrontation than they had been at any time since the Cuban missile crisis of 1962.

11. The Year 1971

The Middle East and the Mediterranean

ON paper, the Soviet relationship with the new Egyptian President began well. In May, four months after the opening of the Aswan High Dam, the financing of which had first been undertaken by the Soviet Government in 1958, Podgorny signed a treaty of 'unbreakable' friendship between the Soviet Union and Egypt,[1] which provided for even closer cooperation between the two governments than did the Soviet–Indian Treaty concluded three months later. But its military clauses were carefully balanced. Article 7 laid down:

in the event of the development of situations creating, in the opinion of both sides, a danger to peace or violation of peace, they will contact each other without delay in order to concert their positions with a view to removing the threat that has arisen or to the restablishing of peace;

while Article 8 stated that military cooperation, developed on the basis of 'appropriate agreements', would:

provide specifically for assistance in training the United Arab Republic military personnel, in mastering the armaments and equipment supplied to the UAR in order to strengthen its capacity, to eliminate the consequences of aggression as well as to increase its ability to stand up to aggression in general.

The phrase 'to eliminate the consequences of aggression' suggested the possible provision of more sophisticated offensive weapons by the Soviet Union than hitherto, while the phrases 'in the opinion of both sides' and 'appropriate agreements' seemed to safeguard the Soviet Union from being drawn into an adventure by Sadat, who had announced that 1971 was to be the Year of Decision.

Despite the treaty, it was a difficult year for the Russians in Egypt. Although Article 2 described Egypt as having 'set itself the aim of reconstructing society along socialist lines', it was in May that Sadat liquidated the pro-Soviet faction in Egypt, led by Ali Sabri. Worse still, soon afterwards the Sudan Government, which was being supplied with Soviet arms, executed the

Sudanese Communist Party leader, Abdel Khalik Mahgoub. (The Chinese profited from the quarrel which arose between the Russians and the Sudanese by signing a 34 million dollar aid agreement with the latter in August.) Already perhaps sensing something of what was to follow in Egypt in 1972, the Soviet Government reinsured elsewhere. In the course of 1971 they supplied Syria with aircraft and surface-to-air missiles, accompanied by military advisers. The first Soviet arms deal with the Lebanon was announced in November, and in the following month the Soviet Prime Minister visited Morocco and Algeria— Morocco's armed forces being then partly, and Algeria's wholly, supplied by the Soviet Union.

Although there were some anxious moments in the Arab–Israeli dispute, the cease-fire was maintained, amid a series of negotiations which were complicated by the fact that they were at times being simultaneously conducted by the Soviet and the US governments bilaterally; by the Russians with the Egyptians and by the Americans with the Israelis; and by Jarring with both the Egyptians and the Israelis. The idea which held the field at any rate in the earlier part of the year, was one which had first been floated by Moshe Dayan the previous October, namely that the Israelis should withdraw a certain distance from the Suez Canal, which would then be reopened by the Egyptians. The negotiations foundered; in November Sadat said that he would go to war by the end of the month; once again both the super-powers were able to exercise restraint on their clients; but the Soviet Union was to pay the price for this in 1972.

Europe

Notwithstanding the importance of the Soviet treaties with Egypt and India, by far the most significant agreement signed by the Soviet Government during the year 1971 was the Quadripartite Agreement on Berlin of 3 September. (The city was described as 'the relevant area' in the preamble and the first article of Part I of the agreement, in order to bridge the gap between the Soviet Government, mindful of its East German ally, and the other three governments.) The agreement,[2] which was expressly stated not to affect the Four Powers' quadripartite rights and responsibilities and their 'corresponding wartime and post-war agreements and decisions', was, like the Moscow Treaty, a compromise. It provided for unimpeded traffic between the western sectors of Berlin and the Federal Republic, for improved communications between these sectors and the rest of Berlin and the German Democratic Republic, and for the maintenance and development of the ties between the western sectors and the Federal Republic. Even though the western sectors of the city were not to be regarded as part of the Federal Republic, it was also agreed that the latter's government might perform consular services for permanent residents of the western sectors and might represent the interests of these sectors in international organizations and conferences; in return, the Soviet Union was authorized to establish a consulate-general in the western sector of Berlin.

In order to overcome the legal difficulty that the German Democratic Republic had not yet been formally recognized by the three Western signatories, or by the Federal German Government, the Quadripartite Agreement delegated the detailed arrangements for traffic and communications to be agreed by 'the competent German authorities'; and it was stated that these arrangements would be brought into force by a final quadripartite protocol when the latter had been concluded. These, broadly, were the legal niceties thanks to which the problem that had bedevilled East–West relations for twenty-three years was now in sight of solution. That the negotiations took eighteen months was, at least in part, the result of the opposition of the East Germans, whose object remained—as it is today—the *Abgrenzung** of the two Germanies.

The Berlin Agreement also opened the way for the first practical steps towards the holding of a European Conference. At their meeting held in Brussels in December, NATO ministers suggested four areas of discussion for an eventual meeting in Helsinki: 'questions of security, including principles governing relations between states and certain military aspects of security; freer movement of people, information and ideas, and cultural relations; cooperation in the fields of economics, applied science

* The concept of two German states, each with a completely different, irreconcilable, social system.

and technology, and pure science; and cooperation to improve the environment'.[3] And, following a remark about tasting the wine made by Brezhnev in a speech at Tbilisi in May (which perhaps helped to defeat the Mansfield amendment calling for US troop reductions), they also appointed Manlio Brosio, the former Secretary-General of NATO, to engage in exploratory talks about mutually balanced force reductions with the Soviet and other interested governments. To this offer there was no Eastern response; and there was no meeting in Helsinki for another year.

In 1971 Western and Eastern Europe each made what, at the time at any rate, seemed important advances towards closer unity. In the West, the enlargement of the European Economic Community was in sight. In the East, the COMECON Council approved in July its 'Complex Programme for the Development of Socialist Economic Integration', with a time-scale of fifteen years for its execution. The lengthy text of the programme made it clear at the outset that socialist economic integration is 'completely voluntary and does not involve the creation of supranational bodies; it does not affect questions of internal planning or of the financial and self-financing activity of organizations'. Given this restriction, which was essential for the Romanians (who had temporarily abstained from the previous year's decision to set up an Eastern European Investment Bank), integration meant the coordination by the member governments of their Five-Year Plans, through agreed decisions on product specialization, and implemented both by trade agreements for an equivalent period and by flows of capital, and in particular by the exchange of scientific and technological information between members. The basis of intra-COMECON trade remained the provision by the Soviet Union of long term supplies of raw materials in return for equipment manufactured by the Eastern European countries under specialization agreements.[4] But in deference to the smaller members of the organization, the programme included a schedule whereby the 1980 unit of COMECON accounting was to become mutually convertible at unified exchange rates. The organization's principal task was defined as being gradually to bring closer and level up the economic development of member countries.[5] By Western

European standards of the time the scope of this Eastern European economic programme was modest; and, in the event, was destined to be watered down still further.

Asia

The language of international relations is the poorer for its wealth of dead metaphors: bombshell, landmark, watershed. None of these is strong enough to describe the effect of the announcement on 15 July 1971, that the United States President intended to accept an invitation from Mao Zedong to visit Peking the following year, with the object of restoring normal relations between the United States and China. This decision, secretly prepared by Kissinger during a 49-hour visit to Peking, which he reached from Pakistan, paved the way for the lifting of the ostracism imposed on the People's Republic of China by the United States for a quarter of a century, and for China's assumption of its seat in the UN Security Council. It was particularly dangerous for the Soviet Union, for which the worst of all possible worlds would be a nuclear China and a unified Western Europe, backed by the United States, in alliance with Japan. The Soviet leadership lost little time in making the best of a bad job. In October of the same year, they invited Nixon to Moscow: the first visit ever paid to the Soviet Union by a US President.

The Soviet response was not as clear-cut as this invitation may suggest. Some idea of the Kremlin's thinking may be derived from a comparison of the speech made by Brezhnev to the XVth Soviet Trades Union Congress, five months after the invitation was announced, with an article that appeared in *Kommunist* in January 1972. Having reaffirmed the need for a collective security system in Asia—a proposal that he had first launched in 1969—Brezhnev spoke with caution about the new Sino-American relationship: only time, perhaps the near future, would show how matters really stood.[6] According to the Chinese, Sino-Soviet relations should be based on principles of peaceful coexistence. This was not a flattering proposal, since in Leninist theory peaceful coexistence applies only to countries 'with different social systems', i.e. between Marxist and non-Marxist countries. So be it, said Brezhnev; and went on to recall Soviet proposals to the Chinese for non-aggression and the settlement of the frontier questions.[7] As for the United States, the key to success in the SALT negotiations was the recognition by both participants of the principle of identical security of both parties and their readiness to abide by this in practice—a Soviet formulation of the American concept of essential equivalence?

There was not yet, however, any public recognition of the responsibilities imposed on the two super-powers by their ability to blow up the globe. On the contrary, the *Kommunist* article repeated to its readers the conventional warning against the ideas, current in the bourgeois scientific world, of super-power, convergence, and bridge-building. None the less, in February 1971 the Soviet Union joined with Great Britain and the United States in signing the Sea-bed Treaty; and on 30 September 1971 the United States and the Soviet Union signed two bilateral agreements, one to improve the hot line, which was converted to communication by satellite, and the other to reduce the risk of accidental nuclear war. Under the terms of the latter agreement, both sides agreed to do everything in their power to render harmless or destroy any nuclear weapon launched accidentally or without authority; each undertook to inform the other not only if its warning systems detected a possible missile attack, but also if warning or communication systems were themselves interfered with; and they committed themselves to give advance notice of any missile flights beyond their national territory.

On the ground in Asia, the Soviet leadership did all that they could to counter the Sino-American *rapprochement*. Whether they did indeed seek to influence some of their Chinese opposite numbers cannot be judged from Soviet sources; but two years later the Chinese Prime Minister publicly accused Mao Zedong's former right hand man, Lin Biao, of treason, plotting an armed *coup d'état* and fleeing 'surreptitiously . . . as a defector to the Soviet revisionists in betrayal of his party and country'.[8] (Lin Biao's death in an air crash in Mongolia in September 1971 was made officially public in August 1972.) Certainly, by the end of the year nearly a third of the two-year-old CCP Politburo had been dismissed by Mao. The number of Soviet divisions stationed along the Chinese frontier (including two in Mongolia) rose to forty-five (from fifteen in 1968)—more than the number in Central Europe. Soviet support for India was given legally binding form by the Indo-Soviet Treaty concluded in August 1971,[9] on the eve of the Indo-Pakistan War, in which China and the United States both found themselves backing Pakistan—unsuccessfully, as it turned out.[10] There was a delicate moment in December when elements of the US Seventh Fleet were sent to the Bay of Bengal and elements of the Soviet squadron were sent northward from the Indian Ocean; but the war ended quickly with an overwhelming Indian victory. Soviet support for India was also diplomatic: two vetoes of cease-fire resolutions in the Security Council, where the representatives of the world's two great communist powers at once became engaged in a slanging match. As a Soviet commentator claimed, 'events in the Indian sub-continent led to the first joint defeat of the USA and China in the struggle with the national-liberation movement'.[11]

The Indo-Soviet Treaty looked like the first link in the Soviet system for containing Chinese power in Asia, which the Russians adopted just as the Americans were in the process of giving it up. (The number of US troops in Vietnam was halved in the course of 1971.) Its preamble affirmed both sides' belief in the principles of peaceful coexistence and of cooperation between states with different political and social systems. Could this have been designed to justify whatever agreements the Soviet Union intended to conclude with the United States in the following year? It was, however, balanced by Article 10, in which the parties declared that they 'shall not undertake any commitment, secret or open, towards one or more states incompatible with the present treaty'. In essence, the treaty provided India with a Soviet umbrella against China for as long as India chose to stay out of the nuclear club: under the terms of Articles 8 and 9 respectively, each party solemnly declared that it would not enter into or participate in any military alliances directed against the other, and undertook to:

refrain from giving any assistance to any third party taking part in an armed conflict with the other party. In case any of the parties is attacked or threatened with attack, the High Contracting Parties will immediately start mutual consultations with a view to eliminating this threat and taking appropriate effective measures to ensure peace and security for their countries.

The message to China was clear enough.

12. The Year 1972

China

THE year 1971 had been a transitional one for Soviet foreign policy. At the outset of 1972—the year in which Peking and Moscow were, each in turn, visited for the first time by the President of the United States—Nixon said: 'I believe in a world in which the United States is powerful. I think it will be a safer world and a better world if we have a strong, healthy United States, Europe, Soviet Union, China, Japan, each balancing the other, not playing against the other, an even balance.'[1] The concept in Washington of the structure of world power emerging in the late twentieth century almost resembled the nineteenth-century concert of the great powers. Nixon visited China from 21 to 28 February only a few weeks after the American rearguard action, fought in New York and many of the world's capitals, in a final attempt to retain Taiwan's seat in the United Nations. The joint communiqué[2] consisted partly of points agreed by both sides and partly of statements of each side's position on the Taiwan question. The Chinese categorically described Taiwan as a province of China; its liberation was a Chinese internal affair; and they were opposed to concepts such as the two Chinas and an independent Taiwan. The Americans acknowledged that 'all Chinese on either side of the Taiwan Strait maintain that there is but one China and that Taiwan is a part of China'; they affirmed as their ultimate objective the withdrawal of all US forces and military installations from Taiwan; meanwhile they would reduce them progressively, as tension in the area diminished. Both sides agreed to conduct their relations on the basis of the Five Principles;[3] neither would seek hegemony in Asia and the Pacific; each was opposed to efforts by any country or group of countries to establish such hegemony; major countries should not divide up the world into spheres of influence; and the Chinese declared that

China would never be a super-power, and that it opposed hegemony and power politics of any kind. Nixon's visit did not 'change the world',[4] not did it quite achieve its aim of normalizing relations between the United States and China (liaison missions were exchanged between the two countries in 1973). But it remains a remarkable feat.

The Soviet Union

This done, Nixon visited the Soviet Union from 22 to 30 May. Any doubt that by May 1972 the Soviet leadership had reached the conclusion that they must agree, at the highest level, the framework of a new Soviet–American understanding, was removed by the welcome that they gave the US President in Moscow, in spite of his decision (announced only a fortnight previously) to mine seven North Vietnamese ports and to attack supply routes from China to Vietnam. Of the Soviet–American bilateral agreements concluded in 1972, by far the most important were the Treaty on the Limitation of Anti-Ballistic Missile Systems (ABMs), the interim agreement (lasting five years) on certain measures with respect to the limitation of strategic offensive arms, both signed during Nixon's visit, and the three-year grain agreement, signed in Washington on 8 July.[5]

The first of the SALT agreements was clear, the second less so. It will be recalled that one of the major destabilizing factors in the nuclear strategic equation by the end of the 1960s was the prospective deployment by both the super-powers of ABM systems. Under the terms of the treaty limiting such systems, each side was permitted to deploy them in two areas only: one centred on its capital and the other, at its own choice, containing some part of its ICBM force. Launchers so deployed must be capable of firing one missile with one warhead only; they must be static, and they must be land-based. These conditions, coupled with restrictions on the associated radar systems, meant that the Soviet Union could expand the existing ABM defences of Moscow to a total of 100 launchers, and also construct another site for the defence of some of its ICBMs.

The interim agreement was a holding operation, designed to set the ring for the second round of SALT talks, which were resumed in Geneva—their venue from then on—in November. Under its terms, each side was permitted a total of ICBM and SLBM launchers based on the number either operational or under construction on 1 July and 26 May respectively, although both sides were allowed to modernize and replace these launchers, subject to certain conditions. Quantitatively, this agreement sanctioned what had in the previous three years become a marked Soviet superiority: about 1,530 operational ICBMs (with another 90 under construction) as against 1,054 American ICBMs; and about 560 operational SLBMs (with another 245 under construction) as against 656 American SLBMs.[6] The Soviet Union had achieved an equally marked superiority in megatonnage, each of its 290 SS–9s having an estimated warhead yield of between 20 and 25 megatons, as opposed to the *Titan* 2's estimated yield of between 5 and 10 megatons. In order to assess the balance of the interim agreement, it is important to bear in mind not only that in strategic nuclear weapons systems accuracy matters more than megatonnage, but also that the agreement mentioned neither strategic bombers—an arm in which the US Air Force had retained its superiority—nor the so-called forward based systems (FBS)—US strike aircraft based on the territory of the United States' allies or on aircraft carriers stationed in the Mediterranean Sea and the Pacific Ocean—between two and three thousand in all—capable both of carrying out conventional attacks and of delivering nuclear warheads on Soviet targets.[7] Moreover, the ceilings on permitted numbers of American missile launchers were based on programmes laid down at the outset of the Kennedy Administration and had been accepted by successive US Administrations since 1967. Five years later, by which time both governments were probably spending about twenty-five billion dollars annually on strategic armament,[8] the US Government was already concentrating its efforts on quality rather than on quantity. In consequence, by 1973 US *Poseidon* submarines and *Minuteman–3* ballistic missiles were being deployed as quickly as possible, equipped with MIRVs, capable of doubling the number of Soviet targets at which, at any rate in theory, American missiles could strike by mid-1977.[9] (MIRVs, which are unidentifiable by satellite, were not mentioned in the interim agreement, which was signed at a time when they had not yet been deployed by the Soviet Union.) And in the same year the US Senate approved the construction of the *Trident* submarine, at a cost then estimated at 1,300 million dollars (since far exceeded). Carrying 24 missiles, each with 10–14 independently targetable warheads with a range of 6,000 miles, it was designed to be both faster and quieter than previous submarines and would have a displacement larger than that of a British cruiser of the same date.

The passage of the interim agreement through the US Senate was not an easy one. Ratifications were finally exchanged by the two governments in October, after the Senate had adopted an important amendment, submitted by Henry Jackson, urging the President to seek a further treaty with the Soviet Union—i.e. in SALT II—'which would not limit the United States to levels of intercontinental strategic forces inferior to the limits provided for the Soviet Union'.

The significance of the two strategic arms agreements of May 1972 was described by Soviet writers as difficult to overestimate.[10] Even though they did not mark a breakthrough towards the kind of disarmament to which both super-powers had been committed since their ratification of the Nuclear Non-Proliferation Treaty over two years previously, they did mark a beginning; and this must be assessed against the new kind of language used in the twelve points of the Joint Declaration on Basic Principles of Relations between the USA and the USSR, which formed part of the agreements signed in Moscow. In this declaration the two sides agreed that in the nuclear age there was no alternative to conducting their relations with each other on the basis of peaceful coexistence; they attached 'major importance to preventing the development of situations capable of causing a dangerous exacerbation of their relations'; they would therefore do their utmost to avoid military confrontations and to prevent the outbreak of nuclear war; they would always exercise restraint in their relations with each other and would be prepared to negotiate and settle differences by peaceful means; efforts to obtain unilateral advantage at the expense of the other, directly or indirectly, were inconsistent with these objectives; and the prerequisites for maintaining and strengthening peaceful relations between the USA and the USSR were 'the recognition of the security interests of the parties based on the principle of equality and the renunciation of the use or the threat of force . . . '

These principles of parity were reaffirmed by Nixon in his speech at the Kremlin banquet given in his honour on 22 May, when he said that there was no longer such a thing as security in a preponderance of strength; the nuclear great powers had a solemn responsibility to exercise restraint themselves in any crisis, to take positive action to avert direct confrontation, and to exercise a moderating influence on other nations in conflict or crisis.[11] As if to play down the closeness of the special relations between the two super-powers implied by such language, he declared in his televised broadcast from the Kremlin on 28 May that it was not their aim to establish a condominium. And the joint communiqué ended by affirming that the Moscow agreements and understandings were not in any way directed against any other country.

Unlike the strategic agreements, the two commercial agreements, one covering the Soviet purchase of American grain and the other setting up a Joint Trade Commission, could be assessed in hard cash. Of these, the former came into immediate effect, whereas the Trade Commission, which held its first meeting in Moscow in July, could not exert its full impact on the Soviet–US economic relationship until Congress was willing to pass the legislation required to grant the Soviet Union most-favoured-nation treatment. Nevertheless, the Commission succeeded in settling the long outstanding Soviet Lend-lease debt to the United States; and the Trade Agreement contemplated that the volume of trade during its three-year period would be at least three times as much as over the 1969–71 period, to an aggregate of at least 1,500 million dollars; American business was on the point of making an assault on the Soviet market, which had previously been largely a West European and Japanese preserve.

The dimensions of the grain agreement were a measure of the Soviet crop failure. During the three-year period beginning on 1 August 1972 the Soviet Union was to buy at least 750 million dollars' worth of US grown food grains, at least 200 millions' worth of which was shipped in the first year. The US Government undertook to make available a line of credit not exceeding 500 million dollars for these purchases, repayable in three years from the date of delivery. This agreement, taken in conjunction with the conclusion six days later of a five-year agreement with the Soviet Government by the Occidental Petroleum Company, for the joint development of Soviet oil and natural gas, seemed to open up a prospect of a longer term economic relationship between the two super-powers.

One subject in the joint communiqué on which the two sides were able only to record their agreement to differ was Vietnam. Did the Soviet leadership use their influence in Hanoi on behalf of the US Government in the closing stages of the latter's painful negotiations with the North Vietnamese? The American bombing was halted while Podgorny visited North Vietnam in June; in August the last US combat unit was withdrawn from Vietnam; and by December (although it did not appear so at the time, when American bombing of the North was temporarily resumed) the end was at last in sight. In his televised address to the American people during his visit to the United States a year later, Brezhnev spoke of Soviet–US cooperation in halting the war in Vietnam.[12] Just how much ice Soviet representations cut with a government that had already held out so long,[13] and with the Chinese offering Hanoi free military equipment and materials for 1973, is questionable. In any case by January 1973, when Kissinger finally reached agreement with Le Duc Tho in Paris, the sigh of relief in the Kremlin must have been as deep as in every other country.

Japan

The political pattern that had been familiar in post-war Asia was beginning to break up. The immediate[14] response of Kakuei Tanaka, the new Japanese Prime Minister, to the American announcement of 15 July 1971 had been to reinsure both with China and with the Soviet Union: in the words of the Japanese Foreign Minister, Japan must adapt to the multipolar age and pursue a foreign policy divorced from ideology. In September 1972 Tanaka visited Peking. The Japanese Government expressed its 'respect' for the Chinese position on Taiwan; the Chinese Government renounced its claims to war reparations; and the two governments re-established diplomatic relations. (In consequence Taiwan broke off diplomatic relations with Japan.) In October the Foreign Ministers of Japan and the Soviet Union began to discuss the negotiation of a peace treaty in Moscow.[15] Although the Japanese Government had earlier agreed to study positively the Soviet proposal for an Asian collective security system (during a visit paid to Tokyo in January by Gromyko), the only territorial concession that the Soviet Government felt able to offer Japan, no doubt with Chinese territorial claims in mind, was the return of two of the four Kurile Islands occupied by the Soviet Union in 1945—not enough for Japan, for whom half a loaf was unacceptable. This deadlock did not prevent a rapid expansion of trade. This had already increased in both directions from a mere 40 million dollars in 1958 to 822 millions in 1970; a new trade agreement concluded in 1971 had provided for an increase of nearly double over the next five years; and in June 1972 the two governments seemed to be nearing agreement in principle to engage in immense projects, the joint development of the Tyumen' oil field in Western Siberia and other areas, including Sakhalin, possibly with American participation, and natural gas resources at Yakutsk.

Japanese–Soviet participation in projects such as the Tyumen' development was viewed with suspicion by the Chinese Government, because this would in their view increase the potential Soviet military threat to China. By the end of the year, during which there had been another alleged clash on the Sino-Soviet border (this time between Kazakhstan and Xinjiang, in which five Soviet border guards were believed to have been killed), China had built up, or was on the point of building up, a nuclear *force de frappe*[16] directed against the Soviet Union: 20–30 MRBMs probably deployed, mainly in north-eastern China, and an IRBM developed and possibly deployed with a range long enough to reach Moscow. No Siberian agreement was to be concluded between Japan and the Soviet Union for another two years.[17]

Europe

This was year of fruition, both within Western Europe and between West and East. On 22 January the new members of the

European Economic Community signed the Treaty of Accession in Brussels; on 18 October Great Britain ratified this treaty; on 19–20 October the heads of the Western European Governments, meeting in Paris, set themselves the goal of Western European unity by the end of the decade; and on 1 January 1973 the Treaty of Accession came into force.

It was against this background that on 17 May the Federal German Bundestag finally approved the ratification of the Moscow and Warsaw Treaties; on 26 May the treaty on traffic questions between the two Germanies was signed in East Berlin, thus opening the way for the foreign ministers of the Four Powers to sign the final Quadripartite Protocol of their 1971 Agreement on Berlin, which then came into force; and the West and East German governments went on—in December—to sign their Basic Treaty on relations between the two countries, which was signed in East Berlin.[18] Like the Moscow Treaty, from which this whole network of treaties stemmed, this agreement was a *de facto* compromise, which did not purport to settle the German problem *de jure*; indeed the rights and responsibilities of the Four Powers (who alone are legally entitled to bring about a *de jure* settlement) were expressly affirmed by both sides. Its most important practical consequences were threefold: preservation for the German Democratic Republic of its privileged position under the European Economic Community's Protocol on inter-German trade, whereby East German exports to West Germany are excluded from the EEC common tariff; the exchange of permanent missions—not described as embassies—between the two states; and application by both for membership of the United Nations (which they finally entered in September 1973).

Towards the end of the year the two conferences that had formed the subject of so many communiqués issued by the NATO Alliance and the Warsaw Pact, at last entered the phase of practical preparation: the Conference on European Security and Cooperation (CSCE) at the level of heads of mission in Helsinki, in November; and in the same month—following Kissinger's discussions in Moscow two months earlier—seven NATO countries invited five Warsaw Pact countries (the USSR, Poland, Czechoslovakia, Hungary, and the German Democratic Republic) to preparatory talks on Mutual Balanced Force

Reductions on 31 January 1973.[19] On 30 November, in a speech[20] delivered during a visit to Hungary, Brezhnev declared his belief that it would be possible to solve the problem of reducing armed forces and armaments in Europe, and in his address to a joint session of the CPSU Central Committee and the Supreme Soviet, on the occasion of the fiftieth anniversary of the formation of the Soviet Union, he raised for the first time the possibility that COMECON and the EEC might cooperate.

The Third World

Soviet multilateral diplomacy was impelled in 1972 both by the momentum which it had gathered during the two previous years and by the Soviet understanding with the United States. In March, the Soviet delegate to the Geneva Disarmament Conference presented a draft treaty banning chemical weapons; in April, the convention banning the production or possession of biological weapons was opened for signature in London, Moscow, and Washington; and in May, the Sea-bed Treaty banning the location of arms on the ocean floor was brought into force by the ratifications of Britain, the Soviet Union, and the United States. But in the Third World the Soviet leadership found their traditional policy hard to reconcile with this new understanding. In the Middle East,[21] Egypt became a test case. Having failed to make 1971 his Year of Decision, Sadat paid two visits to Moscow in February and April 1972, doubtless in the hope of securing arms that would enable Egypt to 'eliminate the consequences of aggression' as defined in Article 8 of the Soviet–Egyptian Treaty of May 1971. The Soviet Defence Minister visited Egypt in May. The Soviet–American agreements concluded in that month induced a mood of despair in Egypt. On 18 July Sadat demanded the withdrawal of all Soviet military advisers and experts, estimated to number about 17,000. The Soviet Government took this blow (the forerunner of Sadat's decision, nearly two years later, to adopt a policy of 'positive neutrality' between the super-powers) on the chin. Within a fortnight the withdrawal had substantially been completed; only a few hundred Soviet advisers were thought to have remained; and the Soviet Union lost the use of Egyptian airfields, although their Mediterranean naval squadron retained some facilities on the northern Egyptian coast, for the time being.

The Soviet response was to reinforce success further north. Soviet naval activity along the Syrian coast increased; the return of Soviet-trained military to Syria was accelerated; further arms were delivered; and a SAM-3 system was brought into operation. On 9 April the Soviet Prime Minister had visited Iraq to sign a fifteen-year Treaty of Friendship and Cooperation.[22] As in the Egyptian model, the friendship was unbreakable. The only military commitment was cautious, being to the effect that each side would assist the other in strengthening its defences and that they would coordinate their positions in the event of a threat to peace. The Iraqi armed forces had been largely dependent on Soviet arms since 1963 and wholly so since 1969. Soviet arms supplies were now increased; and a few SAM-3 sites were brought into operation by the end of the year. Equally important, the Soviet Union undertook to help to distribute oil from the Iraq Petroleum Company field at Kirkuk, which the Iraqi Government had at last nationalized on 1 June, and to bring the North Rumaila oil field into large-scale production (Soviet imports of oil from Iraq appeared for the first time in the statistics of Soviet foreign trade in 1972, published one year later). This tightening of Soviet-Iraqi relations suggested that the Soviet Government was seeking to make the Gulf, from which British troops had been withdrawn at the end of 1971, a new focus of its policy in the Middle East. Diplomatic relations had already been established with Kuwait, although not yet with the Union of Arab Emirates that had been formed after the British withdrawal. The Soviet Union also needed to remain on good terms with Iran and in October the Shah, while on a visit to Moscow, signed a fifteen-year treaty of economic cooperation and trade.

The Soviet dilemma in the Third World was presented to the Kremlin personally by the leaders of the two Latin American Marxist governments, those of Cuba and Chile, both of whom visited Moscow in December 1972, in order to seek financial aid. The Soviet answer to their requests for aid was given in blunt terms: to Cuba, a great deal, to Chile, very little. Cuba had five months earlier become a full member of the COMECON, thus qualifying—like Vietnam—for aid within the socialist common-

wealth. By any standards the terms of the deal[23] secured by
Castro were generous: deferment of the repayment of the Cuban
debt (estimated at nearly three billion dollars, excluding military
aid) until 1986, after which it would be repaid free of interest;
Soviet credits to cover Cuban trade deficits in 1973–6, also to be
repaid after 1986 without interest; and a 330 million dollar
development loan, to be repaid at a low rate of interest after 1976.
The Russians also agreed to buy Cuban sugar and nickel for the
rest of the decade at prices well above the world prices then
obtaining.

The joint communiqué[24] issued after Allende's visit to the
Soviet Union could hardly have offered a greater contrast. It had
much to say about the two governments' identity of views on the
problems of the rest of the world and little about either Chile itself
or Latin America—a recognized Moscow method of dealing
politely with a distinguished visitor who has not been granted
what he hoped for. Having made it clear early in his presidency
that he would not accept a Soviet military presence in Chile,
Allende did not seek military aid. But by the end of 1972 he was
in desperate financial straits, with agricultural production
lowered in the wake of the Chilean agrarian reform, and inflation
already soaring at a rate of 160 per cent per annum. (The World
Bank, the Export-Import Bank, and the Inter-American
Development Bank had all suspended lines of credit to Chile,
mainly because of the Chilean Government's decision to
nationalize, without compensation, US copper interests in Chile.)
Having received Soviet trade credits the previous June worth 260
million dollars and obtained Soviet agreement to import 130,000
tons of Chilean copper (despite the fact that the Soviet Union is a
net exporter of copper itself), Allende was believed at the time[25]
to have come to Moscow in search of 500 million dollars in hard
currency loans. The paragraph in the joint communiqué relating
to Soviet aid was not explicit, referring to Soviet agreement to
extend aid to Chile for a number of stated purposes, but subject
to the conclusion of 'corresponding agreements' reflecting the
'concrete measures for implementing this agreement'. All that
Allende seems to have received by way of immediate help was 30
million dollars' worth of credit for Soviet deliveries of food and of
cotton for the textile industry, and agreement to reschedule the

repayment of Chile's debt to the Soviet Union, amounting to 103 million dollars.

Once bitten, twice shy; after the Cuban experience, the Soviet leadership did not, as *Le Monde* gently put it, consider that the Chilean experiment should be defended by all available means. A Soviet apologist for his government's treatment of Allende—the CPSU Central Committee responded to the military *coup d'état* that overthrew his government with no more than a brief expression of sympathy—would no doubt recall the fact that, instead of heeding the economic advice given him by the Chilean Communist Party, Allende followed the ruinous path preferred by the extremists of his own, socialist, party. Yet if he had accepted communist advice and thus strengthened his claim to Soviet support (which even then would have had to be on a huge scale in order to keep Allende's regime afloat), would this claim have been met, given the Soviet experience in Cuba and the new Soviet understanding with the United States?[26] As it was, the award of the Lenin Peace prize, although a compliment to a septuagenarian socialist, cannot have been much consolation to Allende as a president who needed far more than that in order to stay in power, or, as it turned out, to stay alive. (He committed suicide after being deposed by the Chilean armed forces on 11 September 1973.)

So ended 1972, a year of great change for the international status of the Soviet Union, now formally acknowledged by the world's first super-power as its equal: a change that was to be reflected in the following spring by the first new formulation in the doctrine of Soviet foreign policy for nearly two decades.

13. The Year 1973

THIS year began looking as though it would become the *annus mirabilis* of the post-war period. Half-way through its course, this promise seemed almost fulfilled. The year ended not only on a note of political uncertainty, but with events that marked the beginning of the deepest economic recession since the 1930s.

At the Moscow summit meeting in 1972 Brezhnev had accepted Nixon's invitation to visit Washington in the following year. This visit was preceded by major developments in Europe, including the first visit ever paid to the Federal Republic of Germany by the General Secretary of the Soviet Communist Party. By way of preparation, on 27 April 1973 the CPSU Central Committee took two major decisions. The first of these was to set the seal of the Committee's formal approval on a foreign policy that had become more and more identified with Brezhnev personally. The second was to make the first important changes in the composition of the Party Politburo for eight and a half years. Two members of the Politburo were dropped: Voronov and Shelest, the latter having already been removed a year before from his powerful post as head of the Ukrainian Communist Party (perhaps because he was opposed to receiving Nixon, just as he had allegedly been the leader of the hawks over Czechoslovakia in 1968). The three newcomers were Andrei Gromyko, the Foreign Minister, Marshal Andrei Grechko, the Defence Minister, and Yuri Andropov, head of the KGB from 1967–82. None of the holders of these three offices would normally qualify for membership of the Politburo. The last time that any of the incumbents had done so had been in the 1950s; only one previous Soviet Foreign Minister had been a member— Molotov, whom Gromyko succeeded as Foreign Minister in 1957. Brezhnev was thus able to embark on his two delicate missions in the summer backed both by the maximum of departmental expertise concentrated inside the Politburo and by a fresh mandate of the Central Committee of the CPSU.

This mandate was expressed in a resolution, to which the Soviet press gave especial publicity, entitled 'On the international activity of the Central Committee of the CPSU regarding the realization of the decisions of the XXIVth Party Congress.' Two years earlier Congress had approved Brezhnev's Peace Programme. The 1973 resolution began by describing the Party's international policy in conventional terms: active and thrusting, relying on Soviet strength, power, and authority. Although imperialist aggression against Vietnam had been brought to a halt, constant watchfulness was required against any intrigues of the aggressive, reactionary circles of imperialism; in particular, the legal rights of the Arab peoples in their struggle against imperialist aggression must be supported. So far, no change. But the nub of the resolution was its emphasis on the principle of peaceful coexistence 'as a general rule' of relations between states with different social systems.[1] From this rule stemmed the switch from cold war to *détente* and the need to 'ensure that the favourable changes achieved in the international sphere should acquire an irreversible character'. That the inclusion of this phrase 'as a general rule' in the resolution was an important doctrinal innovation, was made clear by its appearance among the officially approved slogans for the October Revolution celebrations six months later. On 26 October Brezhnev described the principle of peaceful coexistence as 'gradually becoming converted into the generally accepted rule of international life'.[2]

Europe

The emphasis on peaceful coexistence as a general rule in this declaration, and the link between foreign and domestic policy, were both pointed up by Brezhnev during his visit to the Federal Republic the following month, when he declared, in the course of his televised address to the German people, published in full by *Pravda* on its front page on 22 May: 'our peace-loving foreign policy is the expression of the very essence of our society, the expression of its deep internal needs . . . our aim is to ensure that the Soviet people live better tomorrow than they do today.' The chief fruit of Brezhnev's visit to Bonn, which lasted from 18 to 22 May,[3] was economic; a ten-year agreement on the development of economic, industrial, and technological cooperation between the Soviet Union and the Federal Republic. (An agreement on cultural cooperation was also signed.) Six months previously the two sides had signed a declaration of intent concerning construction of an integrated steelworks using the direct reduction process of the Kursk ore-fields in central Russia, the largest Soviet-West German project so far; a further long-term agreement for the supply of Soviet natural gas to the Federal Republic had been signed in 1972. The total cost of the steelworks project was estimated at DM3,000 million, including orders from West German firms worth at least DM2,000 million, to be financed by long-term credits granted by a West German consortium, which were to be repaid by the supply to West Germany of the product

of the plant. The joint statement[4] issued on 21 May welcomed the
current negotiations on industrial projects, including the Kursk
steelworks; agreed to promote cooperation in the development of
advanced technology and the creation of new production facilities
in the USSR: while, for its part, the Federal Government
declared its interest in receiving large supplies of crude oil from
the Soviet Union.

At the opening banquet on 18 May, the Federal Chancellor
made it clear where he stood politically: 'the Federal Republic is
a member of the Atlantic Alliance. It is embedded in the
community of Western Europe, which has now grown beyond the
Common Market.' As for Berlin, it was still not all plain sailing.
Although both the Ten-Year Agreement and the Cultural
Agreement contained clauses applying them to West Berlin 'in
accordance with the Four Power Agreement of 3 September
1971', the joint statement referred to a detailed exchange of views
on questions concerning that agreement, and the two sides agreed
that strict observance and full application of the agreement were
essential to lasting *détente* in Central Europe and to the
improvement of relations 'between the states concerned', especially between the Federal Republic and the Soviet Union.
Speaking in the Bundestag afterwards, the Federal Chancellor
denied that there was any question of altering the Four Power
Agreement on Berlin, or of giving it a special interpretation for
the Federal Republic's bilateral relationship with the Soviet
Union. It had become clear as the result of Brezhnev's visit that
practical difficulties existed between the two governments regarding the application of the agreement, which must be, and indeed
could be, solved, by using the facilities offered by the agreement.
Brandt went on to say that the situation in Berlin was the
touchstone of West German-Soviet bilateral relations, and that so
far as economic relations were concerned, no negotiations on
specific projects had been conducted or decisions taken.
The difficulty to which Brandt referred concerned the precise
nature of the consular representation of West Berlin to be undertaken by the Federal German authorities under the terms
of the 1971 Agreement. This was not resolved until November, when a compromise was agreed in Moscow between
the Federal German and Soviet Foreign Ministers.[5]

In June, after five months of preparatory talks in Vienna, the NATO and Warsaw Pact governments concerned agreed to begin negotiations on 30 October, again in Vienna, regarding 'mutual reduction of forces and armaments in Central Europe', with what amounted to an open agenda. Thus the adjective 'balanced' that had occurred in every NATO pronouncement on this question since the ministerial meeting at Reykjavik in 1968, was dropped, although the communiqué[6] recorded agreement that specific arrangements would have to be carefully worked out in scope and timing in such a way that they would in all respects at every point conform to the principle of undiminished security for each party. On the NATO side, the participants did not include France; and the Warsaw Pact side succeeded in securing agreement to the exclusion of Hungary, which would have only observer status, along with Romania, Bulgaria, Norway, Denmark, Italy, Greece, and Turkey. A few days later, when the thirty-five foreign ministers—from all Europe, except Albania, and from the United States, and Canada—convened in Helsinki to prepare for the Conference on Security and Cooperation in Europe, they adopted an agenda which bore a closer resemblance to what NATO ministers had suggested in the past than to what had been put forward by the ministers of the Warsaw Pact, although it was they who had launched the idea of a conference in 1965 and persisted in promoting it ever since. In particular, although the third section of the agenda, entitled 'cooperation in humanitarian and other fields', did not explicitly refer to the freer movement of ideas, it did contain several phrases which, if translated into action, would have that effect. The preparatory talks were notable both for Soviet resistance on this sensitive issue, and for a Romanian attempt to secure the inclusion of the phrase 'irrespective of membership of military and political groupings' in the list of principles which each participating country was committed to respect and apply in its relations with other participating states, by the terms of the first section of the agenda, entitled 'questions relating to security in Europe'. In the end, the words used were 'irrespective of their political, economic, and social systems'—less than the Romanians wanted and more than the Russians were at first prepared to concede. In his speech on 3 July, Gromyko tried to claw this back, saying that cultural cooperation should observe fully 'the principles designed to govern relations between states', particularly those of sovereignty and non-intervention; and he pressed for a rapid conclusion of the conference before the end of the year. It was none the less agreed that the second stage of the conference should meet in Geneva on 18 September.[7]

Thus, after years of bargaining, the Soviet Union and its allies got their European Conference and the United States and its allies got their negotiations on the reduction of forces in Central Europe, although both had to make concessions in order to secure their objectives. Meanwhile, Western Europe began 1973 with a bang—as the Treaty of Accession for the three new members of the European Economic Community, Britain, Denmark, and Ireland, came into force—although by the end of the year the Community had been thrown into disarray. In Eastern Europe, COMECON's target of economic integration by 1985 had receded. This target, and the Complex Programme, remained a slogan, but in the course of 1973 the time-scale began to lengthen to twenty or twenty-five years. This was not simply the result of the fourfold increase in world oil prices at the end of the year, against whose effects Eastern Europe could not be immunized. The old idea of a crisis-proof Eastern European monetary system was beginning to give way to a new concept of Eastern European cooperation, commercial and financial, with the Western economic community. The impulse for this change came from the needs of the Soviet economy, as much as from the desire of Eastern European governments for greater freedom to pursue their national interests. The old basis of the COMECON structure—broadly, an exchange of Soviet raw materials for Eastern European manufactured goods—weakened as the Soviet Union looked increasingly to the United States, Japan, and West Germany for help in the joint development of its natural resources, especially those located in Siberia. In consequence, Eastern European countries were, for their part, beginning increasingly to look westwards for sources of raw materials, for technical assistance in modernizing their industries, and for finance. Romania had become a member of the International Monetary Fund in 1972; Hungary joined Czechoslovakia, Romania, and Poland as a member of GATT; Eurocurrency loans to Eastern European countries rose sharply; the COMECON clearing bank itself raised loans in Western Europe; and in August 1973 the COMECON Secretary-General proposed the discussion of economic cooperation to the Chairman of the EEC Council of Ministers. By the end of the decade Eastern European gross liabilities in convertible currency would total over 80 billion US dollars—a tenfold increase from 1971.

The Washington Agreements

The contrast between the circumstances in which Brezhnev visited the United States, from 18 to 25 June 1973, and those of Khrushchev's visit could scarcely have been greater. In the intervening fourteen years the brave new communist world prophesied by Khrushchev had not materialized—the broad gap in living standards and gross national product between the two countries remained. Militarily, however, the dialogue between the two leaders was now conducted between equals; and it was not just a dialogue, but—as in Moscow the year before—a negotiation expressed in written agreements. Moreover, by the time Brezhnev arrived in Washington, events there had reached a point where the visit of the most powerful leader in the communist world served to strengthen domestically the most powerful leader in the capitalist world, by diverting the attention of the American public for one week from the televised hearings of the Senate Watergate Committee, which suspended its activities while Brezhnev was in the United States as the government's official guest. This irony was unknown to the rank and file of the Soviet public, who learned nothing about the Watergate scandal from Soviet sources until the second half of August, when Moscow radio broke the official silence by attributing it to the fears of Nixon's opponents that he might 'go too far in his steps towards the relaxation of international tension'.[8]

The keynote of the Washington agreements was the use of the word 'permanent'. The preamble of the communiqué issued on 25 June[9] recorded the decision of both sides to turn the development of friendship and cooperation between their peoples into a permanent factor for world-wide peace; and the United

States President accepted Brezhnev's invitation to pay a second visit to the Soviet Union, in 1974. In spite of the constraints of Watergate, the 'broad network of constructive relationships' between the two super-powers—the aim of the new American diplomacy—was further strengthened. Three nuclear agreements were signed, one relating to the peaceful use of atomic energy and the other two to the prevention of nuclear war and to the limitation of nuclear weapons respectively. Under the terms of the first, for a duration of ten years, both sides agreed to expand and strengthen their cooperation in the fields of controlled nuclear fusion, fast breeder reactors, and research on the fundamental properties of matter, and to set up a joint committee to this end. The second agreement[10] is of unlimited duration; its second article binds the Soviet Union and the United States to 'proceed from the premise that each party will refrain from the threat or use of force against the other party, against the allies of the other party and against other countries, in circumstances which may endanger international peace and security'. These last nine words provide a possible loophole, which Kissinger was at pains to close when, in an explanatory news conference held after the agreement's signature, he urged that the document should not be approached with the eye of a sharp lawyer; and he conceded that in the light of history, if either signatory wanted to go to war, it would, as before, find an excuse to do so. Article IV of the agreement defined the special relations between the super-powers in the strategic field in the following terms:

If at any time relations between the parties or between either party and other countries appear to involve the risk of a nuclear war between the USA and the USSR or between either party and other countries, the United States and the Soviet Union . . . shall immediately enter into urgent consultations with each other . . .

Kissinger said that this agreement did not make the United States an arbiter between the Soviet Union and China. Zhou Enlai described it as a 'scrap of paper'. The third nuclear agreement signed in Washington committed the two governments to make serious efforts to work out the provisions of a permanent agreement on the limitation of strategic offensive arms, with the objective of signing it in 1974. They described the prospects for reaching a permanent agreement in 1974 as favourable.

In the commercial field, American firms had governmental encouragement to work out concrete proposals on specific projects involving the participation of American companies, including the delivery of Siberian natural gas[11] to the United States. A sign of the times was the front page of *Pravda* on 24 June, which devoted a few lines to the CPSU General Secretary's meeting with American Communist Party leaders, but the whole of the rest to his meeting with American businessmen, whose names and firms were spelled out in full. It was on this occasion that he spoke with candour both about the origins of the cold war—leaving it an open question which side had been responsible for it in the first place—and about deficiencies in the Soviet economy generally and in the handling of Soviet foreign trade in particular. In his televised address to the American people, which took up the front page of *Pravda* of 25 June, Brezhnev reverted to the question of the cold war, describing it as 'a miserable substitute for real war', whose 'sombre influence is unfortunately preserved to some extent even to the present day'. He emphasized that both the Soviet Union and the United States respected the fact that each had its own allies and obligations to other governments. But the chief significance of what he and the President had discussed and agreed was the determination of both sides to make good relations between the USSR and the USA a permanent factor of international peace. He might well have added that this new relationship between the super-powers was symbolized by the plan for the meeting of their astronauts in space in July 1975.

Apart from the Watergate affair and related scandals, whose drama was resumed as soon as Brezhnev left America, two other shadows hung over the visit: the failure of the two governments to make any headway over the Middle East, their only point of agreement being that it caused both of them deep concern—with good reason, as events were soon to prove—and the question whether Congress would approve the granting of most-favoured-nation treatment to the Soviet Union. Two months later, a Soviet periodical[12] carried an abridged version of an article entitled 'USSR–USA and the Contemporary World', written by the chief

editor of the Soviet journal *USA*, who had remained in the United
States for some time after Brezhnev's visit, in order to sound the
opinions of leading figures across the whole range of the
American political spectrum. Basing himself on the premise that
the changes both in Soviet–American relations and in the world
as a whole were due to the decisive change in the Marxist
correlation of world forces, which had obliged the leaders of the
capitalist powers to carry out ' "an agonizing reappraisal" of
their foreign policy doctrines', the writer of this article went on to
observe that the question that now interested many people both
in the United States and in other countries was whether stability
in US–Soviet relations was possible. So far as the Soviet side was
concerned, the answer was clearly affirmative. As for the
American side, it was not merely a matter of the good will of the
present Administration or of external factors, but also of internal
political problems in the United States, which had necessitated
new approaches and concepts both in the international and in the
domestic field. The conclusions drawn were that the Administration's policy towards the Soviet Union had bipartisan support to
a remarkable degree and that there were grounds for hoping that
the world really was entering an era of *détente*. What was
significant in this article was the evident anxiety that this
assessment should prove to be correct. Soviet anxieties were
deepened by the dramatic news of the President's dismissal of the
Watergate Special Prosecutor and the consequent resignation of
the US Attorney-General on 12 October. *Novoe Vremya* gave the
Soviet public this news at the end of October—by Moscow
standards, promptly—but it was not until this periodical
appeared on 2 November 1973 that Soviet readers were informed
for the first time of the possibility that Nixon might be impeached
by Congress, the word 'impeachment' being transliterated into
cyrillics.

The dissidents

By that time pressures were building up in the Western world
with the object of making any concessions to the Soviet Union in
the field of foreign policy dependent on Soviet willingness to
modify internal policy—this in spite of the appeal of Kissinger,

newly appointed Secretary of State,[13] for a fresh consensus behind US foreign policy and Brandt's statement that his government would have pursued the same *Ostpolitik* even if Stalin had still been head of the Soviet Government.[14] In the United States these pressures focused on the clause* in the Trade Reform Bill granting most-favoured-nation treatment to the Soviet Union, that is to say, the termination of the existing tariff discrimination against Soviet goods to which the Administration stood committed by the Moscow commercial agreement of 1972. Under the leadership of Jackson and Vanik, overwhelming support was secured in Congress for withholding not only MFN treatment but—more important—American credits and credit guarantees backed by the US Government, from countries denying free emigration or imposing more than nominal taxes on emigrants. This support was reflected in a non-binding resolution, passed in the Senate by an unopposed vote of eighty-five on 18 September, condemning Soviet treatment of political dissidents and calling on the President to use current negotiations to secure its end.[15]

The last edition—the twenty-seventh—of the *Samizdat* chronicle of current events had appeared in October 1972. At the end of August 1973—just before the second stage of the European Conference on Security and Cooperation was due to open in Geneva—two Soviet dissidents, Yakir and Krasin, pleaded guilty to offences under Article 70 of the Russian Federation's penal code, allegedly linked with the activities of organizations in the West. In the course of this trial, the names of Sakharov and Solzhenitsyn were implicated by the defendants. Both reacted forcefully. Solzhenitsyn said in a press interview in August that so long as permission to print his works in the Soviet Union was withheld, he would continue to have them printed by Western publishers; on 21 September he announced that he had begun underground circulation in the Soviet Union of two hitherto unpublished chapters of *The First Circle*;[16] and in the same month he decided to publish, in Paris, the most damaging attack on the

* The object of this bill was to give the US Administration a mandate to negotiate further liberalization of world trade with other countries in the GATT framework. The clause relating to MFN treatment for the Soviet Union was tacked on to the bill by the Nixon Administration as an afterthought.

Soviet system that he had ever written—*Gulag Archipelago*—for this reason:

> with an uneasy heart I refrained for years from printing this book that was already completed; my duty towards those still alive outweighed my duty towards the dead. But now that the State Security has in any case seized this book nothing remains for me but to publish it at once.[17]

Adding what must have seemed to the Soviet leadership insult to injury, on 5 September Solzhenitsyn sent them a letter,[18] which was later published in the West. In this he put forward a programme of proposals aimed at preventing war with China, which he regarded as the chief danger facing the Soviet Union abroad, and at preserving the Russian environment and the Russian nation: these proposals included repudiation of official support both of Marxism as a state ideology and of national liberation movements, termination of Soviet tutelage over Eastern Europe, permission for national republics to leave the Soviet Union, a Soviet agrarian reform on the Polish model, and concentration of Russian effort on domestic problems, especially development of the Siberian north-east. Five months later Solzhenitsyn was arrested by the KGB, and deported to the Federal Republic of Germany, on 12 February 1974.

For his part, Sakharov gave a long press conference on 21 August 1973 in his flat in Moscow, the full text of which was published in the West.[19] In the course of this he lamented the much stronger reprisals taken against Soviet political dissidents during the previous two years; he described the Soviet élite as having a 'sort of separate thinking' which prevented them from reacting differently from the way in which they did; and he declared:

> a *rapprochement* while the West accepts our rules of the game . . . would be very dangerous . . . would not solve any of the world's problems, and would mean simply a capitulation to our real or exaggerated strength. It would mean an attempt to trade, to get gas and oil from the US, neglecting all other aspects of the problem . . . *détente* without any qualifications would mean the cultivation and encouragement of closed countries . . . no one should dream of having such a neighbour, especially if this neighbour is armed to the teeth.

The subsequent campaign in the Soviet press against the two

world-famous figures caused a wave of indignation in the West. Ironically, this happened at a time when, following the outcry aroused by the Leningrad trials[20] of December 1970, an unprecedented number of Soviet Jews received permission to emigrate to Israel (70,000 in the period from 1971 to September 1973), and when the stiff emigration tax on Soviet Jews applying for exit visas was suspended, in deference to American pressure in April 1973. Moreover, in Marc Chagall's old age an exhibition was at last allowed of his works, which had lain for years in the cellars of Soviet museums; and just before the Geneva Conference opened, the Soviet authorities stopped jamming Western broadcasts in Russian.

China

The *rapprochement* between the super-powers came under even heavier fire from the Chinese. On 28 July the Chinese Prime Minister said that both the contradictions between the two super-powers and their contention were ceaselessly intensifying, and that their temporary compromise and collusion would in no way change the nature of either of them. In a speech delivered on 15 August in Central Asia, at Alma Ata, Brezhnev repeated the offer that he had made to the Chinese Party leadership two years earlier at the XXIVth CPSU Congress (to normalize Sino-Soviet state relations and restore good-neighbourliness and friendship). Speaking on 24 September[21] at Tashkent, he revealed that as recently as mid-June the Chinese Government had not even replied to a renewed Soviet offer of a non-aggression pact; they also rejected a suggestion that they should confirm the validity of the 1950 Treaty, by which China was still theoretically bound. The Chinese response to the Soviet Union was not encouraging. At the end of August, the New China News Agency, after accusing the Soviet Union of having dismembered Romania and subjugated Bulgaria, concluded: 'The Romanov dynasty and the Khrushchev–Brezhnev dynasty are linked by a black line, that is, the aggressive and expansionist nature of Great Russian chauvinism and imperialism. The only difference is that the latter dons a cloak of "socialism"—"social imperialism" in the true sense of the term.' The Chinese radio broadcast at length a speech made by the Chinese Prime Minister at the Xth CCP Congress, in the course of which he went so far as to compare Brezhnev with Hitler and accused him of trying to get money from capitalist countries as a reward for opposing China.

The strength of the language used by the Chinese, who again spoke of the danger of a Soviet pre-emptive nuclear strike, was clearly dictated by the fear that Kissinger had sought to allay in June. It may also have been partly attributable to trouble on the Sino-Mongolian border (little more than 300 miles from the Chinese capital). In September a fresh element was injected into the Sino-Soviet dispute by a Mongolian press allegation that China had been violating this frontier.[22] But the two major attacks on Chinese policy that appeared in *Pravda* in August over the pen-name Aleksandrov provided enough explanation in themselves. The second[23] of these left nothing unsaid. The CCP, which represented the Soviet Union as its principal enemy, preached:

a reactionary pseudo-theory borrowed from bourgeois ideologists, according to which the march of historical development allegedly determines a 'conflict' of all small and medium states of the world with the two 'super-powers' . . . the absurd thesis of the 'two intermediate zones',[24] according to which the oppressed peoples of Asia, Africa and Latin America (the 'first zone') are allegedly not only 'linked by common interests' with certain basically capitalist countries of West and East (the 'second zone'), but they should and can unite with this 'zone' in a struggle against the 'super-powers'.

According to *Pravda*, China portrayed itself as the defender of the interests of small and medium countries and the leader of the Third World, to which it claimed to belong, instead of to the communist world, and at the same time the Chinese leadership were said to be forcing forward their country's conversion into a 'nuclear super-power', with the object of controlling the destinies of other countries. The chief proof of China's ideas of hegemony cited by Aleksandrov was Chinese policy in South-East Asia, where the Chinese aim was to establish a group of states under the aegis of Peking. China had aligned itself in an opportunistic alliance with the most aggressive circles of imperialism against the socialist countries, and had reoriented its foreign trade at the expense of its links with the communist world. China not only opposed the Soviet Union's European policy—the Moscow and Warsaw Treaties and the European Conference—but even pronounced panegyrics of NATO and the 'principles of Atlanticism', and favoured the maintenance of the American military presence in Europe and a new Atlantic charter.[25] While opposing the Soviet suggestion of Asian collective security, China was described as supporting the US–Japanese security agreement and the US nuclear zone in the Far East; it had also tried to propagate the illusion in Tokyo that China had chosen Japan as its permanent partner for the joint decision of all Asian issues; it had encouraged Japanese territorial claims[26] against the Soviet Union; and had sought to dissuade Japan from pursuing a policy of peaceful coexistence with the socialist commonwealth.

China was further reproached by Aleksandrov for its refusal to sign the nuclear treaties;[27] for its refusal to consider the Soviet proposal for a treaty renouncing the use of force, and its rejection of repeated proposals for the settlement of frontier questions. The claims to broad areas of Soviet territory, allegations about plans for a Soviet pre-emptive nuclear strike, and insinuations about an alleged 'threat from the North' were all spread by the Maoist leadership not only in order to work up a war fever and to justify the nuclear arms race, but also to divert popular attention from internal difficulties. Maoist ambitions of great power hegemony were described as being in contradiction with the needs of the Chinese people, whose interests did not coincide with the great power chauvinism of its leaders—a clear appeal to Chinese public opinion over the heads of the party leadership.

The Arab–Israeli War

In September Jackson had remarked, in support of his resolution in the Senate: 'now, at the beginning of the road to *détente*, is the time to test the direction in which we are asked to travel'. Three weeks later the super-power relationship was subjected to a severe test, of a different kind. On 6 October Egypt and Syria launched a combined attack on Israel, which achieved complete tactical surprise. The course of this war has been described in detail by other writers.[28] The war, which lasted until 25 October, was longer, more evenly balanced, more bitterly contested, and

more costly in loss of life and of material than any of the three
previous Middle Eastern wars. The Arab attack was launched on
two fronts: the northern, on the Golan Heights, and the southern,
in the Sinai Peninsula, both of which had been occupied by
Israeli forces since the Six Day War of 1967. In the north, the
Syrian forces were helped by Arab allies from as far afield as
Morocco. Both attacks achieved initial success. But by 12
October the Israeli counter-attack on the northern front had
reached a point twenty miles from Damascus, and on the
southern front their counter-attacking force west of the Canal was
about fifty miles from Cairo when the fighting stopped. Nevertheless, in strong contrast with previous Arab–Israeli wars, in this
one neither side emerged as the victor; and because Israel had won
the wars of 1948, 1956, and 1967 outright, this time it was the
Arabs who acquired a new feeling of military confidence on the
battlefields, whereas Israel's invincibility was called in question
for the first time. This war also differed from earlier Middle
Eastern wars in two other, highly significant ways: the use of
economic warfare by the Arab oil-producing countries, and the
involvement of the two super-powers, which culminated in the
nearest approach to a nuclear confrontation between them since
the Cuban missile crisis, exactly eleven years before.

In October 1973, for the first time, the Arabs used the power of
their oil resources to apply political pressure to Israel's principal
protector, the United States: an embargo on oil supplies to the
United States, a cut-back in production and—above all—an
increase in oil prices, which led to the world energy crisis of 1974
(a crisis which the war did not cause, though it hastened its
onset).

The super-powers' intervention took two forms. As adversaries, the Soviet and United States governments each delivered
vast supplies of arms by air to the combatants in the Middle East,
to replace the losses incurred in battle. As partners, they
conferred, both with each other and with their allies. At any rate
so far as the public record is concerned, the Soviet leadership's
first reaction to the Arab attacks, the date of which was
communicated to them only on 4 October, was one of reserve. On
8 October the Soviet Union was warned by the United States that
it could not disregard the principles of *détente* in any area of the

world 'without imperilling its entire relationship with the United States'.[29] Brezhnev responded the following day with a message to the Algerian President suggesting that all possible aid should be sent to Egypt and Syria; and on 10 October the Soviet airlift of military supplies to the Middle East began. The American airlift to Israel was announced on 13 October; and on 19 October a bill was presented to Congress seeking 2.2 billion dollars military aid for Israel.

The day after the Israeli bridgehead had been established on the west bank of the Suez Canal, Kosygin arrived in Cairo, where he spent three days. On 20 October Kissinger visited Moscow, where agreement was reached between the two governments to sponsor jointly a resolution in Security Council calling for an immediate cease-fire and for the implementation of the Council's Resolution 242 of November 1967. After Kissinger had flown from Moscow to Tel Aviv, both sides accepted the resolution, which brought the cease-fire into force on 22 October. The cease-fire soon broke down, with the prospect that the Egyptian Third Army, established in force on the east bank of the canal, would be cut off by the Israeli force that had by then reached Suez. After the super-powers had co-sponsored a second resolution in the Security Council, calling for a withdrawal to the positions of 22 October, the Egyptian Government pressed the Soviet and US governments to intervene militarily on the spot to ensure Israeli withdrawal. This was followed on 24 October by a personal message from Brezhnev to the US President, which was interpreted in Washington as a Soviet threat to intervene unilaterally in Egypt unless Israel observed the cease-fire of 22 October. For a few hours, in the early morning of 25 October, the American response took the form of a world-wide Defence Condition Three alert. Later on the same day, a third Security Council resolution[30] was passed, which finally brought the war in Egypt to an end. It was agreed to send a United Nations Emergency Force to the Middle East, from which troops not only of the super-powers, but of all five permanent members of the Security Council were excluded. On 28 October the first meeting between Egyptian and Israeli officers for seventeen years took place, at Kilometre 101 on the Suez–Cairo road. Thus Soviet military intervention in Egypt was prevented; the encircled

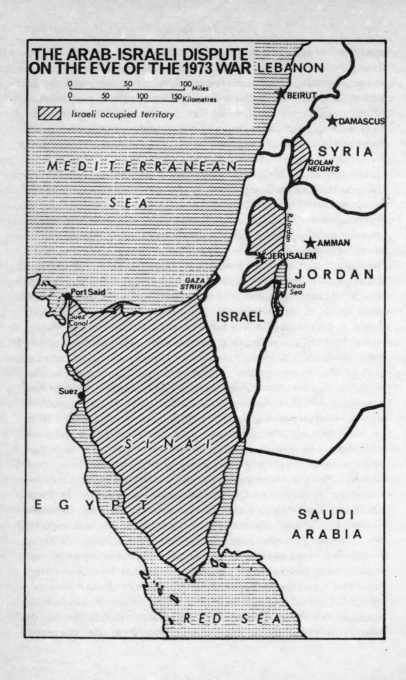

THE ARAB-ISRAELI DISPUTE
ON THE EVE OF THE 1973 WAR LEBANON

0   50   100 Miles
0   50   100   150 Kilometres

Israeli occupied territory

BEIRUT

DAMASCUS

SYRIA

MEDITERRANEAN

GOLAN
HEIGHTS

SEA

R. Jordan

AMMAN

JERUSALEM

JORDAN

GAZA
STRIP

Dead
Sea

Port Said

ISRAEL

Suez
Canal

Suez

S I N A I

E G Y P T

SAUDI
ARABIA

RED SEA

Egyptian Third Army was saved; and Sadat succeeded in making 1973 his year of decision.

To this brief account must be added a complicating factor: that the Middle Eastern crisis coincided with major developments in American domestic politics. On 10 October Spiro Agnew resigned as Vice-President under threat of indictment; two days later Gerald Ford was appointed Vice-President in his place; and on 12 October, by dismissing the Special Watergate Prosecutor, Nixon took a decisive step on the road that was to lead to his resignation nine months later as President of the United States.

Future historians will no doubt seek to provide the answers to four questions arising from the October war. First, in their attitudes towards the Middle East, where the temperature mounted steadily during the three and a half months that followed the signature of the Agreement on the Prevention of Nuclear War in Washington, to what extent did the Soviet and the US governments 'act in such a manner as to prevent the development of situations capable of causing a dangerous exacerbation of their relations, as to avoid military confrontations, and as to exclude the outbreak of nuclear war between them'? Second, once unmistakable signals that the Arab attack on Israel was imminent were received in Moscow (earlier, but not much earlier, than in Washington), did the Soviet Government act in the manner prescribed by the Treaty of June 1973, in relation both to the Arab governments concerned and to the US Government? Third, once the war had begun, how quickly did the Soviet and US governments 'enter into urgent conversations with each other'? (The meeting between the US Secretary of State and the Soviet leadership in Moscow did not take place until after two weeks of fighting and after both the Soviet and the US governments had started their air-lifts.) Fourth, what was the precise chain of events between the meeting in Moscow and the second cease-fire five days later; and in particular did the Soviet and United States governments misunderstand each other's intentions at any point during that critical period?

Without awaiting the full evidence[31] required to answer these specific questions, some general conclusions can be drawn. Although the strain to which the Middle Eastern War subjected the new relationship between the super-powers was intense, their relationship survived the test. Even in the early hours of 25 October what Soviet theorists call the *nekontroliruemyi element** in crisis management was contained. Each of the two governments achieved its immediate aim on that day. Moreover, the political outcome of the war was something new: agreement to open negotiations between Arabs and Israelis—in December, in Geneva, under the co-chairmanship of the Soviet and US governments. The contrast between the crisis of 14–28 October 1962 and that of 6–25 October 1973 spoke for itself.

* Literally translated, 'the uncontrollable element'—the factor of miscalculation—quoted from V. V. Shurin and E. M. Primakov, *Mezhdunarodnye konflikty*, Moscow, 1972, p. 21, by Hannes Adomeit in *Adelphi Papers*, no. 101, p. 5, IISS, London, 1973.

14. The Concept of the Super-Power Relationship

THE contrast between October 1962 and October 1973 was indeed vivid. And not only did the super-power relationship survive the test of the Arab–Israeli War, but the tempo of the second phase of the negotiating process between the Soviet Union and the United States, which began in 1974, was no slower than that of the first. This momentum was maintained unabated until the middle of the decade. From then onwards a gradual erosion of the super-power relationship set in—the combined effect of the 'variables' to which the introductory chapter alluded. The chapters that follow will examine the successive stages of this second phase. With hindsight, its ultimate failure takes on a fatally inevitable look. This was not how it appeared at the time, however. On the contrary, as early as the turn of the year 1973/4, the newfound intimacy of the super-power relationship was already causing anxiety among many in the West—not to mention China, whose fierce reaction has already been described.

Western doubts arose partly from conceptual confusion and partly from differing perceptions of national interest. The whole idea of a close bilateral relationship between the United States and the Soviet Union became identified in many people's minds, particularly in the United States, with the increasingly controversial concept of *détente*: a word taken over from the French diplomatic vocabulary and saddled, in English, with a broader and weightier significance than it is logically capable of sustaining. In the process, *détente* came to represent not the consequences of US foreign policy, or of the foreign policies pursued by the two super-powers, but the foreign policy itself. On the other hand, in Soviet usage *détente*[1] retained its traditional meaning in the language of international diplomacy: the relaxation of political tension.

In reality, the aim and the consequences of a policy are not the same as the policy itself. Yet the words *détente* and the super-power relationship itself came increasingly to be used as shorthand for each other, as though they were one and the same thing. This confusion gave rise to further misconceptions: that in the Western relationship with the Soviet Union all that mattered was a commitment to *détente*—to relax political tension—which would dispense with the need to pursue a coherent overall policy, including the maintenance of a balance of military power, and that the state of the world could somehow be changed overnight. The blurring of these critical distinctions may perhaps be excused on the ground that by 1974 a series of sudden changes had made the structure of world power much harder to understand. In any event, we have only to look back to the Harmel Report on the future tasks of the North Atlantic Alliance of December 1967, to find an expression of clarity and, incidentally, a concept of *détente* closer to the Soviet definition—that military security and *détente* are not contradictory, but complementary. This report spoke of 'realistic measures designed to further a *détente* in East West relations' not as the final goal, but as 'part of a long-term process to promote better relations and to foster a European settlement'. Had this earlier distinction between ends and means been preserved by the North Atlantic allies, and if the recognition of the need for a long-term process had been maintained, the Great Debate on *détente* might have been more dispassionate, especially in the United States, and the wood less often mistaken for the trees.[2] This confusion may have suited those who see the world, and especially the Soviet Union and the United States, in black and white. The task of those who do not share this view, and who do not believe that the sole outcome for super-power rivalry is an ultimate choice between Armageddon and a Grand Reconciliation, is made harder by the fact that no one has yet succeeded in winning general acceptance for a succinct definition of the super-power relationship. Bilateral relations between the Soviet Union and the United States may, at any given moment, be good or bad, taken overall. What remains constant, since they are the only super-powers, is that their relations with each other are qualitatively different from their relations with their allies and with the rest of the world. In 1974 it was generally referred to as a special (in French even stronger—*priviligié* or *exclusif*) relationship. Or as Kissinger put it, at a highly charged moment[3]—'The Soviet Union and we are in a unique relationship. We are at one and the same time adversaries and partners in the preservation of peace': an echo of the term *frères ennemis* used by Raymond Aron to describe the Soviet Union and the United States over ten years earlier.[4]

The elegance of these definitions reflects, in my view, an accurate observation of the lonely eminence of the two super-powers.[5] This clarity was not shared by many in the West. In the academic world, again it was Kissinger who first defined the problem, as early as 1968: 'to develop some concept of order in a world which is bipolar militarily, but multipolar politically'.[6] Unlike many politicians, academics were aware that the international order in the 1970s had entered a decade of profound change. Yet the explanations offered at the time by some distinguished scholars now—only ten years later—have a strange ring. Alastair Buchan, for example, gave his BBC Reith Lectures in 1973 the title of *Change without War*. Both he and Andrew Shonfield, who gave the same lectures in the previous year, argued that military power was becoming increasingly irrelevant; and in the United States Joseph Nye and Robert Keohane similarly ascribed a declining role to military power in international relations.[7]

The increasing closeness of the US–Soviet relationship was hard to tolerate for some of the United States' European allies, particularly for Britain and France, the two European countries most directly affected by the claim that the relationship between the United States and the Soviet Union was special.* The French Government had insisted on conducting an independent foreign policy since the mid-1960s, so that by the end of the decade a close Franco-Soviet relationship had been developed as a balance to France's continued membership of the Atlantic Alliance. By then the British Government, though it no longer claimed its

---

* The Federal German Government was far from indifferent, but in the first half of the decade its *Ostpolitik* was compatible with the policy being pursued by the US Government towards the Soviet Union.

historical 'special relationship' with the United States Government across the board, still continued to enjoy a position in Washington that could be described as special in certain fields, particularly defence. When confronted in the 1970s with the evolution of a new super-power relationship, successive British Governments preferred on the whole to work quietly in order to maintain the alliance on what they regarded as an even keel, while publicly behaving as though little had changed. On the other hand, the French Government made its view forcibly clear. Unimpressed by Nixon's assurance that it was not the aim of the United States and the Soviet Union to establish a condominium, this is just the word that Pompidou and Jobert (then Foreign Minister) did use publicly in the following year. French anger was directed particularly at the conclusion of the US–Soviet Nuclear Agreement and at US–Soviet collaboration in bringing the Fourth Arab–Israeli War to an end.[8] The Nuclear Agreement of 22 June 1973 had set up a 'veritable condominium of the super-powers' and reduced the EEC to impotence; the US and the Soviet Union had committed an error in 'brutally brushing aside' France and Europe while imposing a Middle Eastern settlement; and Europe, 'treated like a non-person and humiliated in its very existence, because of its dependence on supplies of energy' was none the less 'the object of the second battle of the Middle Eastern War'.[9]

European anxieties were compounded by the passage in the statement about the so-called Year of Europe, delivered on 23 April 1973 by Kissinger on behalf of the US President, in which a distinction was drawn between the global interests and responsibilities of the United States and the regional interests of its European allies: interests which were said to be not necessarily in conflict, but in the new era not automatically identical. Although in a formal sense the US–European quarrel caused by this statement was made up at the Ottawa and Brussels meetings of the North Atlantic Alliance in June 1974, the scars have remained; and five years later, in a speech delivered in Brussels, it was Kissinger (by then no longer in office) who took the knife to the old wound.[10]

There must have been a corresponding debate at this time in Moscow, and now that Brezhnev is dead, we may begin to learn something more about the differing views then taken on these issues. However that may be, their firmly established ideological vocabulary, though it cannot accommodate the word 'super-power', enabled the Soviet leadership to avoid the conceptual muddle over *détente*, which they saw as the consequence of the policy of peaceful coexistence between communist and non-communist states—not as the policy itself. Thus in speeches made in 1973 Brezhnev defined the *aim* of Soviet foreign policy as being 'to render irreversible the phenomenon of *détente*',[11] and in October of the same year he described the principle of peaceful coexistence as 'gradually becoming converted into the generally accepted rule of international life'.[12] Notwithstanding the events of the closing months of 1973 in the Middle East and the dramatic changes in the international economic system, the Marxist-Leninist lens did not distort the Soviet view of the paramount importance of maintaining stability in Soviet–US relations. Thus, even on a highly ideological occasion in January 1974[13] the assessments offered, by Suslov and Ponamarev, of the effect on the Western world of the quintupling of OPEC oil prices were not far off the truth. Three months later, in a joint communiqué issued in Moscow, the Soviet and the US Governments expressed their determination 'to pursue . . . the established policy aimed at making the process of improving Soviet–American relations irreversible'[14]—an objective that was to be endorsed personally by Nixon during his second visit to Moscow in June. This third Soviet–US summit meeting was followed by a fourth, held in Vladivostock on 23–24 November 1974. And in August of the following year Brezhnev and Ford were the principal signatories, in Helsinki, of the Final Act of the Conference on Security and Cooperation in Europe. In retrospect, however, this twentieth-century Field of the Cloth of Gold was the high noon of the super-power relationship.

15. High Noon

On 9 August 1974 Richard Nixon resigned the Presidency of the United States and was replaced by Vice-President Gerald Ford. This climax of the long drawn-out Watergate affair was regarded at the time as proof of the vitality of the American Constitution and particularly of the ultimate effectiveness of its system of checks and balances. So it was. The Government of the United States was carried on, but so far as the Executive was concerned, this was done for nearly two and a half years by a President and a Vice-President (Nelson Rockefeller), neither of whom had been elected to the office which he held. True, Ford lost no time in confirming Kissinger as his Secretary of State; and Ford's assurances of the continuity of US policy were swiftly accepted in a speech delivered on 25 September[1] by Brezhnev, who offered the same assurances about Soviet policy towards the United States. But even Kissinger's undiminished energy could not disguise the fact that the authority of the Republican Administration was gravely weakened. To no field of policy did this weakness apply so much as to that of foreign relations; and on 30 April 1975 a further blow to the US Government's strength at home and to its influence abroad was dealt by the fall of Saigon.

In the wake of Nixon's downfall the US relationship with the Soviet Union suffered a backlash from American public opinion. This was inevitable given the way in which, as President, Nixon had overplayed the benefits of the new relationship ('peace in our time') in general and of the SALT agreements in particular. The lengths to which he went to underline his personal links with Brezhnev ('able to meet together as friends'), in speeches made during his last visit to Moscow, did not help his successor. The first casualty was the US–Soviet Trade Agreement of October 1972. Although the terms of the (1973) Jackson–Vanik Amendment[2] regarding Jewish emigration from the Soviet Union were accepted[3] by the Soviet Government, the form finally taken by the US Trade Bill on 20 December 1974 and the publicity given to the emigration issue were too much for the Soviet Govenment, which cancelled the 1972 Agreement on 14 January 1975. At the time this tortuous sequence of events was submerged in the general relief that in this bill the US Government had secured from Congress its mandate to negotiate a new GATT round. Although the Soviet Government coupled its cancellation with a reaffirmation of its commitment to the Soviet–US relationship (and the two governments signed a five-year Grain Agreement on 20 October), in fact this outcome was a major blow against the relationship: a blow struck—significantly—by the US Congress.* As Kissinger subsequently described this episode in his memoirs, 'we ended by achieving the worst of all results'.[4]

The backlash both after Watergate and after Vietnam was directed not only against Nixon, but also against the highly personal and secret methods of diplomacy used by Kissinger. Although these methods helped to ensure his and Nixon's greatest triumphs—the US *rapprochement* with China and the first US Presidential visit to Moscow in 1972—they also made it exceedingly difficult for Kissinger to establish a consensus in Washington after Nixon had resigned. At the beginning of 1974 Kissinger stood at the height of a seemingly unassailable popularity. By the autumn he had been thrown on the defensive. In his statement[5] to the Senate Foreign Relations Committee on the new Administration's policy towards the Soviet Union, he had to assure the Committee that American interests would not be sacrificed to *détente*; and he maintained that the issue 'is not whether peace and stability serve Soviet purposes, but whether they serve our own'. Two years later, at the beginning of an American electoral campaign, the very word *détente*—let alone serious negotiations with the Soviet Government—was perceived by President Ford as damaging to his own electoral prospects and those of his supporters.

It is against this background of American politics that the two US–Soviet summit meetings of 1974 have to be assessed. It will be recalled that the Strategic Arms Limitation agreement reached in Moscow during Nixon's first presidential visit to the Soviet Union in 1972 took the form of a holding operation; and that during Brezhnev's visit to Washington in 1973 the two governments committed themselves to work out the provisions of a permanent agreement on the limitation of strategic offensive arms, with the objective of signing it in 1974.[6] The timing of Nixon's second presidential visit to Moscow could hardly have been worse—six weeks before his resignation. The Soviet leadership must have decided that, although the visit had to go

* Congress also thwarted the Administration by cancelling military aid to Turkey, following the Turkish invasion of Cyprus in July 1974, and refused to vote military aid for South Vietnam and Cambodia.

ahead, they could not expect to do serious business with a US president whose days in office were numbered. In the West fears were expressed either of a 'quick fix' or of a deadlock on the issue of strategic arms limitation. In the event this third summit was not a 'quick fix' for either side; and something was achieved, though certainly not enough to warrant the CPSU Central Committee's description: a 'massive landmark in the history of relations between the Soviet Union and the USA'.

Despite the constraints imposed on both sides by the US domestic political crisis, the documents published at this summit meeting covered the three essential elements that together made up the super-power relationship: arms limitation, economic cooperation, and crisis management. *Pravda*[7] carried on its first pages the agreements reached between the two governments during this visit: among others, the ten-year agreement on economic, industrial, and technological cooperation, signed on 29 June; the Treaty[8] of 3 July banning underground nuclear weapon tests having a yield exceeding 150 kilotons, with effect from 31 March 1976; the Protocol (also signed on 3 July) to the 1972 Treaty on the Limitation of Anti-Ballistic Missile Systems, whereby the two governments bound themselves not to exercise their right, under the Treaty, to deploy an ABM system in the second of their two deployment areas; the agreement to open negotiations on environmental warfare; and—in the text of the joint communiqué of 3 July—the governments' conclusion that the 1972 Interim Agreement on Offensive Strategic Weapons should be followed by a new agreement between the Soviet Union and the United States on the limitation of strategic arms, covering the period until 1985. This agreement should deal with both quantitative and qualitative limitations, and should be completed at the earliest possible date, before the expiry of the present agreement, the SALT delegations being reconvened at Geneva 'in the immediate future on the basis of instructions issuing from the summit'.

In their communiqué the two governments also agreed to consider a joint initiative in the Conference of the Committee on Disarmament for the conclusion, as a first step, of an international convention regarding chemical warfare; they favoured an early date for the final stage of the CSCE conference; and they 'proceeded from the assumption that the results of the negotiations will permit the conference to be concluded at the highest level'. They considered it important that the Geneva peace conference should resume its work as soon as possible; and they agreed 'to remain in close touch with a view to coordinating the efforts of both countries towards a peaceful settlement in the Middle East', which should be based on UN Security Council Resolution 338, taking into account 'the legitimate interests of all peoples in the Middle East, including the Palestinian people, and the right to existence of all states in the area'.

Strategic Arms Limitation

Reduced to its simplest terms, the problem which confronted the two governments in SALT II was twofold; how to agree on a written set of militarily intelligible rules, valid in international law, that would be binding on two arsenals of strategic* weapons which, though they possessed in common the power to blow up the planet, were fundamentally asymmetrical; and how to verify the future development of these arsenals in ways that commanded the confidence of both governments and—in the case of the United States—of public opinion. The problem was compounded by the fact that the Soviet Union claimed the need to deploy strategic nuclear forces against another strategic nuclear power— China—and that two of the United States' allies—Britain and France—had themselves possessed nuclear deterrent forces for many years.

This is no longer the arcane subject that it seemed to many people ten years ago. Today, newspaper articles about it abound in both West and East; and Brezhnev even gave a detailed interview himself to a Western newspaper in 1981.[9] However, the central question of asymmetry is one which the apologists of both sides, in a welter of self-justifying statistics, usually prefer to ignore. The truth is that whereas the United States from the outset—under both the Eisenhower and the Kennedy Administration—sought to strike a balance of land, sea, and air (the

* The word *strategic*, or intercontinental, is important. The so-called theatre nuclear balance in Europe is a separate matter, discussed later in this book.

so-called triad of strategic nuclear forces), the Soviet Union concentrated its earlier strategic nuclear effort on land-based missile launchers. The development of the Soviet *Backfire* bomber and Admiral Gorshkov's naval expansion notwithstanding, this asymmetry remains. Thus, at the end of 1980 Soviet land-based intercontinental ballistic missiles still carried three-quarters of Soviet nuclear megatonnage and over 5,000 of the 7,000 Soviet nuclear warheads; whereas the equivalent US missiles carried 35 per cent of US megatonnage and about 20 per cent of the 9–10,000 US warheads. By contrast, in the same year, about twenty US ballistic-missile submarines (with over 3,000 nuclear warheads) were at sea at any given time; whereas not more than ten such Soviet submarines were kept permanently on station.[10]

If this asymmetry obtained at the beginning of the 1980s, it will be clear how much it weighed in 1974 in the minds of the SALT negotiators, who—broadly speaking—were seeking to strike some kind of bargain between Soviet quantity (mainly land-based throw-weight) and US quality (MIRV-equipped missiles combined with constantly increasing accuracy). In the end what they decided in Moscow in July 1974 was to go for a ten-year framework agreement. The basic elements of this agreement— SALT II—were agreed four months later at Vladivostock. Subject to detailed negotiation, the agreement was expected to be signed in Washington at a summit meeting in 1975 and to be in force from 1 October 1977–31 December 1985. Since the SALT II Treaty ultimately signed in Vienna was the lineal descendant of the Vladivostock Accords, a summary of the basic elements agreed at Vladivostock is relevant to what followed. Each side was to limit its strategic missile delivery vehicles (land, sea, and air-based) to 2,400. Of these a maximum of 1,320 could be equipped with MIRV (at that time the US had about 850 MIRV-equipped missiles and the Soviet Union had none that were operational). Both the American forward-based systems and the nuclear forces of the United States' allies were again, as in SALT I, excluded from the terms of the Accords. Within the terms of the Accords and subject to the numerical ceilings, each super-power was free to pursue all the strategic nuclear development programmes that were already under way.

Although the SALT II agreement envisaged at Vladivostock set limits to strategic nuclear weapons, they were limits established at a high level—a criticism levelled against the Accords from both ends of the American political spectrum as soon as they were made known. Nevertheless, they did at least spell out, publicly and by agreement between the governments of the two super-powers, the course to be followed by the Soviet Union and the United States in developing and deploying the next generation of nuclear weapons—that is to say, from the mid-1970s to the mid-1980s. In this sense, the official Soviet description of the Accords as 'a great contribution to the cause of peace' was less of a hyperbole than Soviet comment on the outcome of the Moscow summit meeting. Nor can either government have been surprised by the kind of development and deployment of strategic arms that has followed. Although the pace, for example, of the Soviet development and deployment of MIRV-equipped missiles may not have been foreseen, nor the speed with which Soviet missile accuracy was improved, the fact is that, with nuclear weapons systems, as with others, the process of Research and Development has an inbuilt momentum that cannot be arrested by a stroke of the pen. As Eisenhower warned, in the valedictory address that made famous the term military–industrial complex: 'we must also be alert to the equal and opposite danger that public policy could itself become the captive of a scientific–technological élite.' The combined power of the two interest groups, in an advanced industrial society, is formidable.

The chief flaw in the Vladivostock Accords was that they did nothing to lessen the vulnerability of the land-based strategic missiles of both sides, which was certain to increase. Given the swings that were already under way in domestic American politics, the fact that it was the US intercontinental ballistic missile force that would become vulnerable first, was bound to affect the super-power relationship. Two super-powers, each armed with vast numbers of strategic nuclear weapon systems that are becoming more and more vulnerable to a pre-emptive first strike, constitute almost an ideal recipe for strategic instability: the exact opposite of the aims generally ascribed to the SALT I agreements two years earlier.[11]

The Helsinki Final Act

The signing of the Final Act of the Conference on Security and Cooperation in Europe (CSCE), signed on 1 August 1975 in Helsinki by thirty-three European heads of state or government, the United States President, and the Canadian Prime Minister, was a unique occasion in post-war history. It represented the culmination of over ten years' sustained diplomatic effort by the Soviet Union and its Warsaw Pact allies. The bargaining which ended in July 1973, with agreement on a three-part agenda, was reflected in the language and the structure of the lengthy document[12], signed by the thirty-five leaders—Albania was the only absentee—two years later. Leaving aside idiosyncratic passages included in the Final Act to satisfy the wishes of certain participants,* the first main section—*Questions relating to Security in Europe*—gave the Soviet Union and its allies broadly what they had been seeking; the second section—*Cooperation in the Field of Economics, of Science and Technology, and of the Environment*—was politically anodyne; and the third main section—*Cooperation in humanitarian and other fields*—contained the concessions which the West had negotiated in return for the first section. On the crucial issue of German reunification, the first section reproduced the formula adopted by the Soviet and Federal German governments in the Treaty of Moscow in 1970. On the one hand, 'the participating states regard as inviolable all one another's frontiers as well as the frontiers of all States in Europe'. On the other, 'they consider that their frontiers can be changed, in accordance with international law, by peaceful means and by agreement'.[13] Moreover, the so-called Brezhnev Doctrine does not fit easily with the paragraph[14] on *Non-intervention in internal affairs* in the first section: '. . . will refrain from any intervention, direct or indirect, individual or collective, in the internal or external affairs falling within the domestic jurisdiction of another participating State, regardless of their mutual relations.' Finally, the first section ended with a useful *Document on confidence-building measures and certain aspects of security and disarmament*',[15] which included

---

* Notably Dom Mintoff, the Maltese Prime Minister, without whom the *Questions relating to Security and Cooperation in the Mediterranean* would no doubt have been omitted.

twenty-one days' prior notification of military manoeuvres involving over 25,000 men and taking place within 250 kilometres of national frontiers, and the exchange of observers at such manoeuvres.[16]

In the third section—*Cooperation in humanitarian and other fields*—the West sought to make life more bearable in practical ways for Eastern Europeans and for people of other countries working in or visiting Eastern Europe. This cooperation is described in the preamble to the section as being 'irrespective of their political, economic and social systems'. Although Soviet caveats are included ('relevant questions must be settled by the States concerned under mutually acceptable conditions'), the participants do 'make it their aim to facilitate freer movement and contacts, individual and collective, whether privately or officially, among persons, institutions, and organizations . . .' Subsequent paragraphs in this section bear titles some of which would have been hardly thinkable even a few years earlier, such as *Contacts and Regular Meetings on the Basis of Family Ties*, *Reunification of Families*, *Marriage between Citizens of Different States*, *Meetings among Young People*, *Improvement of the Circulation of*, *Access to*, *and Exchange of Information*, *Improvement of Working Conditions for Journalists*, and *Access and Exchanges in the academic and scientific fields.*[17]

The Final Act ended by committing its signatories to a Follow-up Meeting in Belgrade in 1977. This meeting ended in deadlock. Inevitably perhaps, the compromises enshrined in the Final Act of 1975 provided ample room for later controversy. This came to a head in Madrid, where the second Follow-up Meeting convened in November 1980, in the wake of events in Afghanistan and Poland, and where, at the time of writing, the debate still continues. In a sense, therefore, Brezhnev's claim in 1975 that the Final Act had given international *détente* 'specific material content' proved to be an accurate observation. At the time of its signature most people in the West found the Final Act's significance hard to assess, not least because it was not legally binding in international law. For their part, the Soviet leadership indicated how they assessed the Final Act by having it printed in full on 2 August 1975 by both *Pravda* and *Izvestiya*. Two years later the new Soviet Constitution reflected the provisions of the Act.[18] Yet the life of Soviet dissidents has grown no easier in consequence. Nor has the Soviet leadership shown any sign of realizing how their practical interpretation of Helsinki principles, both at home and abroad, has affected other countries' views of the Soviet Union in the years since the Final Act was signed.

In 1975 the Final Act's main value for the Soviet Union was symbolic. The meeting and the signatures illustrated in the plainest available way the *de facto* peace settlement whereby the consequences of the second European civil war fought in the twentieth century had been resolved—a settlement already embodied in a series of treaties and international agreements from the Moscow Treaty of 1970 onwards, and now jointly witnessed by the two most important signatures of the CSCE Final Act: those of the United States President and of the General Secretary of the CPSU. As it turned out, this meeting at Helsinki also marked the high noon of Brezhnev's 1971 Peace Programme. For Soviet foreign policy, the next seven years were to be a period first of drift, then of crisis.

16. Drift

A SOVIET apologist might argue at this point either that his country's foreign policy did not falter at all; or alternatively, that during a period where there was almost a vacuum of power in Washington, brought to an end by the Democratic victory in the Presidential election of November 1976, the Soviet leadership had little option but to hold on and hope for the best. For the first view he might cite as evidence the proceedings of the XXVth CPSU Congress, which opened in Moscow on 24 February 1976, and confirmed both Brezhnev personally and his policies without reservation. For the second he need only point to the fact that US foreign policy-making in almost all important fields was frozen throughout 1976 and that thereafter Carter's conduct of affairs exasperated America's allies as much as it did the Soviet Union. Although both these arguments would be partly true, they overlook one Soviet decision in the field of foreign policy taken in the autumn of 1975 regarding a part of the world which had not hitherto loomed large in the calculations either of the Soviet Union or of the United States—Southern Africa.

Angola

In the African regional setting, in terms of CPSU political doctrine regarding countries of the developing world,[1] and in the context of Sino-Soviet rivalry, this decision was understandable. But in geopolitical terms, on the assumption that the Soviet relationship with the United States remained the first priority for the Soviet leadership in late 1975, the decision to send Soviet arms and to transport Cuban troops to Angola was a costly mistake. When Portugal* withdrew from Angola on 11 November 1975 it left the country independent, but in the grip of a civil war. Of the two rival governments, the Soviet Union supported that of Agostinho Neto, whose *Movimento Popular para a Libertaçao de Angola* (MPLA) had been receiving Soviet help since armed resistance to Portuguese rule began in 1961, while the United States supported that of FNLA/UNITA.[2] For world opinion, the FNLA/UNITA cause was not helped by the fact that their force included a substantial number of South African troops. (It is relevant that Brazil was one of the countries that recognized the Neto government immediately.) Indeed, South African intervention in Angola in October, before independence, almost succeeded in driving the MPLA out of the capital, Luanda; but the tide was turned in November/December by the arrival of 11,800 Cuban troops and 200 million US dollars worth of Soviet aid given to the MPLA between March and December 1975 (both these figures are US Government estimates). This build-up, coupled with the arrival in Luanda of an estimated 400 Soviet advisers in November, spurred on the US Government to seek Congressional approval of increased aid for the FNLA/UNITA; Congress refused; even CIA assistance was cut off by a vote of both Houses. By 11 February 1976 the MPLA had, with the help of some 15,000 Cuban troops, grown so strong that the Neto Government was recognized by the Organization of African States; Western European governments followed suit.[3]

* After almost half a century, the Portuguese armed forces restored democratic rule by a *coup d'état* in Lisbon in April 1974; decolonization followed.

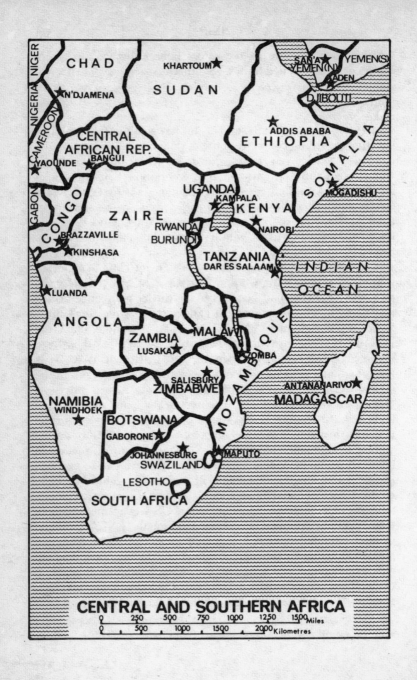

CENTRAL AND SOUTHERN AFRICA

Although it achieved its immediate objective, Soviet intervention in Angola, direct and indirect, can scarcely be said to have
enabled the Soviet Union to establish a sphere of influence in
Southern Africa. Put in the crudest terms, the United States
backed a loser in Angola, rather as the Soviet Union did in
Zimbabwe—but in dubious[4] company. Neither the United States
nor the Soviet Union had any real reason to regard what was
happening in Angola at the turn of 1975–6 as a zero-sum game.
There is no evidence that the Soviet leadership took this view; nor
did the US Congress at the time. However, the fact that the
initiative in Angola was probably Cuban, rather than Soviet, and
that Soviet troops did not themselves take part in the Angolan
fighting made little difference to the US Government's view.
Cuban troops could not have reached Angola in such numbers
without Soviet logistic support; and in any case, against the
troubled background of US–Cuban history from 1960 onwards,
the fact that this expeditionary force came from the Caribbean
was a stinging reminder of the past. The Angolan operation
awakened many people for the first time to the fact that—
strategic nuclear power apart—the Soviet Union was now
capable of projecting its conventional power across the world, like
the United States. Moreover, this realization coincided with a
growing acceptance in the West that the proportion of Soviet
GNP devoted to defence had, if anything, been underestimated
by Western sources; and by the end of 1975 these estimates
ranged between 11 and 13 per cent.[5] Not all at once, but
gradually, the Soviet intervention in Angola also came to be
regarded as a political watershed. Whether the Soviet leadership
miscalculated the effect that this intervention would have in
Washington, or whether they simply did not calculate its effect on
the Soviet–US relationship at all, is not clear. Either way, they
seem to have attached dangerously little value to the advice on
developments in American domestic politics which they must
have received from men like Dobrynin and Arbatov at the time.

Paradoxically—and indirectly—Soviet–Cuban intervention in
Africa led to one beneficial result: the reversal of United States
policy towards Southern Africa in April 1976—a U-turn that was
the more remarkable in that it was undertaken during an
electoral campaign at a moment when Ford was under pressure

from the right wing of the Republican Party. Kissinger began by delivering a speech[6] in Lusaka insisting on the need for a change of racial policy in South Africa and promising US support for black majority rule in Rhodesia and Namibia, economic aid to 'front-line' Southern African states affected by the economic sanctions imposed on Rhodesia, and repeal of the Byrd Amendment (whereby the United States imported Rhodesian chrome in defiance of the sanctions). He went on to meet the South African Prime Minister in June and September, followed by a shuttle round the capitals of Southern Africa, including meetings with Ian Smith in Pretoria, where he persuaded him to announce publicly his government's acceptance of the principle of black majority rule within two years.[7] In reality none of the problems of Southern Africa—in South Africa itself, Namibia, and Rhodesia—was simple enough to yield a solution to this final Kissingerian whirlwind. Yet the fact that he brought a fresh mind to these problems at least provided an impetus, previously lacking, that continued long after he himself left office in January 1977. If the Soviet Union had not intervened in Angola in late 1975, would this have happened, or would it have happened as soon as it did?

Be that as it may, contrary to the declared expectations of both Ford and Brezhnev after their meeting at Vladivostock in November 1974, no summit meeting was held in the following year. At first they were to meet in the spring of 1975 in order to sign SALT II; then in the autumn; then before the end of the year. In November 1975 Kissinger told a press conference that the strategic arms limitation talks were in a state of stagnation. There were indeed problems—notably the strategic potential of the Soviet *Backfire* bomber and the American cruise missile— which had caused the SALT negotiations to drag on through 1975. But agreement was not very far off when Soviet intervention in Angola, in my view, made it politically impossible for the Ford Administration to conclude a second strategic arms limitation agreement. True, Kissinger made one more journey to Moscow—in January 1976—to discuss the agreement (and also events in Angola); but by March, when Ford felt obliged to drop the word '*détente*' from his political vocabulary, there was no hope of further progress during that American electoral year.

To the question—did this failure matter?—one answer is that at the time both sides believed that it did and said so. Later on in the 1970s it became fashionable to remark that too much had been expected of the SALT process, on which the burden of sustaining the super-power relationship came increasingly to depend as the decade went on. To some extent this was inevitable, given the fact that until 1972 this relationship had centred on nuclear issues: hence the Nuclear Test Ban Treaty, the Non-Proliferation Treaty, the ABM Treaty, and SALT I. But in 1972–4 the super-power relationship had been deliberately expanded by the two governments to include other forms of arms control (notably the MBFR talks in Vienna), trade, and crisis management. In all these three fields the super-powers achieved little in 1975–6. In Vienna—though the MBFR talks were not bilateral—no progress whatever was made during these years.[8] In the economic field, the setback of January 1975 was significant not just for the development of Soviet–US commercial relations, but also for that of Soviet–Japanese commercial relations, since Japanese agreement to take part in the largest ventures in Soviet Asia, all of which required concessionary financial terms, depended on the assurance that there would be American participation as well. In 1976 the Soviet Government made further efforts to sign a trade treaty with the US on terms (including MFN treatment) satisfactory to the Soviet Union, without success. As for crisis management, at different moments during the years 1974–6 both super-powers behaved as though the Joint Declaration on Basic Principles of Relations between the USA and the USSR had never been signed in Moscow during the first summit meeting in June 1972.[9] If in this respect the Soviet Government was at fault in Africa, it is hard to absolve the US Government in the Middle East.

The Middle East

The 1974 agreements on the disengagement of forces on the Suez Canal and on the Golan Heights were followed by the Sinai Agreements of 2 September 1975;[10] and on 31 October for the first time in twenty-seven years a ship carrying an Israeli cargo passed through the Suez Canal (the Canal had been reopened in

June). These fruits of Kissinger's shuttle diplomacy marked the beginning of a realignment of political forces in the Middle East. As Egypt drew closer to the United States, with whom diplomatic relations were restored in June 1974, so it drew further away from the Soviet Union; in March 1976 the Egyptian People's Assembly voted to abrogate the treaty of 'unbreakable' friendship with the Soviet Union signed only five years earlier; and the Egyptian Government withdrew from the Soviet Navy the port facilities that had survived the Soviet exodus of 1972. Simultaneously with the Egyptian–US *rapprochement*, the Palestine Liberation Organization won an increasing measure of international recognition: in August 1974 from the Soviet Government, which allowed the PLO to open an office in Moscow and supported its claim to take part in the Geneva Conference[11] on an equal basis with other participants, and in October 1974 from all the states attending the Arab summit conference at Rabat, which unanimously—in the end, including even Jordan—resolved that the PLO was the 'sole legitimate representative of the Palestinian people on any Palestinian land that is liberated'. (The PLO became a full member of the Arab League two years later.) In the following month Yassir Arafat, the PLO leader, addressed the UN General Assembly for the first time; and in January 1976 the PLO attended a UN Security Council meeting on the Middle East.

Part of the price exacted for the Sinai Agreements of September 1975 by the Israeli Government was a written undertaking by the US Government that it would not 'recognize or negotiate with' the PLO as long as the PLO did not recognize Israel's 'right to exist' as well as the UN Security Council resolutions 242 and 338. In January 1976, before the Security Council met, Israel announced that if the PLO participated in the meeting, it would boycott the Geneva negotiations; and the US vetoed a Security Council resolution calling for a Palestinian State. This brought the Geneva Peace Conference process to an end. In fact US support of the Egyptian cause and Soviet support of the PLO's had already reduced Middle East cooperation between the US and Soviet Governments to a minimum. It was not until October 1977 that the new US Administration partly reversed its predecessor's Middle East policy, which by the end amounted to exclusion of the Soviet Union from the Middle-East peace-making process. On 1 October Gromyko and Cyrus Vance, the new US Secretary of State, agreed in Washington on a joint US–Soviet statement, based on UN Resolutions 242 and 338, which called for a reconvening of the Geneva Conference before the end of the year. In this statement both governments recognized the 'legitimate rights' of the Palestinians; the Soviet Government explicitly recognized Israel's 1967 frontiers; and it pledged responsible cooperation with the US Government for a comprehensive Middle East settlement.[12] This lucid interval in the madness of super-power rivalry in the Middle East lasted only a few weeks. (In the euphoria that followed Sadat's historic journey to Jerusalem in November 1977 and the Camp David Agreements of September 1978, the US–Soviet Joint Declaration was jettisoned by the US Government—events which will be discussed in a later chapter.) Had a US–Soviet agreement like the one of October 1977 been reached one or two years earlier, the threshold of Middle East crisis might not be quite as low as it is today.

The XXVth CPSU Congress

A Soviet reader of the proceedings and resolutions of this Congress, as of the Conference of European Communist Parties held in Berlin in June–July, would have observed few signs of the drift described in this chapter. On the contrary—in Brezhnev's own summing up[13]—the international position of the Soviet Union had never been more stable; 'facts' had borne out the timeliness and realism of the Peace Programme that he had presented five years earlier to the XXIVth Congress, which had shown 'the realistic way to end the cold war and set clear objectives in the struggle to replace the danger of war by peaceful cooperation'; and the development of peaceful relations between the USSR and the USA was reflected in a 'whole system of Soviet–US treaties, agreements, and other documents', among which Brezhnev described as 'unquestionably the most important' the Basic Principles of 1972, the 1973 Agreement on the Prevention of Nuclear War, and the Strategic Arms Limitation Agreements. The Soviet Government was trying to carry out the Vladivostock Accords and to 'prevent the opening of a new channel for the arms race, which would nullify everything achieved so far'. Little was said about Angola, which had been supported by the world's progressive forces because, from the first day of its independence, it had become an object of foreign intervention—'the handiwork of imperialism and South African racists'. True, there were influential forces in the United States that were trying to impair US–Soviet relations and international *détente* as a whole, by referring to an 'imaginary Soviet threat'; there had also been attempts to interfere in Soviet domestic affairs related to US discriminatory measures in the field of trade. This was 'not the kind of language that one can use with the Soviet Union'. The Soviet threat was 'a monster lie from beginning to end'.

On the economic front, the new Five-Year Plan, which Kosygin presented to the Congress, ushered in a 'quinquennium of productivity and quality': a recognition of the fact that the growth both of the Soviet labour force and of resources for capital investment would be much slower between 1976 and 1980. In terms of the projection of growth rates, the Tenth Five-Year Plan was more modest than any previous plan in Soviet economic history. There was no sign of economic reform. Nevertheless, by comparison with the problems faced in 1976 by the industrialized democracies of the West, the percentage goals laid down by the Soviet economic planners did not seem unimpressive at the time: national income (in the Soviet definition) in 1980 to be 26 per cent higher than in 1975; total industrial output to be 36 per cent higher; industrial consumer goods to be 32 per cent higher; and agricultural output to be 16 per cent higher—to take only a few of the Plan's projections.[14]

The heavy emphasis laid at this Congress on the continuity and the stability of policy on all fronts was reflected in personal terms in the Soviet leadership. Brezhnev's position as 'the recognized leader'[15] of the CPSU was confirmed. Moreover, having announced his chairmanship of the Defence Council,[16] he was appointed Marshal of the Soviet Union in May; in June 1977 he assumed the Presidency (following Podgorny's resignation); and in November 1977 he added the title of Commander-in-Chief of the Soviet Armed Forces. The one office which Brezhnev— unlike Khrushchev—did not assume was that of Chairman of the

Council of Ministers, which Kosygin retained until 24 October 1980, when Tikhonov succeeded him (Kosygin died in December of that year).

The CPSU Congress was followed three months later by the Conference of European Communist Parties, which opened in East Berlin after preparations that had lasted over a year. It was attended by all the East European parties, by the Yugoslav (but not the Albanian) party, and by the principal communist parties of Western Europe. To ensure Yugoslav participation, Brezhnev was reported to have sent Tito a note on 15 May accepting the principles of Communist Party equality and independence.[17] The Berlin Conference provided a refreshing contrast to the monolithic tedium of the Congress in Moscow. Some delegations criticized the CPSU—including the French,[18] Italian and Spanish—and the final communiqué[19] did not refer to the doctrine of proletarian internationalism. Behind all this lay the development of 'Eurocommunism': the loosening of the umbilical cord between Western European communist parties and the CPSU, which had begun with the posthumous publication of Togliatti's memorandum in 1964.[20] What gave this development particular importance for the United States was the possibility that a Western European ally of the US might be governed by a cabinet that included members of its Communist Party—a possibility exemplified by the Italian Communist Party's *compromesso stórico* with Christian Democracy, the French Communist Party's relationship with the French Socialist Party, and the re-emergence of left-wing parties in newly democratic Portugal and Spain. Embattled in Washington, Kissinger took the line that communist participation in a Western European government would be unacceptable to the US Government and incompatible with the obligations of the Western alliance. As subsequent events[21] in France have shown, he was wrong. The CPSU's attitude was perhaps more pragmatic. In my view, what mattered in 1976 for the Soviet leadership was first, that the Western and Eastern European Communist Parties should meet, and secondly, that they should all agree to put their signatures to the same document at the end of the conference. This they did.

In December 1976 it was Brezhnev's seventieth birthday. A sick man, but fortified by the outcome of these two communist gatherings, confirmed in a multiplicity of offices, and surrounded by a group of colleagues of many years' standing, in the second half of 1976 he had to deal with new leaders, first in China, following Mao's death on 9 September, and then in the United States, following Carter's victory in the Presidential elections. With neither country did he succeed in improving Soviet relationships over the years that followed. On the contrary, three years later the Chinese Government announced that it would not renew the Sino-Soviet Treaty of Friendship, Alliance, and Mutual Assistance when it expired in 1980;[22] and by the end of 1979 Carter described his opinion of the Soviet Union as having 'changed more drastically in the last week than in the previous two and a half years'.[23]

17. Nuclear Weapons Negotiations

The Proposal of March 1977

In one of his first speeches after the 1976 US presidential election, Brezhnev described a satisfactory outcome of SALT II as 'fully possible, the more so because its basic content has already been agreed'. In his inaugural address in January 1977, the new US President expressed the hope that 'nuclear weapons would be rid from the face of the earth'. He went on to plan his initial approach to SALT II according to two new principles. First, SALT was to be an objective on its own, separate from other US policy objectives. High on the list of these objectives was the need to distance himself from what he regarded as the *Realpolitik* of the previous Administration, and instead, to set the conduct of American foreign policy on a firm moral basis. One of the opening shots of Carter's human rights campaign, therefore, was to write a letter[1] to Sakharov—an action seen as irrelevant to the SALT proposal which his Secretary of State, Cyrus Vance, was to take to Moscow two months later. The second new principle was that SALT II should not remain enmeshed in the argument about the so-called peripheral[2] weapons systems, such as the American cruise missile and the Soviet *Backfire* bomber, which had been central to the US–Soviet strategic weapons negotiations from the Vladivostock summit meeting onwards. Instead it should focus on 'real' arms control: deep cuts in numbers of missile launchers, sub-limits on particular weapons systems, limits on weapons tests, and a ban on the deployment of new weapons.

The US proposal[3] of March 1977 was a diplomatic disaster. Hastily put together and publicly announced by the President himself in Washington before the US negotiators reached Moscow, it invited the Soviet Government to choose between two options: either the option of 'deferral', whereby the Vladivostock ceiling of 2,400 on ICBM, SLBM and 'heavy' bombers would be accepted, while the cruise missile and *Backfire* issues would be deferred until a later round of talks, or the new 'comprehensive' option, which was the one that the Carter Administration preferred. Under the terms of this 'comprehensive' option, ceilings for overall strategic missile launchers were to be reduced to between 1,800 and 2,000; the number of MIRV-equipped launchers was to be reduced to between 1,100 and 1,200, not more than 550 of which were to be ICBM, with a sub-ceiling of 150 imposed on the Soviet MIRV-equipped SS–18 'heavy' ICBM; ICBM and SLBM tests were to be limited to six a year; and although a 2,500 kilometre limit was proposed on the range of air-launched cruise missiles, the range of sea and ground-launched missiles was to be restricted to 600 kilometres.

The 'deferral' option had already been rejected by the Soviet Government in 1976. The 'comprehensive' option might have been negotiable if the Soviet Union had possessed the ability to switch the main thrust of its strategic nuclear effort to the sea, and if the proposal had been presented differently, after the ground had been diplomatically prepared in the way to which Soviet SALT negotiators had been accustomed. Whether or not this may one day prove to be the answer to the increasing vulnerability of all land-based strategic nuclear systems, in 1977 the Soviet sea-based ballistic missile force was technologically inferior to the United States equivalent, quite apart from its geographical disadvantages, which are permanent. The Soviet Government was therefore bound to regard the 'comprehensive' option as aimed directly at the heart of its strategic nuclear force, and particularly at its new generation of MIRV-equipped

SS–17s, 18s, and 19s. Carter's public announcement of his two alternative proposals therefore met a public Soviet refusal to discuss either of them. At a press conference called on 31 March—a rarity for the Soviet Foreign Minister—Gromyko described the aim of the US proposal as being to 'obtain unilateral advantages for the USA to the detriment of the Soviet Union'.[4] It is difficult to disagree.

Subsequent negotiations

This inauspicious first encounter did not prevent the two governments from opening SALT II talks in Geneva, where on 18 May a joint communiqué announced agreement on what was described as a common framework for further negotiations. The framework, which foreshadowed the text of the treaty finally signed two years later in Vienna, consisted of three parts: an eight-year treaty setting an overall ceiling on launchers and a sub-ceiling on MIRV-equipped launchers; a three-year protocol limiting the deployment of new systems (the cruise missile and 'heavy' ICBMs); and a statement of principles looking to the future—an eventual SALT III. In September 1977 both governments agreed to continue to abide by the provisions of the 1972 SALT I, which expired formally on 3 October.

The SALT talks dragged on, as they had after the summit meeting at Vladivostock three years earlier. This time, however, the debate was shriller; even *Pravda* took part; and the area of the debate was significantly broadened—from the 'central' (strategic) nuclear balance to that of the 'theatre' nuclear balance in Europe. As time went on, for most American critics of SALT II its signature meant virtually conceding the attainment of strategic nuclear superiority (a term now resurrected) to the Soviet Union in the mid-1980s. In the eyes of Soviet critics,[5] the US Government was hiding behind its Congressional opponents, such as Jackson. In Europe the reaction of political leaders was more complex and influenced, among other things, by some fresh developments which became apparent in 1977.

The European Dimension

These developments included Soviet deployment in Europe not only of the *Backfire* bomber, but also of SS–20 mobile missile launchers, which because of their intermediate range lay outside the scope of SALT II; the possibility of Western Europe being affected by a US–Soviet trade-off (restrictions on US cruise missiles against Soviet qualitative improvements); and the fact that the SALT II treaty was to contain a 'non-circumvention' clause, whereby both sides committed themselves not to evade the provisions of the treaty through third parties, even though this was a watered-down version of the tougher restriction for which Soviet negotiators had been pressing (a 'non-transfer' clause, which would have ruled out Western European use of US cruise missile and other technology). If faced with a choice, on broad political grounds Western European governments preferred SALT II to no SALT treaty at all: hence the support for the SALT II Treaty expressed by the British, French, and Federal German leaders at the Guadeloupe summit meeting in January 1979. But they became increasingly concerned by the way in which certain provisions of SALT II were beginning to spread over the line of demarcation previously separating the central strategic from the European theatre nuclear balance. By September 1977 the Foreign Ministers of the two super-powers had reached a point[6] in these negotiations which made the Europeans anxious lest SALT II should, in effect, 'decouple' Western Europe politically from the United States by separating US security from that of Western Europe. These anxieties were expressed in October 1977 by the West German Chancellor, Helmut Schmidt,[7] when he delivered the Alastair Buchan Memorial Lecture for that year in London:[8] by magnifying the military imbalance within Europe in the field of conventional and non-strategic nuclear weapons, 'strategic arms limitations confined to the United States and the Soviet Union will inevitably impair the security of the West European members of the Alliance'. Thus, before SALT II had even been signed, Western Europeans were beginning to wonder what SALT III might be like. A SALT III treaty seemed bound to affect in some degree the US forward-based systems and the British and French nuclear forces so far excluded from the SALT negotiations. It was important for Western European security that SALT II should offer no hostage that would have to be ransomed in a later negotiation.

The SALT II Treaty

This treaty was finally signed by Brezhnev and Carter at a one-day meeting in Vienna on 18 June 1979. It could have been signed in 1978 if the general climate of relations between the two super-powers had not worsened steadily as that year went on. (It would certainly have been signed in January 1979 but for the timing—in the same month—of the opening of full diplomatic relations between the US and China, followed almost at once by Deng Xiaoping's visit to the United States.) Even though SALT II was, in the event, destined never to come into force—the Senate debate on the Treaty was halted in January 1980[9]—its main provisions are central to the continuing debate on strategic and 'Eurostrategic' issues in the 1980s.

As agreed in 1977, the 1979 treaty consisted of three parts: an eight-year treaty to last until 1985; a protocol to last until the end of 1982; and a statement of principles and basic guidelines for SALT III. The numbers of launchers was not far off those agreed at Vladivostock nearly five years earlier: 2,250, with a sub-ceiling of 1,320 for MIRV-equipped ballistic missile launchers and air-launched cruise missiles (ALCM). Neither side was to build new 'heavy' missiles; the Soviet Union was allowed to equip its existing force of 308 'heavy' missiles with MIRV; and the deployment of ALCM was prohibited on other than heavy bombers. The problem of verifying MIRV was finally overcome by agreement that, once a launcher had fired a MIRV-ed missile, it would be counted as a MIRV-ed launcher from then onwards. Both sides agreed to notify each other of missile testing, to exchange information on their nuclear arsenals, and to refrain from interfering with each other's 'national technical means' of verification—primarily satellites. The US–Soviet Standing Consultative Commission in Geneva was given an expanded role. The ambiguous 'non-circumvention' clause, referred to above, was duly included.

The protocol placed no restriction on cruise missiles launched from heavy bombers, but the deployment (as opposed to testing) of ground and sea-launched cruise missiles with ranges of more than 600 kilometres was prohibited. The problem of *Backfire* was covered in an informal letter from Brezhnev to Carter, giving an assurance that the bomber's range and payload would not be increased and that it would not be produced at a rate of more than thirty a month. Finally, the statement of principles embodied in the third part of the treaty held out a hope—but not a commitment—that Salt III might limit both the number of launchers and further qualitative improvements. Unlike the nuclear agreements signed with the United States earlier in the decade, this treaty was not greeted with extravagant praise in the Soviet Union. It was simply a 'reasonable compromise, respecting the interests of both countries, based on the principle of parity and equal security'.[10] In the United States successive votes in Committee during the last half of 1979 showed opinion in the Senate to be in favour of the treaty on balance—but only just. One of the clearest victories for the US Administration was the defeat in Committee (by 9 votes to 6) of amendments to the treaty's verification provisions that would have obliged the Administration to renegotiate the treaty. It is an open question whether in the end the necessary two-thirds of senators present and voting would have voted for the treaty; and the question also became academic in the last week of December, when Soviet forces invaded Afghanistan.

With the advantages of hindsight, the most powerful argument in favour of the hundred-odd pages that constituted the SALT II Treaty is the fact that over the next three years both the Soviet and the US Government observed their provisions, even though the Treaty had never been ratified (the three-year protocol duly expired in 1982, however). That each of them did so, in spite of the bitterness of the polemics exchanged between the two governments in other contexts from December 1979 onwards, puts paid to some of the criticism levelled against the treaty at the time. And it is particularly significant that the incoming Republican Administration, having first described the SALT II Treaty as 'fatally flawed', in practice treated it in the same way as the preceding Democratic Administration had done—that is to say, almost as if it had been ratified and was therefore binding in international law. Moreover, the ABM Treaty of 1972 seems likely—at the time of writing—to survive the review which officials of the two governments duly began in Geneva in August 1982. This said, the sombre record cannot be ignored: through the five years that separated the Vladivostock Accords and the invasion of Afghanistan, both the Soviet Union and the United States roughly doubled the number of deliverable warheads in their nuclear arsenals. Equally important, each super-power dramatically improved the accuracy of its warheads—in the case of land-based missiles, down to a CEP[11] of 600 feet. The main reason why Brezhnev and Carter put their signatures to the Treaty in Vienna, and why—three years later—the governments of both the super-powers publicly announced their intention of adhering to its provisions, is that this agreement represented the lowest common denominator between the super-powers in strategic nuclear terms. Because of the lead-time of Research and Development, neither government has so far been prevented by SALT II from doing anything in the strategic nuclear field, either in the 1970s or in the opening years of the current decade, that it had planned to do. Their initial decisions to finance the Research and Development of the weapons systems of the 1980s were already taken around 1970, and the decision to commit resources of men, money, and materials to their mass production and development not later than 1975. (The process of Research and Development can best be defined as combining basic and applied research with the development of research into the new products and processes, up to and including the prototype stage.) Without SALT II, however, they might have felt obliged to do even more than they did; their reactions to each other's moves across the board of international politics might have been even less well judged than they were during this period; and the world might have become even more insecure in the process. As the principal American architect of the Treaty, Cyrus Vance, put it one year afterwards, 'we cannot in our approach to Moscow afford wild swings from being too trusting to being hysterical'.[12] What is certain is that the SALT II Treaty was signed five years too late.

The European nuclear balance

As SALT II, overtaken by events, limped towards its end, the wheel came full circle in Europe. The steady pace of the modernization of Soviet conventionally-armed forces had already led NATO governments to commit themselves in 1977 to 3 per cent annual increases in their defence expenditure in real terms, and in 1978 to endorse the so-called Long Term Defence Programme. These decisions were followed by NATO agreement, in December 1979, to modernize the European theatre nuclear force. This agreement foresaw the deployment in Western Europe of 108 *Pershing II* and 464 US ground-launched cruise missiles by 1983—a deployment to which the Alliance remains committed at the time of writing. For a Western European such as Schmidt, who had made public his view two years earlier, the Soviet decision to replace with (mobile and modern) SS-20s the aged intermediate-range missile force that had been targeted on Western Europe for two decades[13] was a decision to alter the military balance in Europe. For the Soviet Union, the NATO agreement would lead to a fundamental change in the opposite sense: if the proposed US nuclear deployment were to take place, it would bring Soviet territory within range of US theatre nuclear missiles for the first time. This view was expressed by Brezhnev, who said in a speech delivered in East Berlin on 6 October 1979[14] that Soviet intermediate range nuclear weapons would be reduced provided that NATO withdrew its decision to go ahead with the proposed deployment of *Pershing II*s and GLCMs. Partly for this reason and partly because of the strength of anti-nuclear feeling in some Western European countries, notably the Netherlands and Belgium, the NATO decision of December 1979 was 'two-tracked', being coupled with an offer to the Soviet Union to establish permanent limitations on (European) theatre nuclear forces through arms control negotiation—in effect an invitation to SALT III.

The uproar caused by the invasion of Afghanistan intervened. In July 1980, however, the Soviet proviso about the NATO decision was waived; in October Soviet and US officials met for preliminary talks on limiting intermediate range nuclear weapons in Europe; and finally, on 30 November 1981 the two governments opened formal negotiations in Geneva regarding intermediate range nuclear forces (INF).[15] On the eve of this meeting, in a speech delivered to the National Press Club in Washington, Reagan, who had by then been in office for ten months, put forward an INF proposal that has become known as the 'zero option': that the United States would cancel its deployment of

*Pershing II*s and GLCMs if the Soviet Union dismantled its SS-20, SS-4, and SS-5 missiles.[16] The Soviet public response, over the signature of the Defence Minister, Ustinov, was that the Soviet Union 'would not proceed to unilateral disarmament' and that the 'zero option' was absurd. 'If the US continues to insist on excluding from the INF negotiations its own FBS and the nuclear systems of Great Britain and France,' Ustinov went on, 'this will prevent progress. Do the Americans want to limit their nuclear weapons in Europe, or is their chief aim to maintain their own existing force of nuclear missiles here and to build it up further by deploying *Pershing* and GLCMs? . . . We shall insist on the inclusion in the framework of the negotiations of the British and French nuclear armaments and we are fully entitled to do this . . .'[17]

On 29 June 1982 the US and Soviet governments began 'official talks on the limitation and reduction of strategic arms' in Geneva. In his speech of 31 May announcing his government's decision to enter into this negotiation, Reagan confirmed that the US Government would 'refrain from actions which undercut' SALT II 'so long as the Soviet Union shows equal restraint'.[18] So far neither set of nuclear weapons negotiations—INF and SALT/START—has made any progress.

In his first speech delivered as General Secretary of the CPSU, Andropov reiterated the statement that the Soviet Union would not disarm unilaterally. He followed this up on 21 December with a long exposition of the Soviet position in both negotiations. The Soviet Union was, he said, prepared to reduce its strategic nuclear armaments by 'more than 25 per cent', or, as he put it in an interview given to an American correspondent ten days later, first to freeze these armaments at their existing level; then to reduce those levels 'by about 25 per cent on each side, leading to equal levels; and afterwards to move further—to fresh cuts.' As for INF, the Soviet Government had already proposed two options: first, that each side, the Soviet Union and the NATO governments, should renounce all types of nuclear weapons in Europe, both intermediate range and tactical; and secondly, that both the Soviet Union and the NATO countries should reduce their INF weapons by more than two thirds. He added the following proposal:

We are in particular ready to agree that the Soviet Union should keep in Europe only as many missiles as Britain and France—and not one more. This means that the Soviet Union would cut hundreds of missiles, including dozens* of the most modern missiles, called SS-20 in the West. So far as the Soviet Union and the USA are concerned, in the sphere of intermediate range missiles this would be a really honest 'zero option'. And if the number of British and French missiles were further reduced, the number of Soviet missiles would also be further reduced by the same amount.[19]

Although this proposal was swiftly given a chilly reception by the US, British, and French governments, it hit the Western headlines. It has been followed by the Prague Declaration issued after a two-day Warsaw Pact summit meeting which ended on 5 January 1983.† This declaration endorsed the Soviet position on arms control and revived the Pact's earlier offer of a non-aggression treaty between the two alliances. It also included one potentially significant innovation: a statement that any agreement on reducing armaments should provide for proper verification measures, 'including, where necessary, international procedures'.

Looking back, it is clear that nuclear weapons negotiations conducted at this desultory pace by the super-powers were bound, sooner or later, to lead to a dilemma of the kind that now confronts both West and East. The reason why these negotiations were so desultory and ineffective, at any rate from 1977 onwards, is fully intelligible only in the perspective of the momentous changes that were taking place in the international scene during these years, which are examined in the rest of this book. These years were largely wasted, so that—at the time of writing—the prospect for both sets of Geneva negotiations is bleak. In my view, however, the SS-20 and the cruise missile have at least served one useful purpose: as catalysts in the wider debate on what Brezhnev himself described a year before his death as the question that matters—'the overall result, the general balance.'[20]

---

* *ne odin desyatok*: literally, 'not one ten'.

† The meeting lies outside the timespan of this book. A summary of the proposals was contained in the *International Herald Tribune*, 7 January 1983. *Pravda*, 6 and 7 January 1983, carried the full text of the communiqué and the declaration respectively.

DEFENCE OF THE PERIMETER

18. The Far East

In Africa and in Asia, the changes referred to at the end of the previous chapter evolved mainly over a period of roughly three years extending from late 1977 onwards. In Africa they included Soviet–Cuban military intervention in the Horn. In the Middle East, in January 1979 the Shah of Iran was driven out by revolution; ten months later sixty-three Americans were taken hostage in the US Embassy in Teheran by Iranian students; and in March of that year the Egyptian–Israeli peace treaty was signed. In the Far East, in August 1978 Japan signed a peace treaty with China; Vietnam invaded Kampuchea on 27 December, six weeks after signing a treaty of friendship and cooperation with the Soviet Union; and in the same month it was announced that the United States and China would enter into full diplomatic relations on 1 January 1979. In that month Deng Xiaoping (reinstated in office for the second time in July 1977) paid an official visit to the United States. In February 1979 Chinese troops began a four-week punitive invasion of Vietnam. At the very end of December Soviet forces invaded—and subsequently occupied—Afghanistan, where eighteen months earlier a pro-Soviet government had been installed by a military *coup d'état*.

To highlight these events is not to suggest that they were the only ones in these two continents that mattered. In Africa, for example, there were other wars and other interventions from outside the continent. Taken together, however, this series of events profoundly affected each super-power's judgement of the other's policy during this period. But the starkest view of all was that taken from Peking, where during these years (and beyond—until 1981) world war was officially regarded as inevitable. On this view, Soviet moves were not reactions to local or regional developments, but part of a gradual attempt to gain control of strategic nodal points, such as the Straits of Hormuz and the

Straits of Malacca—a process which would lead ultimately to Soviet encirclement of China.* The view looking outwards from Moscow was very different. For a Soviet leadership whose constant endeavour was to resist internal change, what was needed on the Soviet Union's Asian frontiers was a ring of stable regimes with which the Soviet Government could develop at least tolerable relationships. Instead, as the 1970s drew to a close, what they saw on the Soviet Union's Asian perimeter and in the countries adjoining it further south was convulsion and change, little of which could be turned to immediate Soviet advantage. For the purposes of a study of Soviet foreign policy, these developments, overlapping in time and not readily susceptible to chronological treatment, may be divided broadly into two chains of events—one affecting Soviet relations with the Far East and the other affecting Soviet relations with the Islamic world— which in the last week of 1979 intersected, in Afghanistan, traditionally the buffer state between the Soviet Union, China, Iran, and the Indian subcontinent.

In 1977 Deng Xiaoping returned to all his posts—membership of the Central Committee and of the Politburo, Vice-Chairman of the Chinese Communist Party, Vice-Chairman of the Military Committee, Vice-Chairman of the State Council, and Chief of the General Staff. In due course he secured not only the replacement of Hua Guofeng (as Prime Minister in 1980 and as Chairman of the Party in the following year), but also a formal reassessment of Mao Zedong by the Chinese leadership. Deng's return marked the beginning of a major programme of reform in China. At home, this programme—the Four Modernizations[1] of 1978—in effect repudiated the legacy of the Eleven Years (1966–76).[2] Abroad, the new leadership pursued a foreign policy which was open to a degree unimaginable at the time when China first emerged from its long period of isolation in 1971. But one aspect of Chinese foreign policy that remained unaltered was the Sino-Soviet relationship: a field in which Deng was personally committed to

* One of the revelations made in 1980 at the trial of the Gang of Four, which included Mao's widow, was that in 1971 Lin Biao (with whom they had close links) had planned to set up a separate state in southern China. After the failure of the plot Lin Biao was on his way to the Soviet Union when his aircraft crashed in Mongolia.

maintaining Mao's line. Indeed, he reinforced it, by drawing China closer to the United States and to Japan. Both these developments—the 'normalization' of Sino-American relations and the Sino-Japanese Peace Treaty—were unwelcome to the Soviet Union.

By the beginning of the 1980s the Soviet Union had become the second largest export market for Japanese steel products and Japan had become the most important single market for Soviet timber and coal. But the great projects for the joint development of Soviet Asia, which had beckoned to both Japan and the Soviet Union in the early 1970s, lay dormant. The reason was partly financial—the Japanese would not accept the risks involved without US participation (which from 1975 onwards was not forthcoming)—and partly political. From 1976 Soviet–Japanese relations were increasingly troubled by the territorial issue of the Kurile Islands.[3] In the Japanese view, this was one of the 'unresolved problems since World War II', on which the conclusion of a Soviet-Japanese peace treaty was described as depending in the communiqué signed in October 1973, when the Japanese Prime Minister, Tanaka, visited Moscow (Tanaka claimed that Brezhnev then assured him that the issue of the Northern Territories was included in the phrase 'unresolved problems'). In 1976 the Japanese Foreign Minister 'inspected' the islands; in 1978 the Japanese Government began to promote tours for the public to view the islands from a distance; and three years later it made 7 February[4] 'Northern Territories Day'.

For its part, the Soviet Government did not help its cause in Tokyo by proclaiming the 200-mile zone beyond the Soviet coastline as an exclusive Soviet fishing zone from 1 March 1977 and by including in it the marine areas adjacent to Hokkaido. Although the Soviet Government made some concessions to Japanese fishing interests in an interim fishing agreement concluded in May 1977, the new Japanese Foreign Minister, Sonoda, was met on a visit to Moscow in the following year with a Soviet refusal to admit that a Soviet–Japanese territorial issue existed at all. On 16 February Japan signed an 8-year, 20 billion US dollars industrial trade agreement and on 12 August, a Treaty of Friendship and Cooperation with China, including the 'anti-hegemony' clause.[5] The Soviet response to its signature was to describe the treaty as 'a threat to stability in Asia' (in Tass's words) and to fortify the Northern Territories. Although the Japanese Government has continued to insist that Japan is committed to neither side in the Sino-Soviet dispute, the Chinese Government supports the Japanese claim to the islands.

Soviet handling of Japanese issues during these years was insensitive, but the hardness of the Soviet political line towards Japan is partly explicable in the context of the Carter Administration's moves, from May–December 1978, to 'play the Chinese card', as Brezhnev himself called it in a speech delivered in Minsk on 25 June, when he described this as a 'short-sighted and dangerous policy, which its authors would bitterly regret'. If the Chinese felt themselves threatened by Soviet encirclement in Indo-China, where the Vietnamese invaded Kampuchea at the end of the year, the growing intimacy of Sino-US relations was a major cause of anxiety for the Soviet leadership. By comparison with the way in which the US President and his National Security Adviser had handled similar issues in 1971–2, US Far Eastern diplomacy in 1978 was hamhanded. Examples are Brzezinski's behaviour during his visit to Peking in May and Carter's unilateral assertion, in December, that Brezhnev had reacted 'positively' to the US decision to normalize its relations with China and to end formal diplomatic relations with Taiwan from 1 January 1979 (a decision that was announced six days before Vance was to meet Gromyko in order to complete the SALT II negotiations in Geneva).[6] But the entry of the US and Chinese governments into full diplomatic relations was bound to get under Soviet skins, however skilfully it had been presented by the US Government. It was followed almost immediately by Deng Xiaoping's visit to the United States—the first visit by a Chinese leader since before the Revolution of 1949—and then by the Chinese month-long invasion of Vietnam. Although the communiqué issued at the end of Deng's visit drew a distinction between US and Chinese security interests, the wording[7] must have struck the Soviet Government as weak, given that during his visit Deng had publicly pressed for a Sino–US–Japanese alliance and declared that China would be obliged to 'punish' Vietnam for its invasion of Kampuchea.

In the event, the Chinese incursion into Vietnam revealed the deficiencies of the Chinese armed forces, which suffered 20,000 casualties; and by the end of the year it was becoming clear that China could not afford both to buy modern defence equipment from Western Europe and at the same time to make the investments required by the domestic economy. Nevertheless, the Chinese went far enough—for Soviet discomfort—down the road towards the purchase of sophisticated equipment from the West: for example, British *Harrier* jump-jet aircraft, which would have been capable of giving the Soviet air force a much harder battle on the Chinese frontier than the Chinese copies of Soviet MIGs[8] with which the Chinese air force is equipped. While the US Government refrained from selling arms to China in 1979, it was content for its allies to do so (subsequently the US Government moved to a position that would enable it to sell 'non-lethal' military equipment to China). In Soviet eyes, China's international alignment under its new leaders, even though it did not amount to the kind of alliance advocated by Deng while he was in the United States, looked something very like it in practice. Against this background the Chinese decision not to renew the Sino-Soviet Treaty (which was theoretically still in force) after its expiry in 1980 cannot have come as a surprise in Moscow. In October 1979 the Chinese Government announced that the bilateral talks with the Soviet Union, especially on the frontier issue, had reached deadlock. In May of the following year China successfully tested its first intercontinental ballistic missile; in October 1982 its first missile was launched from a submarine.

To the Soviet contention that China's armed forces represent a threat to the Soviet Union, of which any Soviet leadership is bound to take account, the Chinese reply is broadly threefold. First, China has neither the wish nor the resources to become a super-power; the aim of its investment in nuclear weapons is minimal nuclear deterrence. Secondly, China will have more than enough problems to solve within its own borders until well into the twenty-first century, without adding the further problem of hostilities across its northern frontier. Thirdly, the size and capability of the Soviet forces deployed along this frontier and in Mongolia are plain for all to see: the number of Soviet divisions almost quadrupled between 1963 and 1982—to about forty-seven, under a *Stavka* (Supreme High Command) responsible for all Soviet forces in the Far East. Since the end of 1977 Soviet SS-20 mobile intermediate range ballistic missiles have been deployed against Chinese targets.[9]

In the Chinese historical perspective, the Russians are comparatively recent intruders into Asia; it was the Chinese who defeated the Russians on the banks of the Amur river as late as 1685.[10] For the Russians, the eight years (1950–8) of an alliance which the West mistakenly called the Sino-Soviet bloc, represented no more than a brief interlude in the centuries of hostility and suspicion generated between the two empires as the Russians moved eastwards across Siberia, compounded by an atavistic trauma deep in the consciousness of every Russian—the memory of the Mongol invasions of the Middle Ages. The fact that Russia was invaded by the Mongols, not by the Chinese (who were indeed invaded by the Mongols themselves) is politically irrelevant—national memory, like individual memory, distorts. By comparison with the eight years of the Sino-Soviet 'bloc', the Sino-Soviet dispute has now lasted for almost a quarter of a century—longer than the Sino-American dispute that began in 1949. The impact on the Soviet leadership of the announcement of 15 July 1971 (that Nixon intended to accept an invitation from Mao to visit China in the following year) has been described in an earlier chapter. But the Sino-US *rapprochement* of 1972 did not, in the event, go quite all the way to restoring normal relations between China and the United States. By the time that their relations were finally normalized, nearly seven years later, this healing of the breach coincided with profound changes inside China. In my view, the political development that caused the Soviet Union the deepest anxiety during this period was the growing intimacy of China's relationship both with the United States and with Japan (not to mention Western Europe), set against the background of the internal Chinese reforms which, from 1977 onwards, brought the domestic paralysis of China to an end.

Whether this anxiety was soundly based is open to question. Could two countries with interests as diverse as China and the United States really have a 'strategic partnership' or a 'parallel strategic outlook'? That the Soviet anxiety is strongly felt, however, is amply attested by both Soviet and Western sources.[11]

The strength of this feeling is, therefore, an important factor in any assessment of the prospect for Sino-Soviet relations during the rest of the 1980s. The Soviet leadership can take some comfort from the degree of the present Republican Administration's susceptibility to the Taiwan lobby in the United States. So long as this remains, the path of Sino-US relations cannot be smooth; judging by the terms of the interim compromise on US arms sales to Taiwan agreed between the US and Chinese governments on 17 August 1982,[12] the US Government seems to take a lot for granted in Peking. As yet, the Soviet Government has not yet taken advantage of the US Government's insensitivity in this field. Such olive branches as Brezhnev offered—for example, his speech in Tashkent in March 1982[13]—do not seem to have been substantial. However, the Soviet Deputy Foreign Minister, Ilychev, returned to Peking in October for talks about talks—the first for three years—and after a conversation with Andropov in the margins of Brezhnev's funeral, the Chinese Foreign Minister expressed his 'optimism' about the future of Sino-Soviet talks. Meanwhile the formal Chinese position is one of opposition to both the super-powers, whose pursuit of global domination was described by Hu Yaobang, in his report to the CCP's XIIth National Congress on 1 September 1982, as 'the main source of instability and turmoil in the world'.[14]

If the Soviet leadership were once to decide that it was worth making serious territorial concessions, they could put together a package of offers both to China and to Japan that their governments might be tempted to accept. Nevertheless, my view remains that the ideological and political issues dividing the Soviet Union and China are still so many and so profound that, for the foreseeable future, a reconciliation at party level—between the CPSU and the CCP—is not practical politics. What is clearly conceivable is an accommodation that would be reached not between the two communist parties, but between the two governments: in effect an agreement to differ, on the model of the Belgrade Declaration of June 1955.[15] This agreement, reached between Khrushchev and Tito following Khrushchev's Canossa journey—admittedly after only seven years of hostility—brought a measure of order to the Soviet–Yugoslav relationship. Although a similar Sino-Soviet accommodation is not yet in sight, the West would be ill-advised not to be prepared for it in advance. By enabling the governments of the Soviet Union and China to devote less effort to preparing for a war that could benefit no one, and would do incalculable harm, it might even contribute to the overall stability of the Far East.

19. The Arc

THESE developments in the Far East overlapped with others, equally momentous, in the Islamic world. Speaking to the Foreign Policy Association in Washington on 20 December 1978, in the midst of these events, Brzezinski, the US National Security Adviser said:

An arc of crisis stretches along the shores of the Indian Ocean, with fragile social and political structures in a region of vital importance to us threatened with fragmentation. The resulting political chaos could well be filled by elements hostile to our values and sympathetic to our adversaries.[1]

Since one end of the so-called arc was in the Horn of Africa and the other in Afghanistan, much of the responsibility for the 'political chaos' in the countries lying along the arc has been ascribed to the Soviet Union. In fact, during these years the Soviet Government, like the Government of the United States, found itself caught up in a sequence of regional events, whose final outcome still—at the time of writing—remains to be seen. Brzezinski's description, quoted above, of the countries lying along the arc could equally well have been derived—with the addition of a little Marxist terminology—from a speech delivered by one of his Soviet opposite numbers. Indeed, for the Soviet Union this has long been 'a region of vital importance' and the Soviet fear that it might be 'filled by hostile elements' is the mirror image of US anxiety on the same score. What alarmed the West was the ease and the speed with which the Soviet Union was now able to project its military power globally: to the African continent, for the second time in two years, and then across its own Asian frontier—the first occupation of a neighbouring country by the Soviet armed forces since the invasion of Czechoslovakia in 1968.

The Horn of Africa

Although the scale and the severity of the conflict in the Horn were unsurpassed anywhere else during these years, they did not come out of a clear blue sky. The fierce ethnic loyalties of this region, uniting people on each side of Ethiopia's frontiers, are old ones; and its frontier disputes were inherited from the imperial era. From its inception, in 1960, the Somali Democratic Republic had been committed by the terms of its constitution to 'liberate' the two million Somali[2] nomads from Ethiopian rule. The collapse of the Emperor Haile Selassie's regime in September 1974, followed in February 1977 by the Marxist Lieutenant-Colonel Mengistu's *coup d'état* in Addis Ababa, seemed to offer the Somalis an opportunity to fulfil this commitment. At the beginning of 1977 the United States was still Ethiopia's principal ally (and provider of arms) outside the African continent, while the Soviet Union had supported Somalia from the beginning of the previous decade and had supplied increasing quantities of arms after the Somali Republic moved to the left following a *coup d'état* in 1969. In 1974 a Soviet–Somali Treaty of Friendship and Cooperation was signed; the Soviet armed forces obtained facilities at Berbera, including the use of the port there by the Soviet Indian Ocean squadron.

Thus the Horn of Africa was highly combustible. Yet paradoxically, when the conflagration came, each of the super-powers found itself supporting the opponent of its traditional ally in the region: the Soviet Union changed sides in the course of 1977, the United States three years later.[3] To begin with, Soviet policy sought to mediate between Ethiopia and Somalia, rather in the way that the Soviet Prime Minister had mediated between India and Pakistan in 1966. This time the mediators were Castro, who met Ethiopian, Somali, and South Yemeni leaders in Aden in March 1977, and Podgorny. The 'progressive' front or federation that Castro tried to form foundered on Somali insistence on occupying the Ogaden. By the autumn Somali forces had not only won control of the Ogaden, but reached

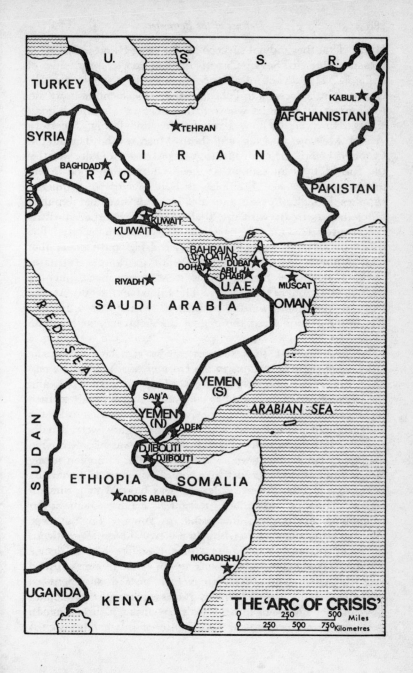

THE 'ARC OF CRISIS'

Harat. That they did not succeed in capturing Harat was in large measure due to Soviet–Cuban intervention on the side of Ethiopia. This switch of alliances was made easier by the US Government's decision in February 1977 to suspend military aid to Ethiopia, as a country whose government was violating human rights. However, there was much toing and froing (Mengistu visited Moscow in May and both Moscow and Havana in October) before Soviet air-lifts to Addis Ababa got under way. By the end of 1977 an estimated[4] 2,000 Cuban and 1,000 Soviet military had reached Ethiopia, as well as large quantities of supplies brought by sea and air. On 13 November Somalia abrogated its treaty with the Soviet Union and expelled all its Soviet advisers. One year later the Soviet Union replaced this treaty by a twenty-year Treaty of Friendship and Cooperation with Ethiopia. After a further attempt to capture Harat in January 1978, the Somali forces were driven back and—by March—right out of the Ogaden. The Ethiopian forces were then able to turn northwards to Eritrea, where the Ethiopian Government announced the end of the eighteen-year revolt in November.

Without Soviet–Cuban support, given on a large scale, the outcome of these operations in the Horn of Africa in 1978 would have been very different. The last word has not yet been said in the Horn of Africa; fighting has continued intermittently in both the Ogaden and Eritrea. As in Angola, the combat role was assigned to Cuban forces, while Soviet military were usually advisers. But the initiative taken in the Horn was plainly Soviet; the Soviet Government won a friend; and the Ethiopian ruling *Dergue* supported the Soviet invasion of Afghanistan two years later. In 1977 the Soviet leadership was faced with a difficult choice. Their Somali allies' territorial claims against their neighbours made them impossible to support (at the time Western governments also withheld military aid from Somalia for the same reason). The Soviet Union therefore had to decide whether it could afford to stand aside while Somali forces, armed over the years with Soviet weapons, attacked and defeated Ethiopia, whose new leadership professed socialist principles. That the decision went in Ethiopia's favour is not surprising. In the long term the political significance of this conflict in the regional context may turn out to be less than it appeared to some observers at the time. It was in any case swiftly dwarfed by events in Muslim countries further north. Nevertheless, Soviet–Cuban military intervention in the Horn—the establishment of a second Cuban expeditionary force in Africa, with Soviet logistic support, two years after their intervention in Angola—made a powerful impact on Western minds.

The Middle East

The gradual realignment of forces in the Arab world from 1974 onwards—the US–Egyptian *rapprochement* and the Soviet espousal of the PLO—has been discussed in an earlier chapter. In 1978–9 this process was given a new dimension by two major events: the Camp David 'framework' agreements[5] and the Iranian Revolution. The Soviet Government had nothing to do with the former, for which the US Government—and the US President in particular—rightly claimed much of the responsibility. The latter event was greeted with dismay by the West. Perplexity may be the best way to describe the Soviet reaction to the Iranian Revolution, for which Soviet policy was in no way responsible. The road towards each of these remarkable events was opened by the leaders of the countries concerned: in 1977 by Sadat's vision and, in 1978, by the folly of the Shah.

Future historians will praise Sadat's courage in undertaking his visit to Jerusalem on 19 November 1977 (Begin reciprocated with a visit to Ismailia). They will also conclude that by signing the 'framework for peace in the Middle East' and the 'framework for the conclusion of a peace treaty between Egypt and Israel' at Camp David ten months later, Sadat virtually helped to sign his own death warrant.[6] A comparison of the five proposals that he put forward in his address to the Knesset on 20 November 1977 with what he settled for in September 1978/March 1979, explains the reason why. Sadat's initial five points were: Israeli withdrawal from all occupied territory, including Jerusalem; acknowledgement of the Palestinians' right to their own state; the right of all states to live in peace within secure frontiers; observation of the principle of not resorting to force; and the termination of the state of belligerency. Even these five points were enough to split the

Arab world; the Arab states confronting Israel rejected Sadat's invitation to negotiate a peace settlement in Cairo; and the Soviet Government rejected the invitation to Cairo as well.

The treaty eventually signed in Washington by Sadat and Begin, in March 1979, was in effect a separate peace agreed between Egypt and Israel: a bargain, whereby Israeli troops were to withdraw by stages from the Sinai Peninsula.* The two countries exchanged ambassadors a year later. The problem of Jerusalem was left on one side. As for the Palestinians, guidelines for future negotiations regarding 'full Palestinian autonomy' were laid down in the first of the two framework documents agreed at Camp David, which was loosely linked with the second. The execution of the second document was not made conditional on the first, however. These guidelines provided for 'transitional arrangements for the West Bank and Gaza for a period not exceeding five years'. In order to negotiate 'the details of a transitional arrangement', the Jordanian Government was to be invited to 'join the negotiations on the basis of this framework'. The 'new arrangements should give due consideration to both the principle of self-government by the inhabitants of those territories and to the legitimate security concerns of the parties involved'. As soon as a 'freely elected self-governing authority (administrative council)' was 'established and inaugurated' in the West Bank and Gaza, the transitional period would begin; and not later than the third year after the beginning of the transitional period, negotiations were to take place to 'determine the final status of the West Bank and Gaza and its relationship with its neighbours, and to conclude a peace treaty between Israel and Jordan by the end of the transitional period'.

Neither Jordan nor any other Arab state agreed to countenance negotiations of the kind envisaged in the first framework document. In the years that followed, these negotiations—between Israel and Egypt—dragged on in fits and starts, with no meeting of minds[7] and with the cracks that had been papered over by the ambiguous Camp David language becoming increasingly obvious as one new Israeli settlement on the West

---

* Israel, who received 2 billion US dollars from the US for the construction of new airfields on its side of the frontier, completed the process of withdrawal in April 1982.

Bank followed another. Moreover, even this limited result was achieved only by prodigious expenditure of American effort, leaving the United States with little leverage for use in any future attempt to bring about a Middle Eastern peace settlement. Not only did the United States President perform personally the role of go-between without which the Egyptian–Israeli bargain would never have been struck, but the Israeli Government also insisted on the signature, by (Vance and Dayan) of a Memorandum of Agreement[8] between the United States and Israel. Vague though the terms of this agreement were, coupled with the Carter Administration's re-endorsement of the previous Administration's undertaking regarding the PLO, they confirmed the fears aroused in the rest of the Arab world by the Camp David agreements six months earlier. Today, it is still argued by some that the first framework document retains an important merit: that it is based on the UN Security Council Resolutions 242 and 338 'in all their parts' and that it specifically recognizes the 'legitimate rights of the Palestinian people and their just requirements'. There can indeed be no doubt about this Israeli commitment; the words are there, in the first document signed at Camp David. But what happened on the ground during the next four years speaks for itself: Israel's gradual annexation of the West Bank *de facto*; the formal annexation of the Golan Heights in December 1981; the air raid on Baghdad in June 1981; a year later the invasion of South Lebanon; the siege and occupation of West Beirut; and the events that followed in September 1982.*

Sadat visited Jerusalem seven weeks after the Soviet and US Governments had issued their Joint Declaration on the Middle East, on 1 October 1977. Confronted by a United States Government that had 'perfidiously broken the agreement established in the Soviet–US Declaration', committed to the PLO, and faced by a Middle East in which Egypt was ostracized by every Arab country—precisely on the Palestinian issue—the Soviet Government could hardly have responded differently to what has since become known as the Camp David process. In the language

---

* At the time of writing, the massacre of Palestinian refugees on 16–18 September was still *sub judice* in Israel, but the Israeli commission of enquiry's interim report had warned Begin, among others, that evidence presented (much of it in camera) was potentially damaging to them: *The Times*, 25 November 1982.

of the official Soviet summary, it 'ignored the fundamental problems of a Middle East settlement and the interests of the other participants in the conflict'; without solving 'a single one of the basic problems . . . on the contrary, it complicated the situation still further'.[9] At the time, the broad sweep of Middle Eastern developments in the autumn of 1978 encouraged most Western observers. The end of the thirty years war between Egypt and Israel was in sight; Begin and Sadat went on to receive Nobel prizes for their part in bringing this about; Camp David was regarded as a personal triumph for Carter; and the United States seemed to have established an unassailable relationship with all three of the leading military powers in the region: Israel, Iran, and Egypt. This imposing triangle outweighed events further south—including those in the Horn. Yet at the very moment when the Camp David documents were being signed, one of the triangle's three sides was already crumbling—in Iran.

The course taken by the Iranian Revolution—from the general strikes of March 1978, through the Shah's departure in January 1979, until the return from exile of Ayatollah Khomeini on 1 February 1979—lies outside the scope of this book, as do its causes. One of the chief reasons for the collapse of the Shah's regime, however, was the closeness of his identification with Western values: an identification compounded by years of praise heaped on the Shah by Western governments as being the military guarantor of stability in the Persian Gulf. All Western governments contributed indirectly to this collapse by their encouragement of the Shah's economic and military fantasies during the 1970s (a very late example was Carter's toast to the Shah in Teheran on 31 December 1977, in which he declared— among other things—that there was no other ruler for whom he felt deeper gratitude or a greater personal friendship).[10] The replacement of the imperial regime in Iran by a fundamentalist Islamic republic—and a Shi'a republic at that—coupled with American inability either to understand[11] what was going on in Iran in 1978, or to forestall it, or to adjust to subsequent events there—an impotence that reached its nadir in the protracted drama of the US Embassy hostages in 1979/80—taken together, all this left the conservative leaders of Saudi Arabia and the Gulf States feeling dangerously exposed. From then onwards it has been US policy to seek to convince these leaders that the primary destabilizing factor in the region is the Soviet threat. To counter it, in his State of the Union speech delivered on 23 January 1980, Carter declared that the United States would be prepared to use force if necessary to protect its vital interests in the Gulf, including the supply of oil. In the preceding month Brzezinski had already spoken of the need for the US to be able to respond 'quickly, effectively and even pre-emptively'. In March 1980 the US Rapid Deployment Force (RDF) was established, primarily for use against Soviet forces, or so-called Soviet 'proxies' in Third World countries, and above all in the Gulf. In November 1981 the US and Israeli governments signed an Understanding on Strategic Cooperation 'designed against the threat . . . caused by the Soviet Union or Soviet-controlled forces . . . '

The Soviet invasion of Afghanistan notwithstanding, this identification of the Soviet Union as the chief threat to the Gulf regimes and the related concept of the RDF are flawed in several respects. To take the RDF first, its name itself is misleading. The setting up of the RDF Headquarters in 1980 did not result in the formation of any new American units. The US ground forces available for a deployment of this kind remained then what they had been before—82nd Airborne Division, 101st Airmobile Division, and two Marine Divisions—of which the airborne division could be deployed in the Gulf in—at best—just under a week. Since then the US Government has been able to negotiate basing facilities in Somalia, Kenya, and Oman (the Diego Garcia base is 2,300 miles from the head of the Gulf); and in November 1980 the US held joint military exercises in Egypt, among other Arab countries. The most significant change in the current decade has been the substantial increase in the US naval task force deployed in the Gulf. However, if the essence of the military problem is which of the two super-powers can get 'combat boots on the ground'[12] first in the Gulf, the advantage clearly rests with the Soviet Union, on whose border the Middle East lies. And the governments of the Gulf region cannot have been encouraged by the failure of Operation *Eagleclaw* in April 1980.[13] In reality, the Soviet Union does not in present circumstances present the main threat to Saudi Arabia and the Gulf States. The sources of instability in the region are of a different order: social, religious, and the region's principal political issue—the Arab–Israeli dispute and the Palestinian problem.

In spite of sporadic expressions of American displeasure, the Arab states have watched the United States become more and more closely identified with its 'strategic partner', Israel, and with Israeli policy towards the Palestinians: a trend, which—if it is to be maintained through the 1980s—must contribute towards Egypt's return to the mainstream of Arab politics. Following the evacuation of PLO and Syrian troops from Beirut in August 1982 (supervized by an international force), on 2 September the US Government undertook its first major initiative in the Middle East for four years. The most significant feature of President Reagan's broadcast statement was the fact that it was not agreed with the Israeli Government, which at once announced that it would not enter into negotiations on the basis of the 'positions of the United States', since they 'seriously deviate from the Camp David agreement, contradict it and could create a serious danger to Israel, its security and its future'. In fact Reagan's statement described the Camp David agreement as the foundation of US policy. But it called for a 'fresh start' and a 'new realism'. In the US Government's view, 'self-government by the Palestinians of the West Bank and Gaza in association with Jordan offers the best chance for a durable, just and lasting peace'. The US Government would support neither the establishment of an independent Palestinian state in the West Bank and Gaza nor annexation or permanent control by Israel. The immediate adoption by Israel of a 'settlement freeze, more than any other action, could create the confidence needed for wider participation' in the peace negotiations—between Israel, Jordan, and the Palestinians—envisaged by the US President.[14] From the opposite end of the spectrum, the Soviet reaction to Reagan's initiative was as critical as that of the Israeli Government: criticism that was followed three weeks later by the description of the Sabra and Chatila massacres as genocide, 'the fruit of strategic cooperation between the USA and Israel, who are seeking, with the help of the so-called Reagan plan, to ensure the continuation of the Camp David policy'.[15]

Through the events of recent years in the Middle East, the United States has been a principal actor, whereas the role of the

Soviet Union has been, by comparison, performed on the margin. Thus, it was not until November 1978 that Soviet vocal support of the Iranian Opposition began; in the same month Brezhnev warned the United States that 'military interference in the affairs of Iran would be regarded as a matter affecting Soviet security interests'; and on 13 February 1979 the Soviet Government recognized the new Iranian Government, expressing its 'readiness to support it and to develop relations between both governments on the basis of the principles of equality, good neighbourliness, the recognition of national sovereignty, and non-interference in internal affairs'. This rather chilly phraseology perhaps reflected the fact that the Soviet Government regarded the 1921 Soviet–Iranian Treaty as still in force (Articles 5 and 6 of this treaty provide the Soviet Union with a legal basis for intervention in Iran). This treaty, like the CENTO Treaty, was revoked by the new Iranian Government. As late as August 1980 Teheran and Moscow radios were broadcasting respectively the Iranian Foreign Minister's demand that the Soviet Government should renounce Articles 5 and 6 and the Soviet Foreign Minister's refusal.[16] So far from benefiting from the Iranian Revolution, the Soviet Union suffered some economic damage as its immediate consequence: one of the first acts of the new Iranian Government was to cancel plans to build a second gas pipeline to the Soviet Union, and to increase the price of gas being supplied to the Soviet Union under the 1966 Agreement. Both in 1978 during the Iranian Revolution and in the subsequent Iraqi–Iranian War, which Brezhnev described as 'senseless', the Soviet posture was even-handed.[17]

In October 1980 the Soviet Government signed a twenty-year Treaty of Friendship and Cooperation with Syria.[18] The intention underlying this treaty, which broadly followed the model of Soviet treaties of friendship concluded with other countries, was stated by Brezhnev at the State dinner given in Moscow on 8 October 1980 in honour of the Syrian President: 'the Gulf, just as any other region of the world, is the sphere of vital interests of the states lying there, and not of some others . . . And no one has the right to meddle from outside in their affairs, to appear in the role of their guardians or self-styled guardians of order.' It must have been a matter of acute embarrassment to the Soviet Government that during the Israeli invasion of the Lebanon in June–August 1982 they did so little to fulfil the terms of Article 6 of this treaty, which obliges the two countries, in the event of a threat to peace, to 'enter into immediate contact with each other with a view to coordinating their position and to cooperate in order to remove the threat which has arisen and to restore peace'.

In December 1980, while addressing the Indian Parliament during his visit to Delhi, Brezhnev put forward a package of proposals regarding the Gulf: foreign bases should not be established in the Gulf area and its adjacent islands, no nuclear weapons should be deployed there, force should be neither applied nor threatened against the countries of the Gulf area, there should be no interference in their internal affairs, their non-aligned status should be respected, and the 'normal commercial exchange and the use of maritime communications linking the Gulf states with other countries of the world' should not be impeded. These proposals were addressed to all interested states, including the United States, Western European countries, China, and Japan.[19] In the light of events that had by then taken place in Afghanistan, they were not well received.

CRISIS

20. Afghanistan

UNDER Brezhnev, Soviet policy in the Middle East, from 1974 onwards, had two principal aims: to ensure stability on the southern frontiers of the Soviet Union and to remain in a position to benefit from any general revulsion against the United States in the region. On the whole the Soviet leadership seemed content to bide its time in order to achieve these objectives. In December 1978, however, the Soviet Government signed yet another Treaty of Friendship[1]—this time with the Government of Afghanistan, where in April 1978 a small group of officers had overthrown the republican government that had been in power since the fall of the Afghan monarchy in 1973. The events that followed this little noticed *coup d'état* and the Soviet Government's uncharacteristically rash decision to sign a treaty with the new Afghan Government at the end of 1978 were, twelve months later, to exercise a profound effect on the Soviet Union's international standing as a whole.

Between 24 and 27 December 1979 the number of Soviet troops in Afghanistan—perhaps 5,000 before that date—was more than doubled by the arrival in Kabul of a substantial airborne force. These troops occupied the presidential palace and Kabul radio and television station on 27 December. At the same time the main invading force, drawn chiefly from units stationed in the republics of Soviet Central Asia, moved southwards into Afghanistan: a total of about 50,000 men, soon to be increased to 85,000[2]—six divisions in all. President Hafizullah Amin was murdered and succeeded by Babrak Karmal, whom he had exiled to Eastern Europe in the previous year. On 29 December the Soviet Government announced that it had been invited by the Afghan Government to protect it against the counter-revolution supported from without by China, Pakistan, and the United States, whose joint aim was described as 'to crush the Afghan revolution and to establish on the Soviet–Afghan frontier a new anti-Soviet *place d'armes* that would replace the US bases lost in Iran'. In the Soviet view, Afghan groups armed by these three countries constituted a 'serious threat to the very existence of Afghanistan as an independent state'.[3]

The Soviet Union inevitably vetoed the UN Security Council resolution calling for withdrawal of Soviet troops from Afghanistan; on 14 January 1980 the General Assembly, in emergency session, passed the resolution by 104 votes to 18 (a vote repeated in November, by 111 to 11); two weeks later, at a meeting in Islamabad, the Islamic Conference condemned the invasion as well; and all its member states were asked to withhold recognition from the new Afghan regime. The General Assembly has repeated its resolution since, most recently in November 1982. So far none of the subsequent attempts made by outsiders to reach a solution has really left the ground: the EEC's proposal for a neutralized Afghanistan, internationally guaranteed; India's proposal that adjacent countries should consult together with a view to a regional solution; Castro's good offices, offered in his capacity as Chairman of the Non-Aligned Movement; and UN participation in a process of mediation.

In spite of the outcry from most of the international community[4]—not least from the Islamic world—the Soviet occupying force has remained in Afghanistan; and it has continued to suffer casualties at the hands of the Afghan resistance groups. These are the same groups that had resisted the Afghan Government from April 1978 onwards; about a million Afghans are estimated to have taken refuge in Pakistan in 1980. The severity of the fighting has been enough to make it impracticable for the Soviet press to gloss it over completely. Soviet readers are accustomed to reading between the lines; *Krasnaya Zvezda* of 23 February 1982, for example, offered them plenty of opportunity to do this.[5] The timing of the invasion could hardly have been worse. As well as being an outrage to Islam, it deflected Middle Eastern attention from American discomfiture in Iran. For the Chinese, it reinforced their 'anti-hegemonist' case against the Soviet Union. In the United States, it stopped the Senate's SALT II debate dead in its tracks and evoked Carter's so-called doctrine regarding the Gulf (among other things, the

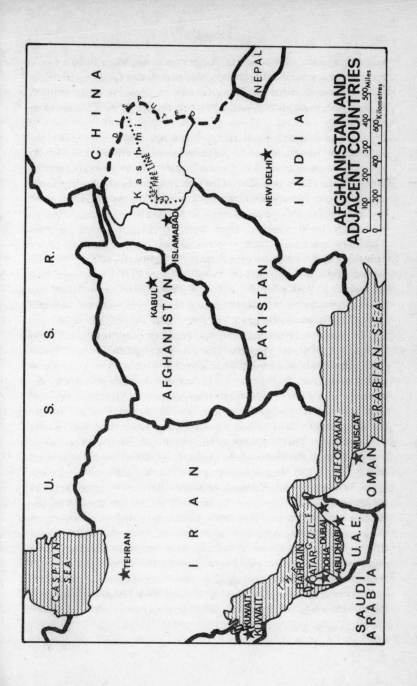

AFGHANISTAN AND
ADJACENT COUNTRIES

US Administration* also cut American grain sales from 17 to 8 million tons, restricted technological transfer to the Soviet Union, refused to attend the Olympic Games in Moscow that summer, and campaigned to persuade other countries to boycott them as well).

It is possible to reconstruct with a fair degree of clarity the successive stages whereby, seven years earlier, the Soviet leadership reached its decision to invade Czechoslovakia, and to measure what the invasion achieved against its objective. In the case of Afghanistan, however, the explanation for the decision to invade is still—three years later—far from clear. The sequence of events inside Afghanistan from April 1978 throws some light on what happened in December 1979, but no more than that. Three points stand out: the measures of agrarian reform hastily introduced and brutally executed by the PDPA[6] government, which took power after the *coup d'état*, were unpopular; the government met such fierce armed opposition that the Afghan army began to disintegrate in 1979; and the PDPA was itself divided into two irreconcilable factions,[7] one led by Karmal and the other by Taraki. However, they do not explain why the Soviet Government should have signed a treaty with such an ephemeral and murderous[8] regime as quickly as it did—only seven months after the *coup d'état* that brought it to power; the Ethiopian regime, with which the Soviet Government had signed a treaty in the previous month, had to wait much longer. Four years afterwards this has been partly illuminated, by the allegation of a Soviet defector[9] that Brezhnev overruled the advice repeatedly offered him by the KGB, in particular, not to back Taraki or Amin; the KGB candidate was Karmal, to whom Brezhnev turned only at the eleventh hour. Instead, at the time of the conclusion of the Soviet–Afghan Treaty Brezhnev went on record as ascribing 'a qualitatively new character' to Soviet–Afghan relations.[10] Once this treaty was in place, it became more difficult for the Soviet Government to resist playing a part in the internal politics of Afghanistan, whose principal supplier of economic aid and military equipment the Soviet Union had become, following Khrushchev's visit in 1955. The fate believed to have been

* President Reagan lifted the US grain embargo on the Soviet Union in April 1981.

suffered by some of the Soviet advisers, at the hands of the Afghan resistance, during the chaos of 1979, may also have contributed.

Since an invasion on this scale could not have been undertaken without careful planning in advance, we must assume that, at the latest, by September 1979 things had reached such a pass in Afghanistan that, seen in the local context, direct Soviet intervention was judged better than waiting for even worse developments. In that month Taraki was got rid of by his rival Amin, whom Soviet sources describe as a traitor, making secret contact with representatives of the United States and China. The wider consequences appear to have been ignored in Moscow: a foolhardiness that gave rise to the question around the world—'if they do these things in a green tree, what shall be done in the dry?'.

At the time several explanations were offered in the West for the invasion of Afghanistan. None of them carry full conviction today. The invasion was said to have brought the Soviet Union one step further towards the warm waters of the Indian Ocean and of the Gulf. Certainly the invasion made a political impact on the Gulf States, though perhaps not exactly in a sense that suited Soviet foreign policy; and the Soviet air forces have the use of (extended) bases in Afghanistan. Militarily, however, the main route from Soviet Central Asia to the Gulf does not lie through Afghanistan, but through Iran. It was also suggested that the Soviet Union wanted to avoid the spread of Muslim fundamentalism into Soviet Central Asia. Again, it is hard to see how this objective could be furthered by converting Afghanistan, by force, into what is now tantamount to a Soviet protectorate. On the contrary, if the Soviet Government does have an Islamic problem in Central Asia, it can only have been compounded by a commitment to conduct a prolonged conflict with Muslim guerilla forces in Afghanistan. Conceivably, though evidence is lacking, the Soviet leadership believed that by invading Afghanistan and installing a government of Soviet choice in Kabul, they might be able to repeat some of the Soviet economic achievement in another neighbouring client state sixty years earlier—the Emirate of Bukhara. Although the Soviet Government can hardly have thought of receiving the Republic of Afghanistan into the

Soviet Union in the way that the Republic of Bukhara[11] was admitted in 1924, the use of the Soviet armed forces in order to crush rebellion, as a prelude to economic change, in a silent state, offers a certain parallel. In any case, the occupation of Afghanistan has not been purely military; Soviet economic and social systems have been introduced on a large scale as well; and the History of Soviet Foreign Policy lays emphasis on Afghanistan's 'broad programmes of economic transformation and social development'.[12]

There remains Brezhnev's own explanation at the time: 'to have acted otherwise would have meant . . . permitting a repetition of what aggressive forces succeeded in doing—for example—in Chile . . . looking on passively while the source of a serious threat to the security of the Soviet arose on our southern border.' This explanation was partly echoed by Leonid Zamyatin, Brezhnev's official spokesman, during an off the record briefing in Delhi in December 1980: ' . . . a state that would be hostile to us, that would endanger our security—a state not thousands of miles away from us, but that is right on our doorstep. Herein lies the crux of the matter'.[13] The reference to what the Soviet Government failed to do in Chile in 1973 is interesting. As for the perceived threat to Soviet security, the same words could equally well have been said of China, seen through Soviet eyes. From the viewpoint of Moscow, in the heart of the Eurasian land-mass, neighbouring countries tend to be divided into geographical groups. For a Soviet observer, therefore, Afghanistan is an Asian crossroads. Was the Soviet invasion of Afghanistan intended as a reminder to the countries of Asia, and to China above all, that the Soviet Union is militarily the most powerful state in Asia? Or—as the Soviet defector referred to above has since put it—the 'real point' was that 'the Politburo was determined to show that the Soviet Union would not be pushed about'.[14] For the time being—until further evidence is forthcoming—Brezhnev's statement coupled with Zamyatin's gloss remains the best available explanation of a decision which Soviet historians will be obliged to acknowledge as a signal blunder. In any case, by the end of 1980 the Soviet Union faced a far greater challenge on its western frontier in Europe.

21. Poland

In the autumn of 1980 the Polish Government was brought down by Polish workers taking to the streets, for the third time in twenty-four years. This followed strikes in the Baltic cities, which were ended on 31 August, when an agreement was signed in Gdansk by the Deputy Prime Minister, Mieczyslaw Jagielski, on behalf of the Polish Government, and a hitherto unknown Pole, Lech Walesa, on behalf of the local interfactory strike committee.[1] As in 1970 (and in 1976), these strikes were triggered by an increase in the price of food. But the changes in the system of meat sales announced on 1 July 1980 were in fact far less[2] than those of 1970 and 1976, and it was not until the middle of August that the strikes became general in the Baltic cities. The extraordinary agreement of 31 August went far beyond issues of wages and prices. Instead it was an attempt to address the fundamental problems of Poland head-on.

Under the terms of this agreement, 'new self-governing trade unions which could provide genuine representation of the working class' were to be set up, to 'defend the social and material interests of the employees'. The new trade unions would 'adhere to the principles laid down in the Constitution of the Polish People's Republic'. They did not 'intend to play the role of a political party'. On the contrary, they recognized that the Polish United Workers Party (PZPR)[3] played 'the directing role in the state' and they did not 'seek to undermine the established system of international alliances'. The Polish Government was to ensure that workers and employees would be guaranteed the 'right of free association in trade unions' under the provisions of the existing Trade Unions Law and the right to strike under those of a new law on trade unions.

The Gdansk Agreement also addressed the question of economic reform. The 'fundamental provisions' of this reform were to be 'defined and published during the next few months'. Meanwhile, gradual wage increases were to be introduced for all groups of employees; wage rises already under discussion were to be completed by the end of September; a programme for rises for the lowest paid was to be submitted by the Government, in agreement with the unions, by 31 October (to take effect from 1 January 1981); and the lowest old-age and disability pensions were to be increased annually, 'in line with the economic capabilities of the country and increases in the lowest wages'. The supply of meat to the population was to be improved by December 1980. By 31 December a programme was to be devised for an increase of work-free Saturdays in 1981. In addition, there was to be an immediate enquiry into the legitimacy of dismissals of Polish workers after the strikes of 1970 and 1976. The Government was to ensure the radio broadcasting of Sunday mass. Radio, television, and the press were, under public control, to 'serve the expression of a diversity of ideas, views, and judgements'.

In the remaining months of 1980 events in Poland moved fast. Walesa was elected Chairman of the new independent trade union, *Solidarnosc*. The union's application for registration as such was made subject by the Warsaw district court to the proviso that the PZPR had the leading role in Poland and to a modification of the right to strike. In November *Solidarnosc*'s appeal against those two provisos was upheld by the Supreme Court. The nation-wide strike that had been threatened was called off, although four months later millions stayed away from work after the Government had announced that the country's economic crisis made the implementation of a five-day, forty-hour week impossible: the first of other nation-wide strikes that were to follow in Poland in 1981. By the end of November 1980 *Solidarnosc*'s membership was estimated to number over eight million, of whom 750,000 were also members of the PZPR. In the wake of the Gdansk Agreement, the PZPR's leader, Gierek, was removed by the party's Central Committee and succeeded by Stanislaw Kania. One year later Kania was replaced by General Wojciech Jaruzelski (Defence Minister since 1968 and Prime Minister from February 1981). In the interval the PZPR had, as a 'democratic centralist' party, virtually disintegrated. At its IXth Congress, held in July 1981, the delegates voted by free and secret ballot; they rejected the proposed agenda and adopted a new one; they attacked some of the Party's existing leaders and quarrelled with others; and in the elections they threw out almost the whole Party apparatus (seven-eighths of the members of the old Central

Committee were not re-elected, including seven of the eleven members of the Politburo).[4]

The Soviet initial reaction to the events of 1980 in Poland followed the pattern of 1968. By December—one year after the invasion of Afghanistan—a force of some thirty Soviet divisions[5] had been assembled on the frontiers of Poland and stood ready to invade the country. When the new First Secretary of the PZPR, Kania, visited Moscow to meet Brezhnev and the other Eastern European leaders on 5 December 1980, he was granted what amounted to a reprieve, in return for an undertaking—in the language of the Soviet–Polish bilateral meeting four months later—to 'reverse the turn of events' in Poland.[6] It was on the model of 1968 that the CPSU Central Committee sent a letter on 5 June 1981 to the PZPR, which spoke of the 'mortal danger threatening the revolutionary gains of the Polish people' and the 'onslaught of the internal counter-revolution', and which concluded by repeating the statement made four months earlier by Brezhnev to the XXVIth Congress of the CPSU: 'we will not abandon fraternal, socialist Poland in its hour of need. We shall stand by it.'[7]

Nevertheless, unlike Czechoslovakia, Poland was not invaded. Instead, the Soviet leadership settled for a compromise—the declaration[8] of a 'state of war' (in effect, martial law, imposed and administered by the Polish armed forces and endorsed by the Council of State). This was welcomed[9] in Moscow after it was announced in the early hours of 13 December 1981, and must have received official Soviet encouragement while it was being planned. The proximate cause of the declaration was the Warsaw section of *Solidarnosc*'s call for mass demonstrations to be held on 17 December, following the storming by the police, on 2 December, of the Warsaw firemen's academy (in order to end a sit-in there). But the precise way in which martial law was imposed showed beyond doubt that the operation had been carefully planned in advance. Walesa was put under house arrest. Thousands were arrested and interned: mainly, but not entirely, members of *Solidarnosc* and their sympathizers—the PZPR itself was pushed to one side for the time being. Even so, the Katowice miners sat in underground for a fortnight and Nova Huta steel workers barricaded themselves in. In the end, all these and other protest strikes were broken, at an officially admitted cost of nine lives.[10] The official and the unofficial figures, both of detainees and of dead, differed greatly. The difference in the number of detainees may have been partly due to the fact that many people were held only for a few hours and then released. Jaruzelski's own figure for the number detained in the first wave, given in January 1982, was 6,309.[11]

To return to the end of 1980, why did the Soviet Government not invade Poland, having invaded Afghanistan, where far less was at stake, only twelve months before? Can the West be absolved from a share of the responsibility for the Polish economic crisis of 1980? And—two years later—can any lessons be learned for the future? The definitive answer to the first of these questions, like the motive for the Soviet invasion of Afghanistan, lies in the Soviet archives. All three, however, become simpler if the condition of Poland, political and economic, in 1980 is recalled.

By the end of 1980 the PZPR leadership was no longer capable of exercising the 'leading role' expected of a communist party. From 1956 onwards, one of the main reasons—perhaps the main reason—why successive governments were able to rule Poland with minimal Soviet interference and a fair degree of individual freedom, was the unwritten understanding existing between the PZPR and the Roman Catholic Church, on whose universally respected, politically conservative Primate, Cardinal Wyszynski,[12] they were usually able to rely for counsels of wisdom. Twenty-four years later the Church remained what it had always been in Poland—the symbol and the interpreter of Polish nationalism—but the PZPR had gradually become an emperor with no clothes. Its leaders were generally incompetent, often corrupt, and—with a few honourable exceptions—devoid of ideas. By contrast, Walesa's fresh approach to the country's problems made him an international figure and won him popular acclaim comparable only to that given to Pope John Paul II[13] when he visited his country during the previous year. Walesa and his colleagues were also helped in formulating their Gdansk programme by members of the intellectual dissident movement which had developed in Poland during the 1970s. Broadly speaking, however, in 1980 the three political forces in Poland were the PZPR, the Church, and *Solidarnosc*. On 16 December representatives of all three united in Gdansk to honour the memory of those killed in the Baltic riots of December 1970. Had it proved possible to preserve this unity in 1981, the outcome at the end of that year might have been different. As it was, the crowd's response to the official delegation at this ceremony was politically indicative: cheers for the military delegates but silence for the party representatives.

All efforts foundered on the PZPR's reluctance to come to terms with Poland's political problem and on *Solidarnosc*'s reluctance to accept responsibility for solving its economic problem. Much of the Gdansk programme, accepted by the Polish Government as the price of ending the strikes (and avoiding worse), was divorced from economic reality even at the time when the Gdansk Agreement was concluded. By the end of 1980 Poland was in effect, though not formally, bankrupt. Unlike other countries that ran into balance of payments difficulties in the 1970s, Poland was not a notable victim of the rise in the world price of crude oil. The price of Soviet oil exported to COMECON countries was indeed gradually increased during this period; but until 1979 Poland had an energy trade surplus; and it is distinguished from the rest of COMECON (excluding the Soviet Union) by the strength and diversity of its natural resources, notably coal. Like all Eastern European countries, however, Poland had borrowed heavily from the West from 1974 onwards. By the end of 1979 Polish gross debt in convertible currency was twenty times what it had been in 1971; the Polish debt-service ratio in convertible currency had reached 92 per cent[14]; and by the end of 1980 Polish debt was estimated at 25 billion US dollars, with a gross financing requirement for 1981 of 10 billion US dollars.[15] In the following year both Western governments and the Soviet Government were, in turn, obliged to reschedule Polish debts then falling due.[16]

In one sense *Solidarnosc* was right to blame others for the country's economic plight. The PZPR's incompetence was nowhere more manifest than in the field of economic planning and management. Polish agriculture suffered from this as much as Polish industry, so that in 1980—admittedly a bad year for weather—over one billion US dollars had to be spent on importing about 10 million tons of grain—over half Polish domestic production. Nevertheless, the West was also partly to blame; it was the West which financed the Polish boom in the 1970s. Western banks continued to lend to Poland large sums[17] long after Poland could be expected to be able to service the loans, let alone repay the principal, except on assumptions that were wholly unrealistic. Western governments were no better, guaranteeing credits at concessionary rates of interest for the export of machinery for use in Polish projects which had no hope of generating the income that would be needed for repayment. (Poland's application for membership of the International Monetary Fund in November 1981 was a belated step in the right direction.) Meanwhile Polish GNP fell by 2.3 per cent in 1979, 4 per cent in 1980, and 15 per cent in 1981.[18] In 1980 and 1981 the increase in money incomes over the previous year was 10 per cent and 20 per cent respectively. Meat was rationed on 1 April 1981, followed by the rationing of butter, sugar, rice, and grains.

Thus in economic terms, the Gdansk Agreement was reaching for the moon. Within *Solidarnosc*, the leadership were aware that this was so, but they never resolved their internal debate about how much, if any, responsibility their movement should assume for restoring the Polish economy. In the sixteen months that followed, *Solidarnosc* made it increasingly clear that its aim was a political bargain. In effect, cooperation in restoring the economy was being offered by the independent trade union, as also by the new independent farmers' union recognized by the Polish Government in February 1981, in return for political reform. In Gdansk, one year after the signature of the Gdansk Agreement, *Solidarnosc*'s first national congress passed a resolution calling for a pluralistic political system in Poland and resolved that a message of support should be sent to workers in other communist-governed countries who wanted free trade unions.

From the Congress[19] onwards, Walesa and the moderate group within the trade union's leadership found themselves outmanoeuvred by the radicals. For the radical wing of the *Solidarnosc* leadership, the crisis was entering its 'revolutionary' phase in the first week of December. According to one of the members of the union's regional committee in Lodz,[20] they were then thinking in terms of an 'active' strike (as opposed to the previous 'passive' strikes), to be declared on 21 December; workers guards would be formed; and production would be put in the hands of strike committees at factory level. Their three objectives were 'struggle against the crisis', realization of the economic reform (delayed by the Government), and the creation of a 'self-administered republic'. Exasperated by the way in which the PZPR sought to claw back or whittle away the concessions made in the Gdansk Agreement, *Solidarnosc* responded by waving a rag at the Soviet bull, as at other Eastern European governments, that was very red indeed.

Neither West nor East reacted imaginatively to the Polish crisis that followed the Gdansk Agreement. Over events in Poland, as over those in Afghanistan, Western governments argued among themselves about what was the right response to the Soviet Union. And all of them were ambivalent. This ambivalence went beyond the contradictions inherent in all Western policy towards Eastern Europe for the past quarter of a century. This time large sums of Western money were at stake. On the one hand, the West praised *Solidarnosc* for its pursuit of the political liberalization of Poland (and hence of Eastern Europe;) on the other, they shared one interest in common with the Soviet Union—that Poland should repay its debts—an interest which Western governments and Western banks pursued firmly through 1980–1. The Soviet attitude was at least candid. The Soviet leadership intensely disliked what they saw unfolding in Poland from the autumn of 1980 onwards—above all, the demonstrated weakness and disunity of the PZPR. They said so, plainly. They avoided—perhaps narrowly—making in Poland the mistake that they had made a year earlier in Afghanistan. Had they repeated their reaction of August 1968 and of December 1979, the Brezhnev Peace Programme would have looked even more threadbare than it does today. Moreover, unlike Czechoslovakia in 1968, in 1980 a Soviet force invading Poland would have had to contend with armed resistance. Once this had been overcome, few Poles would have been prepared to form a government while their country remained under Soviet occupation—and those that were would have been shown up for what they were: a Soviet-protected minority within the PZPR. Equally important, in my view, was the economic factor—another radical difference from 1968. As the lender of last resort to COMECON countries, the Soviet Union would have found an occupied Poland a financial millstone round its neck. Soviet calculations at the end of 1980 must have taken account both of the difficulty of servicing the Polish debt after an invasion and of the damage that would be done to COMECON credit, including the terms on which the Soviet Union could itself borrow in the international financial market, in the event that the Polish debt was disowned. In economic terms, a Soviet invasion of Poland would simply have been counter-productive.

Since 1939 the Soviet Union has tried one solution after another for the Polish Question—in that year, yet another Russo-German partition of Poland; after the Second World War, the shifting of Poland bodily westwards (at Germany's territorial expense), followed by the imposition of a Stalinist regime in Poland; and after the Polish 'October' of 1956, a series of Polish Administrations (Gomulka, Gierek, Kania), through which the Soviet Government exercised a kind of indirect rule, which by the standards of the rest of Eastern Europe was liberal.[21] All these attempts have ended in failure. The solution of martial law was adopted at the climax of a prolonged crisis that was really a crisis of confidence in Polish political institutions. The attempt to resolve this crisis by force could only be transitional. Arguably, it achieved its immediate aims with tolerable success in the twelve months December 1981–December 1982. Soviet military intervention was averted; a measure of economic order was restored; *Solidarnosc*'s underground leadership became less and less able to influence the course of events; on 8 October the *Sejm* passed a law rendering *Solidarnosc* illegal; a month later Jaruzelski met Archbishop Glemp and it was announced that the Pope would visit Poland again in June 1983, provided that the country remained calm; Walesa's release followed on 13 November. Finally, martial law was 'suspended' by the *Sejm* on 30 December 1982.

Nevertheless, the days are now over when Soviet leaders could repeat to the Poles (and through Poland, to the rest of Eastern Europe) the words of the Tsar Alexander II in Warsaw— 'Gentlemen, let us have no more dreams.' There is now an identifiable *de facto* Opposition in Poland, which no Polish

Government and no Soviet Government can ignore. Seen from Moscow, there are vital Soviet interests at stake in Poland: the politico-military cohesion of the Warsaw Pact, on which the Soviet military position in Central Europe critically depends, and the lines of communication between the western Soviet Union and the crucial Soviet forces stationed in the German Democratic Republic. Sooner or later the Polish Question demands a new approach. In my view, it cannot be purely Eastern European. Stability in Central Europe is a Western interest as well.

22. The Economic Dimension

The XXVIth CPSU Congress

AT the XXIInd CPSU Congress in 1961, Khrushchev claimed that in twenty years the Soviet Union would overtake the per capita standard of living of any capitalist country and that it would reach 80 per cent above the 1960 American standard of living. In the event, it was almost exactly twenty years later that the decline of Soviet growth rates, already beginning to be apparent in 1976, became crystal clear. Yet, as we have seen, the Soviet Government continued to devote to defence about 13 per cent of its gross national product—two-thirds the size of American GNP—and maintained its support for some expensive allies, such as Cuba, Ethiopia, and Vietnam (these three countries together cost the Soviet Union a sum of the order of 5 billion US dollars per annum). The decline in the rate of Soviet growth affected every major sector of the economy, with the important exception of natural gas. The two crucial sectors were agriculture and energy (gas again excepted). And all projections looking forward to the end of the twentieth century had also to take account of the demographic problem illustrated by the results of the Soviet census of 1979.

At this stage of Soviet economic development, and hard on the heels of events in Afghanistan and Poland, 23 February 1981 was not an easy date on which to convene the XXVIth Congress in Moscow. Moreover, it closely followed a major event in

Washington: the inauguration as President of Ronald Reagan, an avowedly right-wing Republican, who had arrived at the White House committed—among other policies—to increasing US defence expenditure by 7 per cent per annum in real terms. Not surprisingly, therefore, this Congress was a fairly muted affair. What was remarkable was that the whole of the Politburo and the Secretariat were re-elected without a single change, for the first time in the Party's history. (The average age of the Politburo members was 69.3.) In his report[1] to the Congress Brezhnev laid the blame for the deterioration of the super-power relationship, during the five years since the XXVth Congress, at the door of the United States. This was predictable. Nevertheless, in spite of the White House's 'bellicose calls and statements'[2], he declared that the Soviet Government wanted 'normal' Soviet–US relations and an active Soviet–US dialogue 'at all levels'. Although 'the pillars of the Polish state were in jeopardy', harsher words on Poland were—perhaps deliberately—left over until after the Congress, whose atmosphere they might otherwise have disturbed. Among the proposals that Brezhnev put forward in his report were: an immediate moratorium on the deployment in Europe, either by the Warsaw Pact or by NATO, of further intermediate-range nuclear missiles; military confidence-building measures applied to the entire European part of the Soviet Union; and talks with 'all interested countries' about confidence-building measures in the Far East. To his Delhi proposal of discussions regarding security in the Gulf, Brezhnev added an offer to include the 'international aspects' of the Afghan problem and to withdraw the Soviet 'contingent' from Afghanistan once the danger from the 'imperialist undeclared war against socialism in Afghanistan' was removed; and the suggestions in his report regarding the Middle East had some features in common with the declaration agreed by the EEC Heads of Government at their summit meeting in Venice in June 1980.[3] These proposals were clearly aimed at West European opinion. Yet a Soviet reader of the published proceedings of the XXVIth Congress would have been barely aware of the intensity of the transatlantic debate, which had by then been going on for over a year.

Economic Sanctions

Among the several different strands of this debate, one of the most contentious concerned economic policy. Within the new US Administration the Defence Secretary, Caspar Weinberger, was the leading proponent of the efficacy of economic sanctions as a response to the 'new *global*[4] challenge' presented by the Soviet Union: a country whose economic system he described as 'struggling, misdirected, and largely inefficient'. The essence of Weinberger's case was expressed in the following year in his annual budget report to the US Congress:

without access to advanced technology from the West, the Soviet leadership would be forced to choose between its military–industrial priorities and the preservation of a tightly controlled political system. By allowing access to a wide range of advanced technologies, we enable the Soviet leadership to evade that dilemma.[5]

Thus the US Congress, which in the early 1970s had thwarted the attempt of the Nixon Administration to impose political constraints on the Soviet Union by involving the Soviet Government in a network of economic agreements intended to benefit the Soviet Union, was being asked to achieve the same political objective ten years later by economic sanctions directed against the Soviet Union. And, paradoxically, one of the first acts of the new Administration was to lift the embargo on American grain sales to the Soviet Union,[6] in fulfilment of one of Reagan's campaign commitments. It is also ironical to reflect that in the days of the earlier challenge to the West, thrown down by Khrushchev, it was precisely the advanced state of Soviet technology (exemplified by the launching of the sputnik) that alarmed the West and provided the impetus for the US *Polaris* missile programme.

At the time that the XXVIth Congress met in Moscow and the Reagan Administration took office in Washington, six Soviet divisions were occupying Afghanistan and five times as many were surrounding Poland. The determination to do nothing either to condone the invasion of Afghanistan or to facilitate an invasion of Poland was shared by the United States and by its allies. Agreed on these ends, they differed on the means. At the centre of the disagreement on economic policy was the Soviet gas pipeline contract,[7] whereby Western companies, financed by Western banks, are to help to build a 2,200 mile pipeline from Urengoi in Siberia to Western Europe, supplying gas to the Federal Republic of Germany, France, Belgium, Italy, and Austria from 1984 onwards. American objections were threefold: the degree of future Western European dependence on Soviet sources of natural gas implied by the contract (30 per cent of the Federal Republic's gas supplies by 1990, for example); the fineness of the concessionary interest rates and the length of the maturities offered to the Soviet Government under the terms of the contract; and the amount of foreign currency that the Soviet Union stands to earn over the whole life of the contract—perhaps 160 billion US dollars in the course of twenty years. The corresponding European counter-arguments were that: the Soviet Union can scarcely be regarded as a less reliable source of energy than the Middle East (and in any case, by 1990 the Soviet Union will account for less than 10 per cent of the Federal Republic's total supplies of energy;) interest rates and maturities are a matter for the governments comprising the OECD 'consensus', not just the US Government; and the Soviet Union is unlikely to kill the goose that lays the golden eggs.

Through 1980 and 1981 the US and Western European governments argued about economic policy towards the Soviet Union. On 29 December 1981, a fortnight after the imposition of martial law in Poland, the US Government took a unilateral decision: a series of economic measures directed against the Soviet Union,[8] but stopping short of the only one that would do real damage—an embargo on the sale of American grain. This debate took a new, still more divisive turn in June 1982, when the US Government extended to the subsidiaries and licensees of American companies abroad its existing embargo on the export to the Soviet Union of oil and gas equipment. By then—grain apart—there was so little American trade with the Soviet Union that only Western European and Japanese economic leverage remained available as an economic sanction: a weapon that the Western Europeans (and the Japanese) were determined not to allow the Americans to use. In the specific case of the Urengoi pipeline, even the British Government (not itself a signatory of any of the pipeline agreements concluded by the Soviet Government and traditionally a bridge-builder in times of transatlantic stress) was obliged to invoke an Act of Parliament in order to prevent British sub-contracting firms from complying with the US embargo. The arrival of George Shultz at the State Department in July, following the resignation of Alexander Haig, enabled wiser counsels to be heard and in the end to prevail in Washington. On 13 November Reagan announced the lifting of the embargo of June 1982, following 'substantial agreement' between the US and its allies 'to a plan of action' regarding East–West trade. This decision was welcomed in Europe, although the French Government at once stated that it was not a party to the agreement announced in Washington.[9]

This attempt by the US Government to compel European governments to renege on contracts concluded with the Soviet Union and already legally in force, did greater damage to the Western alliance than it could ever have inflicted on the Soviet Union. Although by the end of 1982 this particular wheel had come full circle, its chief significance was more political than economic: it threw into sharp relief the growing difference between the US and the European view of how policy—not just economic policy—towards the Soviet Union and Eastern Europe should be conducted. So far as economic policy is concerned, the transatlantic debate has been in effect referred to committee, not concluded. Measures adopted by governments in order to canalize or to restrict the flow of international trade, which is essentially conducted for mutual commercial advantage, are notoriously hard to carry out successfully in the circumstances of an industrial democracy—still more so where several governments are concerned, and above all in the middle of a recession in world trade. There are exceptions: in time of war adversaries must seek to damage each other's economies, while in time of peace a government may decide to deal with its allies and friendly countries in terms not justified by a strict calculation of profit and loss (the Marshall Plan is the outstanding example in recent years). Between these two ends of the spectrum there is room for varying shades of international economic behaviour. One of these is the economic relationship between two rival super-powers, during a period of intense political strain, when the urge to register political points through economic measures is at its most powerful: a grey area, which in the present instance has been convincingly occupied neither by the thrust of Californian logic nor by the conventional wisdom of Europe. The weak point of the former is that American farmers are being allowed by their government to continue to earn substantial sums by exporting grain to the Soviet Union (admittedly for cash, but the defence of these sales—that they oblige the Soviet Union to use up scarce convertible currency resources—is unimpressive). The weak point of the European position is that their governments are using their taxpayers' money to subsidize Soviet imports of capital goods; until the increase agreed in October 1981 the Soviet Union was able to obtain interest rates from OECD countries comparable with those granted to countries of the developing world.

It will be clear from earlier chapters that my sympathies lie with a different economic approach towards the Soviet Union: that of the US Administration during 1972–5. Political pressures prevented this approach from proving its worth. In the different political circumstances of the 1980s, however much a European (or a Japanese) may deplore the current attitude of the Reagan Administration towards this question, he should also perhaps pause to reflect what other outlet for its political frustration the Administration might seek if this one were not to hand. Be that as it may, he would be a bold man who would say what effect any one of these economic policies (US policy of ten years ago, current US policy, current European policy) may have had, or may have, on the Soviet leadership. That the Soviet economy is overstretched and that the Soviet leadership—and their successors—face an economic dilemma in the 1980s is clear. So do Western governments. But in any future 'guns and butter' discussion within the Soviet Politburo, Western imports will be, in my view, a significant factor, but only one among several. The idea that this factor may by itself be decisive is—on any reading of history, Soviet or Russian or both—fanciful.

The State of the Soviet Economy

The figures of the Eleventh Five-Year Plan published before the Congress spoke for themselves. The Tenth Plan had been underfulfilled by a wide margin. The national income, which should have increased by 26 per cent over the previous five years, had in fact increased by 20 per cent. It was planned to increase by 19 per cent during 1980–5, but the fulfilment of this programme depended on an increase in overall efficiency, in which it was extremely hard to believe.[10] The one outstanding success was natural gas: as planned, production over the previous five years had risen from 289 to 435 billion cubic metres and a further increase—to 620 billion—was planned between 1980 and 1985. By contrast, coal output fell in absolute terms both in 1979 and in 1980; and the planned figure (785 million tons) for 1985 was lower than that originally planned for 1980 (805 million). The crude oil target for 1985—632 million tons—was also lower than that planned for 1980—640 million (against 604 million actually produced).

None of these figures alters the fact that the Soviet Union remains the world's largest producer of oil and coal, and that it will outstrip the United States as a producer of natural gas before the end of the century—thus disposing of predictions[11] made in the late 1970s that the Soviet Union was on the eve of an energy crisis. Nevertheless—natural gas apart—the Soviet era of rapid expansion is coming to an end. In energy terms, this constitutes a threat not to the economy of the Soviet Union itself, but to that of its COMECON allies. By the middle of the current decade these countries, most of whose energy needs have hitherto been met by importing from the Soviet Union, are likely to be obliged to import substantial quantities of crude oil from other countries—for payment in convertible currency. Even this prospect—let alone the prophesy of some analysts that the Soviet Union would itself become a net importer of crude oil during the 1980s—has been enough to arouse the fear of a Soviet military expansion towards the Gulf undertaken for economic reasons. In my view, what the Soviet Union needs in the Gulf is stability—not the burden of another army of occupation; and the graver danger to the West lies in the political consequences within Eastern Europe if COMECON countries were unable to afford to import the energy required for the development of their economies.[12]

For the Soviet Union the crucial sector of the economy was—and remains—agriculture. By the time of the XXVIth

CPSU Congress, Soviet agriculture absorbed, directly and indirectly, one-third of all Soviet investment; and the agricultural subsidy exceeded the officially declared level of Soviet defence expenditure.[13] In four successive years there has been one bad harvest after another. Few Soviet readers of the Eleventh Five-Year Plan can have believed that the productivity of agricultural labour would really increase by 23 per cent in the period of 1980–5. And on 24 May 1982 Brezhnev himself presented to the Central Committee his *Prodovol'stvennaya programma*: a Food Programme with the object of securing reliable supplies of foodstuffs over the period up to 1990, which he described as not only a top economic priority, but also 'an urgent socio-political task'. It is an indication of the degree of urgency that Brezhnev's speech of 24 May and the Central Committee's resolutions were published, in full, in the national and regional press on the following day, as well as on television and radio.[14] It is also a measure of the magnitude of the problems to be solved that, according to a Soviet source, the number of persons 'mobilized' to help with the 1979 harvest was 15.6 million—half of them 'workers from productive sectors'.[15] The 1982 *Prodovol'-stvennaya programma* will be expensive; it may help to alleviate the long sickness of Soviet agriculture; but it will take drastic measures of reform to cure it within the timespan of the current decade.

The facts of Soviet demography compound the difficulty of developing the Soviet economy over the next twenty years with anything like the same speed as over the last twenty. In the past, in spite of the losses suffered during the Great Terror and the Second World War, Soviet industry enjoyed one immense advantage: vast resources of labour. In future, the exploitation of Siberian mineral wealth will require not only finance and technology, but also a massive application of human resources. Yet the figures of the 1979 Soviet census[16] showed that the country's seemingly inexhaustible supply of labour was at an end. The republics with the highest birthrate in the Soviet Union, whose population almost doubled between 1959 and 1979 and may number not far short of one hundred millions in twenty years' time, are the traditionally Muslim republics of Central Asia—the Soviet citizens who least want to move to other parts of the country. As Brezhnev put it in his report to the XXVIth

Congress, people 'prefer to move from north to south and from east to west, although the rational location of productive forces requires movement in the opposite directions'. By contrast, during the same twenty years the population of the Russian Republic increased by only 17 per cent, and those of the Ukrainian and of the Belorussian Republic by 19 per cent. The political significance[17] of this problem, particularly the projected size of the number of Soviet citizens of Islamic origin at the turn of the century, is at the moment unclear; hard evidence is lacking; but the economic implications are already manifest.

The Economic Outlook in 1982

The slowdown in Soviet economic growth was further confirmed two years after the publication of the current plan. On 23 November 1982 the Head of *Gosplan*, Nikolai Baibakov, told the Supreme Soviet that the target for industrial growth in 1983 was 3.2 per cent—the lowest since five-year plans were instituted in the Soviet Union in 1929—and even this target was predicated on a three per cent growth in the productivity of labour. In 1982, again according to Baibakov's statement, the growth in labour productivity was expected to be two per cent, instead of the 3.7 per cent planned, and industrial growth was therefore not expected to be 4.7 per cent, as announced to the Supreme Soviet twelve months earlier, but 2.8 per cent—the lowest growth in Soviet peacetime history. For the second year in succession the size of the current year's harvest has not been announced; according to Western sources, it may be around 180 million tons—55 million tons below the target.[18] The principal weaknesses of the Soviet economic system—Alec Nove's 'diseconomies of scale'—have been discussed in an earlier chapter. Apart from Kosygin's half-hearted attempt in the 1960s, no economic reform of any importance was introduced during the Brezhnev years. Today the obvious target for sweeping reform is the country's agricultural system. Perhaps Brezhnev himself recognized this when Mikhail Gorbachev was admitted to the Politburo in October 1980, as its youngest member (forty-nine at that time). A new Soviet leadership now face this challenge. What they will in the event decide to do (or not to do) will depend on a complex of

personal rivalries within the Soviet political structure that is still
at the moment unforeseeable. Meanwhile, for the purposes of the
present study what matters is Lenin's observation quoted at the
outset of this book, that what determines Soviet foreign policy is
'the economic interests of the ruling classes of the state'. If the
foreign policy of the Soviet Union is an extension of the CPSU's
economic interests, it follows that its foreign policy will be as
much liable to change during the rest of the twentieth century as
its economic policy—but change from within, not change
imposed under threat from without.

23. The Succession Accomplished

IT is a commonplace of Western writing about the Soviet Union
that the Soviet system makes no provision for legitimate
succession to the highest party office *inter vivos*. It is indeed true
that with the single exception of 1964—the removal of Khrushchev from office by his colleagues, subsequently approved by the
Central Committee—each transfer of Soviet power has been
carried out as the result of the death of the leader. In 1982 there
were rumours that Brezhnev would set a new precedent by
stepping down voluntarily at the end of the year. In the event, he
died on 10 November. He was succeeded as General Secretary of
the Soviet Communist Party not by his closest surviving political
associate, Konstantin Chernenko, but by Yuri Andropov,
who—according to *Pravda*[1]—received the Central Committee's
unanimous vote at an extraordinary session held on 12
November.

For Andropov, delivering the funeral oration in Red Square,
where Brezhnev was buried on 15 November next to the grave of
Stalin, Brezhnev was a 'consistent, passionate, and tireless fighter
for the peace and security of the peoples of the world'; for the
Chinese Foreign Minister, he was an 'outstanding Soviet
statesman'; and in the words of the leading article published by a
distinguished British periodical,[2] 'the most appropriate monu-
ment for him would be a multi-warhead missile linked to a
stopped clock'. Of these three epitaphs—Soviet, Chinese, and
Western—the second may prove to be the nearest to the truth, in

spite of a quarter of a century of Sino-Soviet polemic. The third is quoted here as being representative of a Western misconception. At home, Brezhnev was indeed a conservative. But abroad he was—by Soviet standards—an innovator, until ill health began to take its toll in the mid-1970s. (Had he died then, his Western obituaries would have been different.) His health notwithstanding, he not only remained General Secretary, but added the other offices which he held for the last five years of his life. Although his holidays grew longer and his physical disabilities were evident, his public performance continued to the last—not just taking the salute on Red Square, followed by the usual Kremlin reception, three days before he died, but also a significant speech on 27 October, delivered in the presence of the assembled Soviet military establishment.

The first chapter of this book ended by quoting the old remark that, where the Soviet Union is concerned, there are no degrees of knowledge, only degrees of ignorance. This is perhaps even more true of the years 1972–82 than it was of the preceding ten years. In time, now that there has been a change of leadership in Moscow, flashes of illumination may follow the change, which will confirm, complement, or alter previous views of the motives underlying particular decisions taken by the Soviet leadership during the past eighteen years. To improve our understanding, these revelations need not necessarily be as dramatic as those made in Khrushchev's speech at the XXth Congress of the CPSU in 1956. But in due course at least some light is likely to be thrown on the differences of opinion that must have been evoked within the Politburo on major issues. Until some illumination of this kind is offered from Moscow, the wise course is to rely only on hard evidence and to refuse to be lured down the track of speculation—for example, on the question of who, at any given moment, have been the hawks and who have been the doves in the Politburo over the decisions to invade Czechoslovakia in 1968, to intervene in Africa in 1975 and 1977, to occupy Afghanistan in 1979, and not to invade Poland in 1980–1. (It is partly for this reason that I have generally used the phrase 'the Soviet leadership' in this book, even in its account of the last five years, during which Brezhnev held every high office of significance in the Soviet Union other than that of Prime Minister.)

Nevertheless, the fact that in time Brezhnev personally will be reassessed by his successors and by Soviet historians, need not prevent an interim balance-sheet from being drawn up.

Historians may record the XXVIth CPSU Congress, which once again showered praise on Brezhnev, as marking the beginning of the end. On present evidence, however, little seems to have changed in Moscow during the rest of 1981; if so, the real break may have been January 1982, when Suslov died. In the following month the news of a series of scandals broke in Moscow, one of which[3] involved Brezhnev's own family. On 21 April Andropov was chosen to deliver the speech on the anniversary of Lenin's birth; his departure from the KGB and his appointment as secretary of the Central Committee followed in May (apparently when Brezhnev was away ill); he thus became one of the two major contenders for the succession.

Whatever the significance of the jockeying for position in the Kremlin that seems to have gone on during Brezhnev's last months, and whatever the verdict of historians on his personal contribution to his country as General Secretary of the CPSU, they cannot overlook the fact that, politically, this period of eighteen years was one of the most stable in Russian history and certainly the most stable in Soviet history. What a Western observer recalls is Brezhnev's treatment of Sakharov and Solzhenitsyn and the political misuse of psychiatry in the Soviet Union. What most Soviet citizens recall is the contrast between the comparative calm of the Brezhnev years and the terror of the Stalinist era.

The Brezhnev years were also a period during which the Soviet consumer lived steadily better, although for this Brezhnev may not be thanked by the Soviet people, on the grounds that— measured against the yardsticks either of the Khrushchevian boasts of 1961 or of the progress made by free market economies during the corresponding period—the Soviet economic achievement was not as impressive as he made out. In fact the economic goals set in 1961, like Weinberger's analysis of the Soviet economy in 1981, overlooked some of the fundamental differences between the Soviet Union and the United States—not least the baselines from which the two economies set out twenty years earlier: whereas the American economy was boosted by the

Second World War, the Soviet economy was devastated by it. Nevertheless, there is no doubt that political stability was maintained during the Brezhnev years in large measure by the leadership's resistance to economic change—an exceedingly high price to pay, whose full cost may only become public knowledge in the Soviet Union now that Brezhnev is dead. Even the lustre of the Soviet attainment of super-power in the late 1960s and the consolidation of super-power status in the 1970s, under Brezhnev's leadership, may in time be dimmed by realization of the ultimate paradox of super-power: that national security can never be absolute—on the contrary, it is like a constantly receding horizon on a march through a desert.[4]

It was this paradox that seems to have been in Brezhnev's mind when, a fortnight before his death, he delivered a speech[5] in the Kremlin, at a meeting of senior officers of the Soviet armed forces and officials of the Defence Ministry, to which he said he had been 'invited' by the Defence Minister. Although the speech contained nothing particularly new, the nature of the audience to which it was addressed made it important. And, as it turned out, it was Brezhnev's last reflection on the state of the world—'not simple' but complicated, and therefore requiring both the 'doubling, trebling of efforts in the struggle for the preservation of peace and for the lessening of the threat of nuclear war hanging over mankind' and a 'constant strengthening of the country's defence'. The CPSU Central Committee would, he said, see to it that the armed forces wanted for nothing. He had harsh words for the United States and soft words for China: an acknowledgement perhaps of the fact that even a super-power needs friends. During Brezhnev's eighteen years, although the Soviet Union acquired some expensive allies, it won very few more friends.

Since Brezhnev's death the Soviet overture towards China has been taken a step further by his successor, who in his first speech to the Central Committee, delivered on 22 November,[6] described the People's Republic as 'our great neighbour'. So far as Soviet international relations were concerned, what Andropov said on the occasion could have been said by Brezhnev, whose foreign policy he undertook to continue. The policy of *détente* was 'by no means a stage that had been left behind'. 'The future', he said, 'belongs to *détente*.' But no one should expect unilateral disarma-

THE PROSPECT AFTER BREZHNEV

24. Soviet Options

SUCCEEDING to the office of General Secretary of the CPSU at the age of sixty-eight, over ten years older than his predecessor was in 1964, and with uncertain health, Andropov can hardly look forward to the eighteen years of power that Brezhnev enjoyed; and perhaps not to Khrushchev's eleven. Indeed it would be understandable if he were to decide, in a shorter term of office, to concentrate his energy on the reform of the Soviet economy, which involves the daunting task of rejuvenating the cadres of the party *apparat*.* But the conduct of foreign policy attracts political leaders, whether of West or East, like a magnet. Moreover, Andropov has firsthand experience of Eastern Europe; he is reported to have disagreed with Brezhnev on both Afghanistan and Poland; some of those who talked to him after Brezhnev's funeral have spoken of an early resolution of the Afghan dilemma; and there is also the next round of the Sino-Soviet talks. Whether these reports' are right or wrong, it would make sense for Andropov to take the opportunity at least to review Soviet options in the field of foreign policy at the outset of his tenure of office. How would some of these options look, if submitted to him by an objectively minded member of his planning staff, set against the geopolitical background of December 1982, and taking full account of Soviet economic and demographic factors in the 1980s?

So far as relations with the United States are concerned, the starting point of 22 November (referred to at the end of the preceding chapter) could hardly have been more unpromising. Nevertheless, a good planning staff would look both further forward and further back. Looking back, the planner might take the view that although the leadership had been right to seek to establish a close bilateral relationship with the United States in the 1970s, without a matching bi-partisan response in Washing-

* He did so decide, but fell ill early in 1983; he died on 9 February 1984.

24. Soviet Options

SUCCEEDING to the office of General Secretary of the CPSU at the age of sixty-eight, over ten years older than his predecessor was in 1964, and with uncertain health, Andropov can hardly look forward to the eighteen years of power that Brezhnev enjoyed; and perhaps not to Khrushchev's eleven. Indeed it would be understandable if he were to decide, in a shorter term of office, to concentrate his energy on the reform of the Soviet economy, which involves the daunting task of rejuvenating the cadres of the party *apparat*.* But the conduct of foreign policy attracts political leaders, whether of West or East, like a magnet. Moreover, Andropov has firsthand experience of Eastern Europe; he is reported to have disagreed with Brezhnev on both Afghanistan and Poland; some of those who talked to him after Brezhnev's funeral have spoken of an early resolution of the Afghan dilemma; and there is also the next round of the Sino-Soviet talks. Whether these reports[1] are right or wrong, it would make sense for Andropov to take the opportunity at least to review Soviet options in the field of foreign policy at the outset of his tenure of office. How would some of these options look, if submitted to him by an objectively minded member of his planning staff, set against the geopolitical background of December 1982, and taking full account of Soviet economic and demographic factors in the 1980s?

So far as relations with the United States are concerned, the starting point of 22 November (referred to at the end of the preceding chapter) could hardly have been more unpromising. Nevertheless, a good planning staff would look both further forward and further back. Looking back, the planner might take the view that although the leadership had been right to seek to establish a close bilateral relationship with the United States in the 1970s, without a matching bi-partisan response in Washing-

* He did so decide, but fell ill early in 1983; he died on 9 February 1984.

dangerous?'. The beginning of the execution of the MX programme was attacked as 'contrary to one of the central provisions of SALT I and II: not to construct additional silos for intercontinental ballistic missiles'. If the MX were deployed, the Soviet Union would 'find an effective response'. Or—as Brezhnev himself put it in an earlier statement—'whatever weapon may appear in the United States of America and in whatever quantity, the Soviet armed forces will deploy the appropriate counterweight to such a weapon'.[9] As though these statements had not been specific enough, on 7 December *Pravda* published a Tass interview with Ustinov, in the course of which he described the MX dense pack programme as a 'crude violation' of Article 1 of the SALT I Treaty and of Article 4 of SALT II. If the MX were deployed, he said, the Soviet Union would 'respond by developing a new ICBM of the same class, whose characteristics will be in no way inferior to those of MX'. This warning was confirmed two weeks later by Andropov, in his address delivered on the sixtieth anniversary of the formation of the Soviet Union; he added a similar warning on long-range cruise missiles.[10]

ment from the Soviet Union: 'We are not naive people.' If Andropov broke any new ground in this speech, it was in his frank admission of the Soviet economy's failure to meet its planned targets in the first two years of the current Plan. This was, however, an admission that Brezhnev, had he lived, would also probably have been obliged to make to the Central Committee on this occasion. What may be a pointer for the future was Andropov's remark: 'There are many problems in our national economy that are overdue for solution. I do not have ready recipes for their solution. But it is for all of us—the Central Committee of the Party—to find answers for them.'

The next chapter will examine some of the options that may be open to the new Soviet leadership in the field of foreign policy. I do this not because, at the time of writing, there is evidence that the leadership intends to make any radically new departures in this field, but because I believe that it is of the utmost importance in the coming years that the West should not be taken unawares by Soviet initiatives which, in today's circumstances, may appear visionary; and also that the West should be ready to come forward with fresh ideas of its own. At the moment there is unfortunately little sign of such awareness or of a readiness of this kind. Reagan chose the day of Andropov's first speech as General Secretary to announce his Administration's decision to deploy the MX intercontinental ballistic missile in the 'dense pack' formation in Wyoming. The total cost of this controversial[7] project, which has been given the bizarre name of *Peacekeeper*, is estimated at 30 billion US dollars. Reagan coupled this decision with a proposal that the two super-powers' Geneva negotiators should consider measures to 'strengthen mutual confidence' between the two governments and reduce the risk of 'surprise and miscalculation' in the nuclear field.[8] The US House of Representatives' decision to delete the MX's production funds makes the MX's future very uncertain. The Soviet response to the President's announcement was categorical, however. A 3,000-word editorial published by *Pravda* on 25 November described Reagan's confidence-building proposals as 'undoubtedly positive', but added the question: 'if for every one hundred MX missiles we add ten telephones directly linking Moscow and Washington, red ones or blue ones, does this make the missiles any less

Second World War, the Soviet economy was devastated by it. Nevertheless, there is no doubt that political stability was maintained during the Brezhnev years in large measure by the leadership's resistance to economic change—an exceedingly high price to pay, whose full cost may only become public knowledge in the Soviet Union now that Brezhnev is dead. Even the lustre of the Soviet attainment of super-power in the late 1960s and the consolidation of super-power status in the 1970s, under Brezhnev's leadership, may in time be dimmed by realization of the ultimate paradox of super-power: that national security can never be absolute—on the contrary, it is like a constantly receding horizon on a march through a desert.[4]

It was this paradox that seems to have been in Brezhnev's mind when, a fortnight before his death, he delivered a speech[5] in the Kremlin, at a meeting of senior officers of the Soviet armed forces and officials of the Defence Ministry, to which he said he had been 'invited' by the Defence Minister. Although the speech contained nothing particularly new, the nature of the audience to which it was addressed made it important. And, as it turned out, it was Brezhnev's last reflection on the state of the world—'not simple' but complicated, and therefore requiring both the 'doubling, trebling of efforts in the struggle for the preservation of peace and for the lessening of the threat of nuclear war hanging over mankind' and a 'constant strengthening of the country's defence'. The CPSU Central Committee would, he said, see to it that the armed forces wanted for nothing. He had harsh words for the United States and soft words for China: an acknowledgement perhaps of the fact that even a super-power needs friends. During Brezhnev's eighteen years, although the Soviet Union acquired some expensive allies, it won very few more friends.

Since Brezhnev's death the Soviet overture towards China has been taken a step further by his successor, who in his first speech to the Central Committee, delivered on 22 November,[6] described the People's Republic as 'our great neighbour'. So far as Soviet international relations were concerned, what Andropov said on the occasion could have been said by Brezhnev, whose foreign policy he undertook to continue. The policy of *détente* was 'by no means a stage that had been left behind'. 'The future', he said, 'belongs to *détente*.' But no one should expect unilateral disarma-

ton this was bound to be an exceedingly difficult task. In the absence of such a response, in retrospect it was not surprising that the ambitious efforts of both governments to establish a durable super-power relationship—of the kind that Brezhnev described in 1974 as 'Soviet US relations . . . really stable and independent of unfavourable combinations of events'[2]—fell foul of the 'wild swings' of American policy. When Cyrus Vance used this phrase in his Harvard Address in 1980 he was referring to the fate of the 1979 SALT II Treaty, but a Kremlin planner would find the fate of the 1972 Soviet US Trade Agreement an even more instructive illustration. He would therefore have no difficulty in arguing the case for the maximum degree of Soviet circumspection in negotiating with the United States. Looking forward, however, he would not rule out the possibility of seeking to restore the super-power relationship, now reduced to a bare minimum, to the level to which it was raised by the Soviet and US Governments in the years 1972–4.

It is no doubt argued by some in the East—as it is by some, whose views command respect, in the West—that the events of those remarkable years were a flash in the pan. Indeed, it was *Pravda* which described this as 'one of the rare moments in history when both sides are ready to admit equality in the broadest sense and to regard this as an initial position for reaching agreement'. It certainly was a rare moment and its consequences lasted only a few years. But it is conceivable that a similar moment will recur. If it did, if both governments were to see this as an opportunity to be turned to their mutual advantage, and if (as was their original intention in 1972) they were to decide to broaden and extend their agreement from the nuclear field to the fields of trade and crisis management, our Kremlin planner would be obliged to add the warning that, however strenuously the two governments might deny any suggestion of condominium (as they did ten years ago), this time accusations of condominium, both from China and from Western Europe, would be far more strident. He might therefore argue that the certainty of this adverse reaction was yet another reason why the new leadership should exercise extreme caution in dealing with the United States Government—even one which, unlike the present Administration, showed signs of wanting to make real progress in reaching agreements with the

Soviet Union. And he might conclude that before embarking on a second attempt to establish a Soviet–US relationship 'based not on a balance of terror, but on the principle of parity and equal security',[3] the first priority for the new leadership was to mend Soviet fences elsewhere in the world.

If the new Soviet leadership were to decide, in principle, to pursue an innovative foreign policy in one geographical area, Asia must be the first choice. It is generally believed that the reason why the Soviet Union has for so long refused to make the slightest territorial concession to any country lying along its immense frontiers is that if one square kilometre were handed over at any point along them, other concessions would be hard to withhold. This consistent policy is indeed logical. But the opposite side of the coin is also valid. If it were once decided in Moscow that the game was worth the candle, the list of internationally significant bargaining counters at Soviet disposal, following nearly thirty years of territorial intransigence, is an impressively long one. This applies above all in Asia, where Soviet obsession with its frontiers recalls that of Imperial Rome with the eastern boundaries of the Empire.[4] The potential concessions in Asia include the Kurile Islands claimed by Japan, the territories ceded by China under the terms of the nineteenth-century 'unequal' treaties, and the presence of the Soviet 'contingent' in Afghanistan. Such concessions would only be sold dearly. But if the economic development of Siberia is to be seriously undertaken, the Soviet Union cannot indefinitely allow itself the luxury of relations with the principal countries of Asia that are unnecessarily bad. This is, in my view, the minimum requirement; a bolder Soviet leadership might go for a comprehensive Far Eastern settlement.

Let us assume that the planner recommended for the time being a step-by-step approach in Asia. This might imply a Politburo directive that the Sino-Soviet negotiations should from now on receive the highest priority and that they should be pursued on the Soviet side with a vigour and a flexibility comparable—for example—with the way in which the Soviet–German negotiations were pursued in 1970. A compromise solution for Afghanistan, involving the withdrawal of Soviet troops, would be the immediate objective. The planner would not

find it hard to argue that it is contrary to Soviet state interests
to maintain forces in Afghanistan, whether in the Asian or in the
Middle Eastern context. A planning paper drafted on these lines
would be more than enough to be going on with; and Soviet state
interests once identified, the task of providing ideological
sanction for such changes in policy would still remain. (Under
the terms of the new Soviet Constitution, approved in 1977,
safeguarding the state interests of the Soviet Union ranks second
among the aims of Soviet foreign policy, immediately after
'ensuring international conditions favourable for building communism in the USSR').[5]

Still more adventurous initiatives would offer themselves to a
Soviet leadership that was prepared to instruct its planning staff
to dust off other old files. It should not be beyond the ingenuity of
the governments of the three countries chiefly concerned—the
United States, Cuba, and the Soviet Union—to work out an
agreement which, even if it did not bring stability to the
Caribbean and Central America, might at least achieve a
measure of damage limitation. The US–Cuban feud and Cuban
support of left-wing groups in Central America are, in the
circumstances of today, an anachronism. Here again Soviet
concessions would not be offered cheaply. More difficult by
orders of magnitude, but a future possibility that should not be
lost sight of, is a fresh resolution of the Polish Question in a way
that preserved both the interests of the Soviet Government and of
the Polish people better than the existing botch-up—the product
of another era—which gives the Soviet Union the worst of both
worlds: a recalcitrant population in Poland and a line of
communication to the German Democratic Republic that is not
really secure. It is only thirty years since Stalin made his offer of a
reunified Germany. The offer was indeed conditional and the
reasons why it was refused by the West at the time now form part
of the history of the Federal Republic. Nevertheless, we would do
well to remember that Soviet foreign policy is officially described
in Soviet texts as 'flexible', as well as 'circumspect'.

At the outset of this chapter the imaginary planner was
assumed to be intellectually objective. We must also assume him
to be a political realist. He would therefore be well aware that the
natural tendency of the politicians, civil servants, and diplomats

of any country is to act on the assumption that the broad course
of their country's international relations will continue more or
less as it is, and to hope that this assumption will be justified by
events. The Soviet Union is no stranger to this rule of the
conventional wisdom. The Soviet national security establishment, like that of the West, has grown accustomed to the system.
They too have their 'sherpas'—senior officials who prepare the
way in advance for the summit meetings of the Political
Consultative Committee, the Council of Foreign Ministers, and
the Council of Defence Ministers of the Warsaw Pact—not to
mention the informal meetings with the General Secretary in the
Crimea. The simplest foreign policy option, therefore, for the new
Soviet leadership is not to move down the roads of change, but to
stay put.

For this 'better the devil we know' course, too, the planner
could make a convincing case. The period of intensive negotiations in the 1970s gave the Soviet Union a *de facto* Central
European settlement, but with this one major exception, Brezhnev secured from these negotiations few of the benefits that he
sought. Arguably, the less negotiating surface the Soviet Union
offers the West in existing circumstances, the better. Finally, the
planning paper might well conclude by reminding readers that to
present Soviet foreign policy options in isolation, however
convenient for purposes of analysis, is an illusion. In the real
drama of world politics the Soviet role will be affected by that of
the other actors on the international stage, above all the United
States and its European allies. Might it not therefore be better to
wait and see?

At the time of writing, Andropov has been in office for under
two months. I shall not, therefore, attempt to prophesy in which
of these several directions the new Soviet leadership will set its
international course. Instead, the last chapter of this book will
seek to draw some conclusions for the European members of the
Western Alliance. I make no apology for ending this book with
Eurocentric conclusions. Europeans have spilled so much of other
peoples' blood, as well as their own, across the centuries, that
they now owe it to the rest of the world to put their own house in
order.

25. An Option for Europe

In a comparable chapter attempting to draw some conclusions for Europe in 1973, I described what was then the best that Western Europe could reasonably hope for in these terms:

The equilibrium between the United States and the Soviet Union withstands all the stresses to which it may be subjected during the next ten years, in particular, those arising from the Middle East; both super-powers keep their present military partners and do not seek others; the Soviet Union finds a means of preserving the effectiveness of the Warsaw Pact, while allowing its members a greater measure of freedom to experiment with internal political reforms; the American military presence in Europe is reduced, but remains credible; a Western European defence entity emerges, including a nuclear capability, despite all the formidable difficulties, both political and technological, which this would involve; Western Europe, without aspiring to the status of a super-power, is none the less able to . . . avoid walking 'naked into the council chamber'.

This prospect—offering the best of all worlds—now looks even more remote than it did then. So what are our practicable options? First, a revival of the super-power relationship is still a theoretical possibility, as the 1980s go forward. On balance, I still believe that, if new life were put into this relationship, and if the relationship could be maintained over a period of years, the world would become a safer place for all of us—not just Europeans— especially if this time the Middle East were included in its scope, and if one of its fruits were to be a fresh approach to this region by the super-powers, which repaired the damage done in the Middle East by the tragically mistaken policies of recent years. Nevertheless, the list of 'ifs' is too long for the purposes of practical politics. It is now also my view that, in the altered circumstances of today, a revival of the super-power relationship based on the early 1970s model, would create as many problems as it would solve. As the imaginary Kremlin planning paper foresaw, any attempt by the super-powers to revive their special relationship would evoke both Chinese and European accusations of condominium that would be even louder than those of ten years ago. For Western Europe, these accusations would be reinforced by the fact that the

Soviet Government has served notice that the British and French nuclear deterrents must be included in any future agreement on nuclear weapons.[1] It seems unlikely that the super-powers would again press ahead, regardless of the opposition both of their allies and of China, along a path which would in any case be strewn with other obstacles. The best that we can hope for from the super-powers is agreement on some self-denying ordinances in the strategic nuclear field. And in present circumstances even that is expecting a great deal.

Secondly, for 'Alice through the looking-glass' reasons, Western governments may be just as reluctant as the Soviet Government to abandon the conventional wisdom. For them, too, the simplest option may well seem to be to carry on as they are. Seen from the West, the principal argument in favour of this 'devil we know' option is that, with all its disadvantages, this is the international system to which Western governments have long been accustomed. Although no one disputes the fact that the underlying political and economic changes of the past ten years have been profound, the international system, particularly that of the Western alliance, has changed remarkably little. Under this system—so the argument runs—the peace has been kept, not least in Europe. So why make changes now—and certainly why make them until we know what, if any, changes the new Soviet leadership may have in mind?

Because this argument is immensely powerful, this option may carry the day. Yet the counter-arguments are powerful too. The crisis today is Western as well as Eastern. Nuclear weapons are, in my view, here to stay, if only because they are, in relative terms, cheaper than so-called conventional weapons, whose escalating cost is one of the central problems of modern defence policy (cheaper, alas, not only for the existing members of the nuclear 'club', but also for the countries of the developing world). But the strength of the revived nuclear disarmament campaign in Europe and of the nuclear freeze and the ground zero movement in the United States represents far more than the views of those who believe that nuclear warfare is morally wrong or politically unacceptable. It is also an indication of the views of people, many of whom were not alive at the time,[2] who do not accept today the premises on which the Western alliance and the NATO doctrine of deterrence were based, over thirty years ago. Any society, above all an industrialized democracy, requires a consensus to back its defence policy. If this consensus is beginning to fall apart in Western countries, it is not only because, in a period of recession, the budgetary claims of defence and welfare compete with each other. And it is certainly not because of any belief that the Soviet Union is in reality what it proclaims itself to be—the world's foremost peace-loving country—although it is a fact that since 15 June 1982[3] the Soviet Union stands committed to 'no first use' of nuclear weapons against all countries, without exception.

The Western consensus has been weakened by the impact of several factors, among which two are of particular relevance to this study. Of these two, one is of comparatively recent date; the other, though it has been recently reformulated, is as old as the Western alliance. The first arises from what might be called the transatlantic rhetorical gap. Of course there have always been differences of opinion among the Western allies, but until recently they were usually manageable; and although one and the same international event, or a particular aspect of international policy, might be differently written or spoken about in various Western countries, the differences were usually of a kind that could be readily understood, and therefore allowed for, in terms of the different languages and traditions of the countries concerned. From 1979 onwards the rhetorical gap has become more and more politically unmanageable. It had already widened, under the strain of events in Iran, well before the Soviet Union invaded Afghanistan in the last week of that year. The United States reacted to this invasion, as it already had to events in Iran, in a radically different way from that of its European allies. For the US Government, the invasion was the worst crisis since the Second World War. For the French Government, for example, it was simply 'unacceptable'. Similar differences, though to an even greater degree, have arisen over Poland. Today, it is no longer possible to avoid the question whether rhetoric should be taken literally, and appropriate conclusions drawn from it, on both sides of the Atlantic.

Did the President of the United States really mean to launch an anti-Communist 'crusade' in 1982; and how should the fact that he proclaimed it on European soil—forty years after the launching of Operation *Barbarossa*—be interpreted? Is it realistic to believe—and to base foreign policy on the belief—that the US land-based intercontinental ballistic missile force is now exposed through the 'Window of Opportunity' to a Soviet pre-emptive first strike, even when the greater part of the US strategic nuclear triad remains invulnerable, and although the absolute minimum estimate of the number of American dead following a Soviet attack concentrated on US land-based missile-launchers is bracketed between 300,000 and 800,000? (The worst estimate is twenty million.)[4] If the appeal to join a crusade is not rhetoric, if the 'Window of Opportunity' is more than a defence staff's worst possible case, if the present US Administration's doctrine of 'prevailing' means not just the determination to survive in battle, but an attempt to achieve the unachievable—nuclear superiority over the other super-power—then the Western consensus will become increasingly hard to hold together as the decade goes forward.

The second factor arises from an anxiety that has haunted the Western Europeans off and on throughout the life of the North Atlantic Alliance. Its intensity has varied in proportion to the degree of general political confidence in the United States felt at any given moment by Western European public opinion. Pinpointed by Kissinger in Brussels in 1979, it is the prospect that, in the last resort, the defence of Western Europe may not be seen in Washington as identical with the defence of the United States—that Europe will be 'decoupled' from America. Kissinger's aim was to concentrate European minds on the need to raise the nuclear threshold and to follow the Soviet example by modernizing their armoury of conventional weapons; and since he delivered his warning,[5] the urgency for Western Europeans to look to their conventional defences has grown more and more intense (as Sakharov himself reminded them, in his message to the 1982 Pugwash Conference). But statements by members of the Reagan Administration have also conjured up the European nightmare: the vision of a nuclear war between the super-powers confined to Europe.

By the turn of the year 1982/3, such was the intensity of the fears aroused by these two factors that in his David Davies Memorial Lecture Michael Howard recorded the fact, inconceivable for the founders of the Western alliance and hardly credible even ten years ago, that for many people on both sides of the Atlantic 'the present threat to nuclear stability comes, not from the Soviet Union, but from the United States'. As he pointed out in this lecture, it is above all the extent to which the present US Administration has accepted the ideas of the possibility of a Soviet nuclear first strike and of a 'limited' nuclear war in Europe which has led us to this pass, although, in my view, the origins of the transatlantic rift lie further back than the Reagan Presidency. We may take some comfort from the thought that Administrations come and go; the United States will not always be led by a President who professes his belief that Soviet communism is 'the focus of evil in the modern world'.[6] Nevertheless, the problem of how to preserve—now almost how to reconstruct—the Western consensus on defence (and therefore on the conduct of foreign policy as a whole) is now so deep-rooted that the transatlantic relationship requires not tinkering with, but a radical rethink.

On the assumption that the Western Europeans would not find directives issuing from a revived special relationship between the super-powers tolerable in the 1980s, the basic strategies between which they now have to choose are reduced to two: either to accept US direction of the alliance, seeking to influence US decisions as best they can, but willing in the last resort to follow the US lead, or—in the alternative—to work out their own salvation. This they could do, if they so chose, by committing themselves to what might be called the European Option. This alternative involves a hypothesis that is not easy to write about[7] in my country, whose military alliance with the United States is older than the North Atlantic Treaty, and whose suspicions of continental Europe go back for centuries. Moreover, it carries risks, which most people on both sides of the Atlantic have long regarded as unacceptable. But in the high-risk world of today there is no such thing as a low-risk policy for national security.

As Nixon and Kissinger rightly reminded the Europeans in 1973, American and Western European interests are 'not automatically identical'. Since the first, unsuccessful, American attempt to put some order into what Brandt described at the time as a 'choir of contradictory European voices . . . of no use to anyone',[8] the transatlantic conflict of interests has increased.

Three of the major fields of conflict between US and European interests have been discussed in this book—nuclear weapons; the Middle East; and, increasingly, the broad question of how policy towards the Soviet Union, on which the current argument about economic sanctions in reality depends, should be conducted. There are others. It is becoming difficult to find good grounds for believing that these conflicts of interest will diminish in the rest of this decade. But if the Americans and the Europeans were once to agree among themselves—calmly, not in the heat of sudden crisis—to admit and to face their differences, the way might then be open to restructure the transatlantic relationship in a looser form consistent with the circumstances of the 1990s, not with those of half a century earlier. The transatlantic relationship is often discussed as though its only, or primary, basis were defence. In fact, defence is one of many threads in a complex relationship. Even if Europe were 'decoupled' from the US tomorrow, the financial and economic links, let alone the ties of history, with the United States would remain.

The present system of Western European defence was established at a time when the countries of Western Europe were incapable of defending themselves—morally exhausted and financially bankrupt—against what was then perceived as the threat of a Soviet dash for the Channel. The idea that, nearly forty years later, when the European Economic Community has a combined gross national product comparable with that of the United States, the countries of Western Europe are still entitled to defence on the cheap, and that they are today incapable of committing to their own defence the resources that it requires, no longer holds water. If these countries were to accept responsibility for their own defence, this would at last dispose of one of the most telling American criticisms of the Western Europeans: that they do not bear their fair share of what is in reality their own burden. New ideas about defence strategy and its implications for the transatlantic relationship are beginning to be aired on both sides of the Atlantic.[9] Most of them do not go far enough. If we now really 'clear our minds of cant' and apply them rigorously to the transatlantic defence relationship and to the North Atlantic doctrine of deterrence—which from the outset has been ambiguous—at best, we may reach the conclusion that, as things stand today 'to manage the ambiguity' is 'in the final analysis, a task of political will, confidence, and skill'.[10] At worst, we may conclude that a transatlantic relationship and a doctrine of deterrence that are based on an obsolescent (or obsolete) American commitment to defend Western Europe by a first use of nuclear weapons in a European war, are not only ambiguous but absurd. As Voltaire said, people who tolerate absurdities will sooner or later commit atrocities.

In the past, suggestions that Western Europe should look to its own defence and that US troops might not be stationed in Europe for ever have met with a double objection: that for the Western Europeans to defend themselves is impracticable, and that, without the presence of substantial US forces on European soil, Western Europe's relationship with the Soviet Union would sooner or later resemble that of Finland. As has been suggested in an earlier chapter, the term 'Finlandization' is unjust to the Finns, whose special relationship with the Soviet Union reflects historical facts that are peculiar to these two countries. This apart, both objections now require a completely fresh scrutiny. The first invites the counter-question: how far can the existing system of Western defence, in reality, be described as practicable? It is surely based on hypotheses which, whatever their original validity, cannot be sustained in the circumstances of today. The second objection begs the question to which this book has attempted to provide part of the answer: following the settlement enshrined in the agreements of 1970–75, what is the fundamental aim of Soviet policy in Europe? Arguably, it is in the interest of neither side to upset this settlement. But there can be no doubt which of the two now has the greater interest in upholding it: the Soviet Union.

The problem that the European option would have to solve is twofold: how to form a fully fledged, credible, Western European defence entity, and how to maintain the Central European settlement. These two aspects are closely related to each other. The difficulties are formidable, but they are soluble, given time. One way of lessening their force would be to establish a transitional period, perhaps lasting to the end of the century, during which both the North Atlantic and the Warsaw Pact alliances would remain in being, followed by a longer period lasting into the next century, during which the Central European settlement would continue to be underpinned by the super-powers' guarantees, though not in their present form.

The transatlantic negotiation involved in the European option would of itself be complicated enough. But it would also involve a prolonged and arduous East–West negotiation. In such negotiations the Soviet leadership's foremost objective, to which they would give the highest priority, would be to secure copper-bottomed guarantees for the Central European settlement. For any future Soviet leadership, as for all their predecessors, Germany will remain the heart of the matter. Purely European guarantees would not therefore suffice; the guarantors would have to include the United States. These negotiations might fail. If they did, at the very least the West would have learned something more in the process about the Soviet Union; and perhaps also about themselves. The attempt would still have been worthwhile. Sooner or later, in my view, it must be made.

Appendix

Extract from the Constitution of the USSR
Chapters 4 and 5

Source: Constitution (Fundamental Law) of the Union of Soviet Socialist Republics (Moscow, 1977)

Chapter 4. Foreign Policy

ARTICLE 28. The USSR steadfastly pursues a Leninist policy of peace and stands for strengthening of the security of nations and broad international cooperation.

The foreign policy of the USSR is aimed at ensuring international conditions favourable for building communism in the USSR, safeguarding the state interests of the Soviet Union, consolidating the positions of world socialism, supporting the struggle of peoples for national liberation and social progress, preventing wars of aggression, achieving universal and complete disarmament, and consistently implementing the principle of the peaceful coexistence of states with different social systems.

In the USSR war propaganda is banned.

ARTICLE 29. The USSR's relations with other states are based on observance of the following principles: sovereign equality; mutual renunciation of the use or threat of force; inviolability of frontiers; territorial integrity of states; peaceful settlement of disputes; non-intervention in internal affairs; respect for human rights and fundamental freedoms; the equal rights of peoples and their right to decide their own destiny; cooperation among states; and fulfilment in good faith of obligations arising from the generally recognized principles and rules of international law, and from the international treaties signed by the USSR.

ARTICLE 30. The USSR, as part of the world system of socialism and of the socialist community, promotes and strengthens friendship, cooperation, and comradely mutual assistance with other socialist countries on the basis of the principle of socialist internationalism, and takes an active part in socialist economic integration and the socialist international division of labour.

Chapter 5. *Defence of the Socialist Motherland*

ARTICLE 31. Defence of the Socialist Motherland is one of the most important functions of the state, and is the concern of the whole people.

In order to defend the gains of socialism, the peaceful labour of the Soviet people, and the sovereignty and territorial integrity of the state, the USSR maintains armed forces and has instituted universal military service.

The duty of the Armed Forces of the USSR to the people is to provide reliable defence of the Socialist Motherland and to be in constant combat readiness, guaranteeing that any aggressor is instantly repulsed.

ARTICLE 32. The state ensures the security and defence capability of the country, and supplies the Armed Forces of the USSR with everything necessary for that purpose.

The duties of state bodies, public organizations, officials, and citizens in regard to safeguarding the country's security and strengthening its defence capability are defined by the legislation of the USSR.

Notes

Introduction

1. For the definition, see p. 10. The mandate is described on pp. 118–19.
2. The new chapters run from p. 137 onwards. The 'parameters' and 'variables' in Chapter 15 of my earlier book covered the period 1973–83.
3. At a plenary meeting of the CPSU Central Committee held on 16 November 1981: see *Pravda*, 17 November 1981.
4. Department of State Bulletin, July 1974, vol. LXXI, no. 1831, pp. 205 ff.
5. Intercontinentally needs underlining, because within the European continent Soviet medium and intermediate range nuclear weapons targeted on NATO countries could have wrought havoc, had the Cuban crisis ended in a nuclear exchange.
6. What these consequences would be for Birmingham are assessed by Solly Zuckerman, *Scientists at War*, Harper & Row, New York, 1966, pp. 55–8.
7. Fallible, but with brains, values, and judgements still perhaps 'superior to the mechanics and processes of electronic computers or guidance systems': ibid., p. 26.
8. *Strategic Survey 1980–1*, IISS, London, 1981, p. 15.
9. One among many examples of the contemporary Soviet view of what has gone wrong and why is the account offered in the concluding chapters of vol. 2 of *Istoriya Vneshnei Politiki SSSR 1945–1980*, Nauka, Moscow, 1981, pp. 672–3.
10. George N. Curzon, *Russia in Central Asia*, Longmans, Green, London, 1889, ch. VIII.
11. In Afghanistan. The force is described by official Soviet sources as a 'limited contingent'.
12. Towards the end, perhaps rather more the latter than the former: see, for example, J. F. Hough, 'The world as viewed from Moscow', *International Journal* (Toronto), vol. 37, no. 2 (Spring 1982).
13. Frederick Engels, *A Polish Proclamation* (1874) in Karl Marx and Frederick Engels, *The Russian Menace to Europe*, eds. Blackstock and Hoselitz, Allen & Unwin, London, 1953, p. 115.

1. Paradox

1. J. F. Kennedy, in the foreword to Theodore C. Sorensen, *Decision-Making in the White House*, Columbia University Press, New York, 1963, p. xi.

2. In *Expansion and Coexistence*, Secker & Warburg, London, 1968, pp. 432 ff., Adam Ulam makes a good case for regarding this as the opening of the cold war. (The Soviet Government subsequently obliged Czechoslovakia, not yet a member of the Soviet bloc, to follow suit.) Soviet historians might prefer March 1947, when the Truman Doctrine was announced. Certainly the great divide must be set somewhere in 1947.

3. Text in *The Times*, 23 June 1973.

4. *Istoriya Vneshnei Politiki SSSR*, Moscow, 1971, eds. Ponomarev, Gromyko, and Khvostov, vol. 2, p. 486. The distinction between 'building socialism' and 'building communism' is that only the Soviet Union is regarded by Soviet theorists as having reached the latter stage of development (as was announced by Khrushchev in 1961).

5. L. I. Brezhnev, *Leninskim Kursom*, Moscow, 1972, vol 3. p. 196. An even more recent, and identical, formulation is given by *Diplomatiya Sotsializma*, Moscow, 1973, p. 17. See also Appendix, p. 231.

6. V. I. Lenin, *Complete Collected Works*, Fifth Russian edition, vol. 36, p. 327, Moscow, 1962. This quotation comes from Lenin's report on Soviet foreign policy of 14 May 1918. (All other quotations from Lenin's *Collected Works* are taken from the English edition.)

7. Op. cit., vol. 2, p. 485.

8. *Pravda*, 5 June 1973.

9. Ibid., 30 September 1965.

10. Although peaceful coexistence is the invariable phrase in contemporary Soviet usage, Lenin himself spoke rather of peaceful cohabitation (*mirnoe sozhitel'stvo*)—see, for example, *Collected Works*, English edition, vol. 40, p. 145; vol. 41, pp. 132–3; and vol. 45, pp. 327–44.

11. *Pravda*, 21 June 1973.

12. The first description is quoted from *Krasnaya Zvezda*, 9 July 1974. The second is from op. cit., vol. 2, p. 480.

13. *The Times*, 25 June 1973.

14. W. T. R. Fox, *The Super-Powers—their responsibility for peace*, Yale Institute of International Studies, 1944, pp. 20–1.

15. For a classic exposition of this doctrine see Ian Smart's 'Advanced Strategic Missiles', *Adelphi Papers*, no. 93, IISS, London, 1969, p. 27. The 'Soviet view of deterrence' was surveyed by John Erickson in his article in *Survival* November/December 1982, IISS, London, 1982.

16. Alexis de Tocqueville, quoted on the fly-leaf of Graham Allison, *Essence of Decision: Explaining the Cuban Missile Crisis*, Little, Brown, Boston, 1971.

17. Harold Guetzkow (quoted by Nigel Forward in *The Field of Nations*, Macmillan, London, 1971) remarks that 'if the use of quantitative methods and scientific analysis were to bring about an improvement of five per cent in the performance of nations in their relations with

one another, he for one would be well pleased'. And Zuckerman, op. cit., p. 25, observes of abstract strategic analysis that these variables 'are of so qualitative a nature that no one could attribute numerical values to them'.

18. Thucydides, *History of the Peloponnesian War*, II, 48.3, translated by Rex Warner, Penguin Books, Harmondsworth, 1954, p. 152. (I have somewhat altered Warner's rendering of this passage.)

19. 'His own', because the Politburo of the CPSU, the supreme decision-making body in the Soviet Union and the hub of the lobbies that make up the Soviet élite, is not given to indiscretion. Moreover, its decisions on foreign policy are not based only on information and advice from the Soviet Ministry of Foreign Affairs. Other important bodies which submit to the Politburo views that are by definition closed to the outside observer, are the foreign departments of the Party's central apparatus and the foreign directorate of the KGB.

KHRUSHCHEV'S YEARS OF ADVENTURE

2. The Theory

1. *Pravda*, 13 March 1954. For an analysis of the differences between Malenkov and Khrushchev at that time, see J. M. Mackintosh, *Strategy and Tactics of Soviet Foreign Policy*, Oxford University Press, London, 1962, pp. 88 ff.

2. Marshal Tito alone dissenting, from 1948 onwards.

3. Thomas W. Wolfe, *Soviet Power and Europe, 1945–70*, Johns Hopkins Press, Baltimore, 1970, p. 130.

4. Quoted in *Problems of Communism*, vol. XI, no. 1 (Jan.–Feb. 1962), p. 40.

5. A. L. Horelick and M. Rush, *Strategic Power and Soviet Foreign Policy*, University of Chicago Press, 1966, pp. 36–120.

6. Ibid., pp. 42, 58, and 88 respectively. Khrushchev also allegedly remarked that he had been obliged to hold down the megatonnage of one of the Soviet nuclear test explosions in the Arctic because it might have 'broken all the windows of Moscow': see Zuckerman, op. cit., pp. 59–60.

7. In fact it was a 'space gap', rather than a 'missile gap', and even this was more apparent than real: see Herbert York, *Race to Oblivion*, Simon and Schuster, New York, 1970, pp. 109–12, and 144–6, and—for American R and D in the fifties—pp. 83 ff.

8. Ibid., p. 127 for Soviet ICBM design, and pp. 94–101 for the dates of deployment of American ICBMs.

9. This remark, taken from Lenin's article 'The Political Significance of Abuse' was quoted in a Chinese statement in the *People's Daily*, 13

September 1963: see William E. Griffith, *The Sino-Soviet Rift*, Allen & Unwin, London, 1964, p. 423.

10. The 'Origin and development of the differences between the leadership of the CPSU and ourselves', dated 6 September 1963, was published in *The polemic on the general line of the international communist movement*, by the Foreign Languages Press, Peking, 1965. For the Soviet view, see Zbigniew Brzezinski, *The Soviet Bloc*, Harvard University Press, Cambridge, Mass., 1967, pp. 399 ff.

11. In Western terms these may roughly be regarded as schools of Marxist thought representing liberal and conservative communism.

12. At the very least, the Soviet Government must have supplied the Chinese Government with the technology required to construct a plant for enriching uranium. See Gittings, *Survey of the Sino-Soviet Dispute 1963–67*, Oxford University Press, London, 1968, pp. 102–5, and Harry Gelber, 'Nuclear Weapons and Chinese Policy', *Adelphi Papers* no. 99, IISS, 1973, p. 13.

13. Gittings, ibid., pp. 158–61 ff., contains a concise summary.

14. Michel Tatu, *Power in the Kremlin*, Collins, London, 1965, p. 367. Suslov's report, like the 'Open letter' of 1963 (see p. 35 below), covered seven pages of *Pravda*.

3. The Cuban Missile Crisis

1. The profession of faith mentioned in the second sentence of Chapter 1; the full text of Castro's speech was carried in *Hoy* (Havana), 2 December 1961. For the evolution of the Soviet-Cuban relationship during this period, see Stephen Clissold, *Soviet Relations with Latin America 1918–68*, Oxford University Press, London, 1970, pp. 47–50.

2. For example, some publicity had been given to a large-scale amphibious exercise which was to take place off the south-east coast of Puerto Rico, with the object of liberating a mythical republic from a dictator named Ortsac: see Allison, op. cit., p. 47. But Allison strains the imagination when he suggests that the importance of the Cuban issue in American domestic politics could have escaped the attention of any observer, Soviet or otherwise, in 1962.

3. See ibid., p. 49, for a fuller discussion of this proposition.

4. Khrushchev's complicated domestic position at this time is described in Tatu, op. cit., Pt. Three, 'The Cuban Fiasco'. For Castro's evidence—that the purpose of the Soviet missiles in Cuba was 'strengthening the socialist camp on the world scale' and 'we considered that we could not decline'—see *Le Monde*, 22 March 1963 (subsequently confirmed in a speech carried by *Pravda*). The idea that at this late hour China could have been prevented from joining the strategic nuclear club may seem far-fetched today, but it may not

have been a pipe-dream for Khrushchev early in 1962: for an exposition of this view, see Ulam, op. cit., pp. 661 ff.

5. He was replaced as Commander-in-Chief of the Strategic Missile Forces by Biryuzov, a Ukrainian who may perhaps have been a political client of Khrushchev; see Tatu, op. cit., pp. 236–7.

6. P. Salinger, *With Kennedy*, Cape, London, 1967, ch. XI; A. M. Schlesinger, *A Thousand Days*, Deutsch, London, 1966, pp. 324–40; T. C. Sorensen, *Kennedy*, Hodder & Stoughton, London, 1965, pp. 543–600.

7. Salinger, op. cit., p. 176.

8. Ibid., p. 182.

9. Sorensen, op. cit., p. 550. There is nothing in the account given by A. A. Gromyko in *1036 dniei prezidenta Kennedi*, Moscow, 1968, to support this legend either.

10. *The Military Balance 1969–70*, IISS, London, p. 55. It is, however, conceivable that Soviet intelligence was less well informed about the relative strategic nuclear power of the two countries than was American intelligence, which had the benefit not only of U-2 but also of satellite reconnaissance—not to mention Penkovsky.

11. Op. cit., pp. 106 ff. In fairness to the Russians, the same book also points out some remarkable American mistakes, for example, the fact that no U-2 flight was directed over western Cuba between 5 September and 4 October: see ibid., p. 120.

12. Statement by Chinese Government spokesman, 1 September 1963, (*Peking Review*, 6 September 1963): text in Gittings, op. cit., pp. 181–3. The Soviet-US agreement over Cuba was not even registered officially at the UN, as was the original intention. For a discussion of the question whether there was also an unofficial US commitment to withdraw the fifteen obsolete Jupiter missiles from Turkey, see Allison, op. cit., pp. 229–30.

13. Allison, ibid., pp. 200 ff., is the best recent example.

14. Wellington's much misquoted description of Waterloo: 'It was a damned nice thing—the nearest run thing you ever saw in your life'; Thomas Creevey, *The Creevey Papers*, p. 142, ed. John Gore, London, 1934.

15. *Pravda*, 13 December 1962. The relevant passage in *Istoriya Vneshnei Politiki SSSR* is in vol. 2, pp. 364–5, to which the chapter concerned in *Mezhdunarodnye konflikty*, Moscow, 1972, eds. V. V. Zhurin and E. M. Primakov, adds little, summing up the outcome of the crisis as being that 'the USA was compelled to agree to renounce its plans of aggression against . . . Cuba' after a 'fairly intensive exchange of messages between the two governments'—pp. 84 and 95. Gromyko told the Supreme Soviet flatly that 'the leaders of the USA brought the world one step, perhaps only half a step, from the abyss'— *Pravda*, 14 December 1962.

16. Anatolyi A. Gromyko 'Karibskii Krizis', *Voprosy Istorii*, nos. 7 and 8, Moscow, 1971.

17. Robert Kennedy, *Thirteen Days, a Memoir of the Cuban Crisis*, Macmillan, New York, 1969.

18. This accusation is borne out by the text of Khrushchev's 'Friday' letter. The 'Trollope ploy', whereby Kennedy replied to the 'Friday' letter rather than to the 'Saturday' letter, is described in Allison, op. cit., pp. 227 ff.

19. In Khrushchev's letter to Kennedy of 27 October 1962, which was broadcast over Moscow radio on that day, he said that agreement over Cuba would 'make it easier to reach agreement on banning nuclear weapons tests' and in his letter of the following day, which was also broadcast, he said that the Soviet Government would 'like to continue the exchange of views on the prohibition of atomic and thermonuclear weapons'. In Kennedy's letter of 28 October, which was released to the press, he suggested that the two governments 'should give priority to questions relating to the proliferation of nuclear weapons, on earth and in outer space, and to the effort for a nuclear test ban'. Macmillan (whose greatest achievement in foreign policy was perhaps the conclusion of the Nuclear Test Ban Agreement) also regarded a ban on tests as a measure that would enable the three governments 'to proceed rapidly to specific and fruitful discussions about the non-dissemination of nuclear power leading to an agreement on this subject': see the joint Anglo-American letter to Khrushchev of 15 April 1963, quoted in his *At the End of the Day*, Macmillan, London, 1973, p. 467. Ibid., p. 480 gives Macmillan's own view about this during the actual negotiations three months later.

20. *Pravda*, 14 July 1963: Griffith, op. cit., pp. 289–325, contains a translation of this document, which covered seven out of *Pravda*'s eight pages.

21. *The Military Balance 1969/70*, loc. cit.

22. In particular, *Pravda* of 2 October 1964, 'On the main directions for drawing up the plan for the development of the national economy in the next period'. In three columns describing Khrushchev's intervention there is only a single sentence on the needs of defence, which must be 'maintained at the appropriate level', whereas the need to make consumer goods top priority is repeatedly mentioned. Khrushchev's clear implication was that heavy industry was now strong enough to sustain both these objectives. This intervention is all the more striking in that it coincided with the publication of an article in the current issue of *Kommunist Vooruzhennykh Sil* which emphasized the continuing role of heavy industry as the economic foundation of the Soviet Union's progress: see the article reporting this in the *Guardian* of 2 October 1964 by Victor Zorza, whose articles in the

Guardian of 18 and 25 September also described the controversy between Khrushchev and the Soviet military about the value of conventional weapons, particularly tanks.

23. T. W. Wolfe, op. cit., p. 464; Khrushchev's decision to subordinate the Ground Forces directly to the Defence Ministry was not revealed until 1968 (by Marshal Zakharov, Chief of the General Staff).

24. As was argued by P. B. Reddaway in his article on 'The Fall of Khrushchev' published in *Survey*, July 1965.

25. Deported from their homes by Stalin's order, for alleged collaboration with the German forces.

YEARS OF CONSOLIDATION

4. Defence Policy

1. *Pravda*, 17 October and 8 November 1964. See also Brezhnev, *Leninskim Kursom*, vol. 3, p. 30.

2. *Krasnaya Zvezda*, 4 February 1965. It is evident from the context that Khrushchev—not Stalin, who is mentioned elsewhere in the article—is the target of this criticism.

3. The first occasion on which he was specifically described by *Pravda* as leading a delegation abroad (to Poland) was on 5 April 1965.

4. So also was Brezhnev, whose assumption of other offices is described in Chapter 16. About this body little is known, but it is presumed to bear ultimate responsibility for strategic nuclear decisions. For a discussion of the present functioning of these three bodies, and also the important role of the General Secretary's personal secretariat, see Alain Jacob's article in *Le Monde*, 12 February 1974, *L'URSS, société socialiste développée*. Finally, Khrushchev was chairman of the Central Committee Bureau of the RSFSR, an office which was abolished in 1966.

5. For an analysis of the three different defence policy objectives of the new Soviet leadership, see the final chapter of Wolfe, op. cit.

6. This argument was put forward by Michael Boretsky, whose conclusions were called in question by Alec Nove in *Survival* of January 1971, particularly those relating to comparative prices. For a discussion, see *The Military Balance 1973/4*, IISS, London, 1973, pp. 8–9.

7. For Brezhnev's allusions, see Chapter 9 below. John Erickson, in *Soviet Military Power*, Royal United Services Institute for Defence Studies, 1971, p. 100, suggests that in macro-economic terms the Soviet leadership is prepared to see military expenditure 'move

ahead at the rate of 4 per cent per annum within an annual growth rate of about 5 or 6 per cent'. The section of the present chapter that follows is indebted to Erickson's book.

8. The Budapest reforms of the Warsaw Pact introduced in 1969 are described in *Survival*, May/June 1974, 'The Warsaw Pact Today' by Malcolm Mackintosh, pp. 123–4, IISS, London, 1974.

9. By 1973 more than half the officer corps of the Soviet Navy also had engineering degrees, according to *Krasnaya Zvezda*; see *The Times*, 30 July 1973.

5. Asia

1. Adam Ulam in *The Rivals*, Viking Press, New York, 1971, has argued that American diplomacy missed the opportunity for such a dialogue after the Cuban crisis had revealed the weakness of the Soviet position. But Khrushchev's personal position had also been weakened at home. Would he have had the authority to go further towards Kennedy than he did during his remaining two years of office?

2. *Istoriya Vneshnei Politiki SSSR*, vol. 2, p. 422, gives the Soviet view. For the Nanning incident, see Stanley Karnow, *Mao and China*, Macmillan, London, 1973, p. 439.

3. *Strategic Survey 1972*, IISS, London, 1973, p. 50, which describes the estimated figures given as rough. For the Chinese view of the North Vietnam War in the sixties, see Karnow's analysis op. cit., pp. 479 ff.

4. In 1966, Carlos Rafael Rodriguez, when asked by the author to which Communist Party Cuban Communists felt closest, replied without hesitation 'the North Korean'.

5. Zhenbao Island for the Chinese, whose account of what they have claimed as a Soviet defeat was given in the *Observer* of 23 September 1973. For Xinjiang, see Karnow, op. cit., p. 135.

6. Chinese ambassadors who had been withdrawn from their posts returned, after years of absence; diplomatic relations were even restored with the capital of arch-revisionists, Belgrade; and Yugoslavia itself resumed relations with the arch-dogmatist Albania.

7. *Pravda*, 14 and 11 June 1969.

8. For details, see *Novosti*, Moscow, and the *World Marxist Review*, Prague, 1969.

6. The Third World

1. For example, the affair of Aníbal Escalante: see Stephen Clissold, op. cit., pp. 294 ff.

2. By 1970 the joint total of military and commercial Indonesian debt to the Soviet Union was still 750 million dollars. The 400 million dollars owned by Indonesia to Eastern European Governments were not rescheduled until 1971–2.

3. The evolution of Soviet aid policy is traced in ch. 6 of W. W. Kulski, *The Soviet Union in World Affairs 1964–1972*, Syracuse University Press, New York, 1973. For the threefold classification, see ibid., p. 161. The Soviet theorist is Ulyanovsky whose article in *International Affairs* is quoted in *The Conduct of Soviet Foreign Policy*, eds. Erik Hoffman and F. Fleron, Aldine and Atherton, Chicago, 1971, pp. 410 ff.

4. This 'illusion' is specifically attributed to the 'late fifties and in particular the early sixties' by V. Tiagunenko in *Nekotorye problemy natsional'no—osvoboditel'nykh revoliutsii v svete Leninizma*, 1970, quoted by Kulski, op. cit. pp. 188–9.

5. These were described soon afterwards by René Dumont, a left-wing writer sympathetic towards the Cuban Revolution, in his book *Cuba: socialisme et développement*, Editions du Seuil, Paris, 1964. In 1961/2, for example, only half the fruit and vegetables available in Cuba were collected by the Land Reform Agency, which was headed by a geographer, Professor Nuñez Jimenez; and in 1963 agricultural productivity on the state farms was less than half that in what remained of the private sector.

6. The Soviet–Cuban political balance sheet has been drawn up by Clissold, op. cit., pp. 42–59, although given the date of publication (1970), he had to end this chapter of his book with a question mark.

7. Ibid., pp. 304–6, which gives the full text. By the time of the Non-Aligned Conference held in Algiers in 1973, Castro had become an out-and-out defender of the Soviet Union against all comers: see *Pravda* of 9 September 1973, reporting his speech of the previous day.

8. The Central Treaty Organization, consisting of Turkey, Iran, Pakistan, and Great Britain. This succeeded the Baghdad Pact, from which Iraq withdrew after the *coup d'état* in 1958, in which both the King and the Prime Minister were assassinated. Its headquarters was moved from Baghdad to Ankara in 1959.

9. Tatu, op. cit., 'Postscript', pp. 532 ff., gives the Soviet aspect of the chronology of the crisis. This particular incident is referred to on p. 536, from which the quotation is also taken.

10. Which is what the French text of the resolution said.

11. Of an estimated Palestinian Arab population of about three million, in 1973 roughly half were outside the 1948 frontiers of Palestine, and a further 600,000 were living in the West Bank area and the Gaza Strip under Israeli rule. 1,300,000 Palestinians were registered as refugees qualifying for United Nations assistance.

7. Europe

1. The Council of Mutual Economic Assistance was established in January 1949, as the Soviet response to the European Recovery Programme. The Soviet proposal of 1962 was abandoned and replaced by the concept of coordination of long-term planning. Some progress was achieved. In the following year *Intermetall*, which began as a programming centre for iron and steel planning, was set up in Budapest; the *Druzhba* pipeline began to bring Soviet oil to Eastern Europe; and in 1965 COMECON established an International Bank of Economic Cooperation and a joint Institute for Nuclear Research.

2. *New York Times*, 13 May 1966.

3. See, for example, *Istoriya Vneshnei Politiki SSSR*, vol. 2, pp. 61 ff.

4. Text in *Keesing's Contemporary Archives 1967/8*, p. 21981.

5. Text of communiqué in *Pravda*, 8 July 1966.

6. Compare *Istoriya Vneshnei Politiki SSSR*, vol. 2, p. 352.

7. The Soviet Government continued to be concerned at this prospect long after the American proposal for a NATO multilateral nuclear force (MLF), first launched in 1963, had been abandoned. Instead, in 1966 the NATO nuclear planning and consultative committee was established, which *Pravda* of 20 July 1965 described as 'perhaps even more dangerous than the MLF'. The NATO MLF nuclear planning proposals may have influenced the Soviet reversal of policy over the Non-Proliferation Treaty.

8. Text in *Keesing's Contemporary Archives 1967/8*, p. 22425. The original reason for the French abstention from the MBFR proposals was partly that French forces no longer formed part of the integrated NATO command and partly that the idea of negotiations conducted *de bloc à bloc* was contrary to French policy. As time went by the French Government also became increasingly opposed to any withdrawal of US forces from Europe in principle.

9. The name of the author, I. Aleksandrov, is a pseudonym used for articles cleared at the highest level of the CPSU. The text of *The 2,000 Words* was published in *East Europe*, August 1968, pp. 25–8. Aleksandrov described its authors as both counter-revolutionary and linked with reaction.

10. For the full text, see *Pravda*, 18 July 1968.

11. For the text of the Cierna communiqué, see *Washington Post*, 2 August 1968.

12. For the text of the Bratislava communiqué, see *Pravda*, 4 August 1968.

13. William Hayter, *Russia and the World: a Study of Soviet Foreign Policy*, Secker & Warburg, London, 1970, p. 37.

14. An excerpt from an article entitled 'The political side to Soviet military doctrine' and published in *Kommunist Vooruzhennykh Sil*, no.

22, November 1968: quoted by C. G. Jacobsen in *Soviet Strategy—Soviet Foreign Policy*, Glasgow University Press, 1972, pp. 191 ff.

15. Presumably, as Wolfe suggests (op. cit., p. 474), to serve notice on NATO that the Soviet Army meant business. But if so, on what possible sources of information did the planning staff base their supposition that any such notice was necessary? Perhaps the units formed part of the forces' establishment and it was simplest not to leave them behind.

16. *Keesing's Contemporary Archives 1971/2*, p. 24935.

17. *Pravda*, 13 November 1968.

18. The Soviet–Yugoslav *rapprochement*, coming after the stresses and strains imposed on Yugoslavia as an ideological pig-in-the-middle during the early years of the Sino-Soviet dispute, was effected at the time of Tito's visit to Moscow in December 1962. For an account of 'hedgehog' defence, see *Survival*, March/April 1973, 'Yugoslav Total National Defence' by A. Ross Johnson, IISS, London, 1973, pp. 54 ff. A further *rapprochement* began with a visit by Gromyko to Belgrade in September 1969, although relations between the two countries have had their ups and downs since then.

19. *Keesing's Contemporary Archives 1969/70*, p. 23750. It stated that 'the use of force and the stationing in Czechoslovakia of Soviet forces not hitherto deployed there have aroused grave uncertainty about the situation and about the calculations and intentions of the USSR'; this uncertainty demanded 'great vigilance' on the part of the Allies.

20. Ibid., p. 23403.

21. As Nixon described it, in his report to the US Congress of 25 February 1971 on 'US foreign policy for the 1970s'.

YEARS OF NEGOTIATION: The First Phase

8. The Turning Point

1. Text in Command Paper 3683, HMSO, London, June 1968, reprinted 1969, which also contains the text of the security assurances given by the three nuclear powers which signed the treaty.

2. *Strategic Survey 1969*, IISS, London, 1969. One megaton = 1,000,000 tons of TNT, in terms of the yield of a nuclear explosion. For the fortuitous origin of the megaton, see York, op. cit., pp. 89–90.

3. *Keesing's Contemporary Archives, 1969/70*, p. 23291.

4. Quoted in *Istoriya Vneshnei Politiki SSSR*, vol. 2., p. 452.

5. This was more of an off-the-cuff statement than the exposition of a new doctrine, but none the less important for that. The difference between American global policy at the beginning and end of the

decade can be seen by comparing the statement, in Kennedy's
inaugural message, that the United States would help anyone, with
Nixon's reformulation, that the United States would help anyone
who would help himself.

6. *Pravda*, 18 March and 1 November 1969.
7. *Keesing's Contemporary Archives 1969/70*, p. 23750.
8. This major contract was concluded by Fiat after Gromyko's visit to
Italy in 1966, when he also became the first Soviet Foreign Minister
to be received in audience by the Pope.

9. The State of the Union

1. *Kniga o sotsialisticheskoi democratii*, Alexander Herzen Foundation,
Amsterdam/Paris, 1972.
2. Circulated first in *Samizdat*; and the translation was published in
London (Penguin), 1969; see p. 66.
3. *Pravda*, 13 January 1970. As late as July, Brezhnev said that the
Party Congress would be held during 1970.
4. Oscar Lange, who used this description in a lecture given in 1957 in
Belgrade, quoted in Alec Nove, *The Soviet Economy*, Allen & Unwin,
London, 1968, p. 162. The closest quotation in Lange's collected
works is in an article entitled *O niektorych zagadnieniach polskiej drogi do
socjalizmu* (1957), reprinted in vol. 2 of his collected works, *Socjalizm*,
Warsaw, 1973, p. 499.
5. The most important measures introduced in 1965 were some
devolution of planning and decision-making to enterprise level and
changes in the success criteria of enterprises, followed in 1967 by a
revision of prices. Much has been written on this subject: see, for
example, Medvedev, op. cit., pp. 287 ff., and Nove, op. cit., ch. 9.
6. *Pravda*, 3 April 1973. *Pravda* of 19 June foresaw the formation of
transnational corporations.
7. Brezhnev, op. cit., vol. 3, p. 66. See ibid., pp. 62–9 for a strongly
worded exposition of the shortcomings of Soviet agriculture. Cf.
Nove, op. cit., p. 335. For an analysis of the 1965–70 Plan, see Nove,
The Soviet Five Year Plan, Hong Kong Economic Papers, no. 6, 1971.
8. Medvedev, op. cit., p. 302.
9. The cult of the gross output, *kul't vala*, is a quotation from D.
Kondrashev, *Tsenoobrazovanie v promyshlennosti*, Moscow, 1956, p. 32.
The translation of *pokazatel'* as 'success indicator' is Nove's: see *The
Soviet Economy, passim*.
10. Quoted by Alain Jacob in *Le Monde*, 15 February 1974: an example
of the defect known by Soviet economists as *raspylenie sredstv*.
11. De Gaulle's own description of the students' revolt of May 1968.
12. For this attack, see Brezhnev, op. cit., p. 215. The description of

Marcuse is in B. Bykhovskii's article *Filosofia mel'koburzhuaznogo buntarstva, Kommunist,* no. 8, 1969, pp. 114–24.

13. In November 1970. The text of the declaration of the programme of the *Committee for the Rights of Man* is given in Medvedev, op. cit., p. 91.

14. This movement in effect performed the same gadfly function for Soviet society as the emigré intellectuals did for nineteenth-century Russia. For a description of *Samizdat* (literally, 'self-publishing house'), see Julius Taleshin's article in *Encounter,* February 1973.

15. An extreme case was *Can the Soviet Union Survive until 1984?* by Andrei Amal'ryk, Harper & Row, New York; Allen Lane, London, 1970.

16. Grigorenko was not released until 1974, despite the publicity given to his case in the West. A reply from a group of Soviet psychiatrists to Western criticism of this method of treatment was sent to the *Guardian,* which published their letter on 29 September 1973.

17. Brezhnev, op. cit., vol. 3, p. 390. All subsequent quotations from, and references to, this speech will be taken from this source.

18. Ibid., pp. 195–6.

10. The Year 1970

1. A Western European, especially from Britain, old enough to recall the events of 1938/9, might expect his Soviet contemporaries to prefer to forget this treaty, rather as he would prefer not to be reminded of the Munich Agreement: yet it appeared in posters displayed prominently in Moscow at this time, with a Nazi boot kicking through it.

2. Text in *Pravda* of 13 August 1970, translated in *Survival,* vol. XII, no. 10, October 1970.

3. Translated in *Survival,* vol. XIII, no. 2, February 1971.

4. The latter point was rammed home by Brezhnev again and again in his subsequent speeches: see, for example, the many references to the Moscow Treaty in Brezhnev, op. cit., vol. 3, indexed on p. 506.

5. Although the Federal Republic did not ratify this treaty for over four years after signing it: a measure of its importance.

6. The question can roughly be translated as 'who is top dog?'. Brezhnev's own answer, given in the course of a speech delivered to the Central Committee of the Azerbaijan Communist Party and the Azerbaijan Republic Supreme Soviet on 2 October 1970, was 'everyone won equally': Brezhnev, op. cit., vol. 3, p. 145. Apart from acquiescing in the legal niceties described, the main Soviet concession, which did not become effective until the conclusion of the Quadripartite Agreement on Berlin, related to the question of West Berlin.

7. The texts of these two communiqués were reproduced in *Survival*, vol. XV, no. 8, August and no. 9, September 1970, respectively.

8. *Keesing's Contemporary Archives 1969/70*, p. 24348. These principles were 'sovereign equality, political independence and territorial integrity of each European state; non-interference and non-intervention in the internal affairs of any state, regardless of its political or social system; and the right of the people of each European state to shape their own destinies free of external constraint'.

9. Op. cit., vol. 2, p. 352.

10. See *The Times*, 20 April 1974.

11. Op. cit., vol. 2, p. 350.

12. In *Krajowa Agencja Informacyjna*, XII–XVI, no. 7/579, pp. 1, 3–13; Gierek's report to the Polish Central Committee, submitted early in February 1971.

13. George Kennan, in his article published in *Foreign Policy*, Summer 1972, p. 21, edited by Huntington and Manshel, National Affairs Inc., New York, 1972.

14. 'The Year 1919, the Mission of William Bullitt', *SShA*, Moscow, January 1970.

15. G. V. Chicherin, *Articles and Speeches*, Moscow, 1961, p. 227.

16. *Izvestiya*, 31 May 1971.

17. *Strategic Survey 1970*, IISS, London, pp. 46–9; the same source estimates the free market value of Soviet military equipment supplied to Egypt since the 1967 War as having increased during 1970 from 2,000 million to 4,500 million dollars.

18. Units of the US Sixth Fleet also moved eastwards towards the Syrian Coast. It is not clear whether this pressure on the Syrian Government was exerted by the super-powers acting in concert or in parallel.

11. The Year 1971

1. Full text in *Pravda*, 28 May 1971. In fact, Egypt was still called the United Arab Republic at that time, but it has seemed simpler to use the shorter form throughout.

2. *The Times*, 4 September 1971.

3. *Keesing's Contemporary Archives 1971/2*, p. 25015. The NATO communiqué was still cautious about the proposal for a meeting in Helsinki, expressing readiness 'to begin multilateral conversations intended to lead to a Conference on Security and Cooperation in Europe'.

4. As examples, Brezhnev mentioned at the XXIVth Party Congress the prospect that by 1975 the *Druzhba* pipeline would ship nearly fifty million tons of oil to Eastern Europe (as compared with 8.3

million tons in 1964), and that a gas pipeline would carry natural gas from Siberia to European Russia, thus facilitating the supply to Eastern European countries.

5. This analysis of the Complex Programme is indebted to Michael Kaser.

6. Brezhnev, op. cit., vol. 3, pp. 495 ff., contains the text of his speech. For the 1969 proposal see ibid., vol. 2, p. 413.

7. At the end of the same year Brezhnev revealed that the proposal for a non-aggression pact with China, including weapons, had been put forward by the Soviet Union as early as January 1971.

8. *The Times*, 1 September 1973 and 4 September 1981.

9. Full text in *Pravda*, 10 August 1971.

10. On the other hand, China supported the Government of Ceylon—as did the Soviet Union, among other countries—against the left-wing rebels there.

11. *Kommunist*, 'The Programme of Peace in Action', January 1972. But, in my view, Soviet policy in the sub-continent was aimed primarily against China. Soviet relations with Pakistan were restored in March 1972.

12. The Year 1972

1. In an interview published in *Time* magazine of 2 January, the President was echoing a remark made by Kissinger in 1968, in 'Central Issues of American Foreign Policy', Brookings Institution, Washington: 'in the years ahead the most profound challenge . . . will be . . . to develop some concept of order in a world which is bipolar militarily, but multipolar politically.'

2. *Keesing's Contemporary Archives 1971/2*, pp. 25150 ff.

3. Respect for the sovereignty and territorial integrity of all states; non-aggression against other states; non-interference in the internal affairs of other states; equality and mutual benefit; and peaceful coexistence.

4. Nixon claimed on 21 and 27 February 1972, at the banquets given in his honour in Peking and Shanghai respectively: 'what we do here can change the world', and 'this is the week that changed the world'.

5. *Keesing's Contemporary Archives 1971/2*, pp. 25309 ff. and p. 25291. Subsequent quotations from other documents signed in Moscow are derived from the same source.

6. *The Military Balance 1972/3*, IISS, London, 1972, Appendix I, pp. 83 ff., analyses the effect of the SALT agreement on the strategic balance.

7. *Strategic Survey 1972*, IISS, London, 1973, p. 15.

8. Ibid., p. 14.

9. Ibid., p. 16.

10. *Diplomatiya Sotsializma*, Moscow, 1973, p. 171.

11. Cf. Brezhnev's remark, quoted in ch. 1, made a year later in Washington.

12. *Pravda*, 25 June 1973.

13. The United States Air Force is estimated to have dropped three and a half times as many bombs on Vietnam as it did on all the United States' enemies in the Second World War. For rough estimates of the cost, in blood and in treasure, of the Vietnam War, see *Strategic Survey 1972*, IISS, London, 1973, pp. 48 ff.

14. For a Japanese assessment of the range of responses open to Japan in the longer term, see Kiichi Saeko, 'Japan's Security in a Multipolar World', *Adelphi Papers*, no. 92, IISS, London, 1972.

15. The Soviet Union had refused to sign the Japanese Peace Treaty negotiated at San Francisco in September 1951, under Article 2 of which Japan renounced all claim to the Kuriles. The state of war between the Soviet Union and Japan was nevertheless brought to an end in October 1956, by the re-establishment of diplomatic relations between the two countries.

16. *The Military Balance 1972/3*, IISS, London, 1972, p. 44.

17. The 1972 agreement in principle led in the end to Japanese participation on a modest scale, a 450 million dollar loan from Japan for the development of Siberia, not including Tyumen': see *The Times*, 23 April and *Pravda*, 27 June 1974.

18. An account of the three-cornered manoeuvres that preceded the momentous vote of 17 May is given in Kulski, op. cit., pp. 428 ff. The text of the Basic Treaty is in *Survival*, January/February 1973, vol. XV, 1, pp. 31–2.

19. At their meeting in Prague in January 1972, the Warsaw Pact ministers had declared that the interests of European security would be served by reaching an agreement on the reduction of armed forces and armaments in Europe, although it could not be 'an exclusive matter for the existing military and political groupings in Europe to consider and determine the way in which to solve that problem'.

20. *Keesing's Contemporary Archives 1971/2*, p. 25676.

21. In Africa south of the Sahara, on the other hand, Soviet policy, although troubled by fierce Chinese competition for influence, notably in Tanzania (whose armed forces were exclusively trained by the Chinese), could afford to be long-term. In Southern Africa the principal source of the supply of arms for the major guerrilla movements remained the Soviet Union. The Soviet Government also made some well-judged offers to African governments: for example, field artillery to Nigeria, which made an important contribution to the ending of the civil war in 1970 (*New York Times*, 21 January 1970: 'Nigeria says Russian help was vital to war victory'); and cash

($7,500,000) to Somalia for the development of the Port of Berbera, which was to become a valuable port of call for the Soviet Navy's squadron in the Indian Ocean. And the Soviet Navy patrolled the coast of Guinea after that country had been attacked from Portuguese Guinea in 1971.

22. In turning to Iraq, the Russians did the same as the British had done twenty-four years earlier, when the future of their Egyptian base began to look insecure.

23. Summarized in *The Economist*, 13 January 1973.

24. Text in *Pravda*, 10 December 1972.

25. For contemporary assessments of his mission, see *The Economist* of 9 December and *Le Monde* of 7 December 1972.

26. For a Soviet posthumous criticism of Allende's economic mistakes, see A. Sobolev's article in *The Working Class and the Contemporary World*, no. 2, Moscow, 1974. The CPSU's expression of sympathy was carried in *Pravda*, 14 September 1973.

13. The Year 1973

1. Text in *Pravda*, 28 April 1973. A literal translation of the three Russian words *v kachestve normy* will not suffice, because of the different significance of the word 'norm' in the two languages. See also Appendix, p.231.

2. The slogans were reported in *Pravda*, 14 October and Brezhnev's speech was reported in *Pravda*, 27 October 1973.

3. Once again, the Soviet leadership took pains to preserve their links with France: Brezhnev received Pompidou in January, before the French parliamentary elections, and he stopped in France for talks on his way back from Washington in June. He also visited the German Democratic Republic and Poland immediately before his visit to the Federal German Republic, and at a meeting of bloc party leaders, held in the Crimea at the end of July, he obtained their approval of his summit diplomacy: see *Pravda*, 1 April 1973.

4. *Keesing's Contemporary Archives 1973*, pp. 25975 ff. The Kursk negotiations came to fruition two years later.

5. As a result of this compromise, the Federal German and Czechoslovak governments were able to sign a peace treaty on 28 November. Signature had previously been held up by this disagreement.

6. Text in *The Times*, 29 June 1973.

7. *The Times*, 2, 3, and 4 July 1973.

8. *The Times*, 21 August 1973, 'Mr Nixon Gets a Little Help from His Friends' by Victor Zorza. Soviet citizens able to listen to foreign broadcasts would of course have followed the affair throughout.

9. Text in *The Times*, 26 June 1973. The phrase was also used by

Brezhnev in his televised address to the American people: see *Pravda*, 25 June 1973. The Russian texts of the Washington Agreements, the Joint Communiqué of 24 June 1973, and Brezhnev's speeches delivered during his US visit were subsequently assembled by Izdatel'stvo Politicheskoi Literatury, as *Vizit Leonida Il'icha Brezhneva v Coedinennye Shtaty Ameriki*, Moscow, 1973.

10. Text in *The Times*, 23 June 1973. This agreement stemmed from a Soviet initiative. Its curious history, including the fact that much of its drafting was British, has since been related by Kissinger in his *Years of Upheaval*, Weidenfeld & Nicolson and Michael Joseph, London, 1982, pp. 274 ff.

11. *The Times*, 22 June 1973, reported that an annual figure of 200 million dollars worth of natural gas, over 20 years, was being mentioned in Washington at the time, together with Export-Import Bank finance for a part of the cost of a 400 million dollar fertilizer plant.

12. Berezhkov in *Literaturnaya Gazeta*, no. 35, 29 August 1973, pp. 9, 14.

13. Kissinger retained his post as Special Assistant to the President for National Security Affairs.

14. *The Times*, 10 October and 13 September 1973 respectively.

15. Kissinger's own account of the Jackson Amendment and of subsequent developments in this field has since been given in his memoirs: op. cit., pp. 249–55 and 985–98.

16. A brief statement made it clear that Solzhenitsyn's purpose was to test how the Soviet authorities would in practice adhere to the international copyright convention, which the Soviet Government had at last signed in May: see *The Times*, 22, 28 September 1973.

17. *Archipelag Gulag*, YMCA press, Paris, 1973, on the fly-leaf.

18. This letter was published in paperback by Fontana, 1974.

19. See *The Times*, 22 August and 5 September 1973.

20. When several Soviet Jews were condemned to death for having tried to hijack an aircraft in order to fly to Israel.

21. *The Times*, 25 September 1973. For other quotations in this paragraph, see ibid., 30 July, 27 August, and 1 September 1973.

22. *The Times*, 13 September 1973.

23. *Pravda*, 26 August 1973. Both articles had been cleared at the highest CPSU level.

24. This concept, otherwise known as the 'changing geographical vortex of the revolution', had indeed been evolved by the Chinese in the early sixties, when they first began publicly to attack what they regarded as a Soviet–American attempt to establish a global hegemony: see Brzezinski, op. cit., pp. 403 ff.

25. A reference to Nixon's proposals for making 1973 the 'year of Europe', put forward on his behalf by Kissinger in a speech on 23 April 1973. By the end of the year the US and its allies were to have worked out 'a new Atlantic charter setting the goals for peace'. For

the nine EEC governments' draft of such a declaration, agreed at Copenhagen in September, see *The Times*, 25 September 1973.

26. On 20 September the Japanese Diet voted unanimously, including the Communist Party, in favour of a demand for the return of the four southern Kurile islands.

27. The text in fact reads: 'the Nuclear Weapons Non-Proliferation Treaty of 1963'. The writer presumably had had both the Non-Proliferation and the Test Ban treaties in mind.

28. For example. *Strategic Survey 1973*, IISS, London. 1974, examined the war in all its aspects. See also *Survival*, May/June 1974, 'Soviet Aims and the Middle East War', pp. 106 ff., by Galia Golan. And since then Kissinger has offered his own account, in *Years of Upheaval*, op. cit., pp. 450 ff.

29. Kissinger's words at the *Pacem in Terris* conference, to which he added 'coexistence to us continues to have a very precise meaning: we will oppose the attempt of any country to achieve a position of predominance either globally or regionally'.

30. For texts of the three resolutions, nos. 338, 339, and 340, see *Survival*, January/February and May/June 1974.

31. Most of what evidence there is has been assembled by Karen Dawisha in 'USSR and Middle Eastern Crises: 1973, 1980', *International Affairs*, Winter 1980–1981, vol. 57, no. 1, RIIA, London, 1981, pp. 43 ff.

YEARS OF NEGOTIATION: The Second Phase

14. The Concept of the Super-Power Relationship

1. In Russian, *razryadka*, or more fully, *razryadka mezhdunarodnoi napryazhennosti*.

2. For the Harmel report see pp. 64–5 above. The same distinction has also been preserved by Kissinger: see, for example, *The White House Years*, Weidenfeld & Nicholson, London, 1979, p. 1143, and *Years of Upheaval*, op. cit., pp. 981–5.

3. His press conference given at the height of the Soviet–US crisis caused by the Fourth Arab–Israeli War, on 25 October 1973. See also Kissinger, *Years of Upheaval*.

4. Raymond Aron, *Paix et guerre entre les nations*, Calman-Levy, Paris, 1962, pp. 527 ff.

5. For the earliest definition of the term super-power itself, coined by William Fox in 1944, see Chapter 1 above.

6. See note 1 to Chapter 12 above.

7. Hedley Bull reminded me of these Reith Lectures: Alastair Buchan, *Change without War: the shifting structures of World Power*, Chatto &

Windus, London, 1975, and Andrew Shonfield, *Europe: journey to an unknown destination*, Penguin Books, London, 1974. He also drew my attention to Joseph Nye and Robert Keohane, *Transnational Relations and World Politics*, Harvard University Press, Cambridge, Mass, 1972.

8. And also at the Energy Conference summoned in Washington by the US Government in February 1974, which led to the formation (without French participation) of the International Energy Agency in October of that year.

9. Nixon gave his assurance about condominium in his televised broadcast from the Kremlin on 28 May 1972. Jobert's remarks were reported in *The Scotsman*, 13 November 1973.

10. The text of the Year of Europe statement is in *Keesing's Contemporary Archives, 1973*, pp. 25933 ff. The text of Kissinger's Brussels speech was reprinted in *Survival*, November/December 1979, IISS, London, 1979, pp. 264–8.

11. *Pravda*, 16 August 1973 (the italics are mine).

12. Ibid., 27 October 1973. In his later years Brezhnev also used *détente* in its fuzzy Western sense, however.

13. *Pravda*, 19 January 1974 reported Suslov's and Ponomarev's addresses to the conference convened in Moscow to discuss the teaching and achievement of Lenin on the fiftieth anniversary of his death. The full text of Ponomarev's address was given in *Kommunist*, no. 2, Moscow, 1974. Suslov spoke of the 'very sharp ideological struggle that is going on in the contemporary world' and Ponomarev of a 'definite qualitative shift in the development of the crisis of capitalism'.

14. *The Times*, 29 March 1974, has the English text.

15. High Noon

1. *Pravda*, 26 September 1974.
2. Described on p. 127 above.
3. *The Times*, 19 October 1974.
4. Kissinger, *The White House Years*, op. cit., p. 1143.
5. Text in *Survival*, January/February 1975, pp. 35–42.
6. See pp. 107–9 and p. 124 above.
7. *Pravda*, 30 June, 4 July, and 5 July 1974.
8. For the further history of the Peaceful Nuclear Explosions Treaty and related developments, see *Strategic Survey 1976*, IISS, London, 1977, p. 107.
9. *Der Spiegel*, 2 November 1981, pp. 34 ff.
10. *Strategic Survey 1980/81*, IISS, London, 1981, p. 15.
11. For the Vladivostock Accords, see *Strategic Survey 1974*, IISS,

London, 1975, pp. 60–4, to which the summary of the agreement given in this chapter is indebted.

12. Her Majesty's Stationery Office's *Conference on Security and Cooperation in Europe Final Act*, Cmnd. 6198, London, 1975 (reprinted 1979), goes to over fifty pages.

13. HMSO, op. cit., p. 3.

14. Ibid, p. 4.

15. Ibid, pp. 9–10.

16. NATO observed these provisions on seven occasions in 1975; the first Soviet notification was in January 1976—see *Strategic Survey 1975*, IISS, London, 1976, p. 57.

17. HMSO, op. cit., pp. 33 ff.

18. See Appendix, p. 231.

16. Drift

1. See the third of the 'basic tasks' of Soviet foreign policy listed on p. 8 above.

2. *Frente Nacional de Libertacao de Angola* and *Uniao Nacional para a Independencia Total de Angola*.

3. This is a summary version of a long and complicated story. For a comprehensive account of the Portuguese decolonization process in 1975, see *Strategic Survey 1975*, IISS, London, 1976, pp. 27 ff. And for the Cuban role in Angola, see Jorge I. Dominguez 'Cuba in the 1980s', *Problems of Communism*, March–April 1981.

4. That of South Africa, which did not withdraw its forces from Angola until March 1976. The Soweto riots took place in June 1976.

5. *Strategic Survey 1976*, IISS, London, 1977, p. 3. But for a detailed discussion, see the 'Soviet Defence Expenditure' section of the *Military Balance*, IISS, London, for any of these years, e.g., 1973–4, pp. 8–9, and 1976–7, pp. 109–10.

6. Text in *Survival*, July/August, 1976, IISS, London, 1976, pp. 171–4. Legislation reimposing the US ban on the import of Rhodesian chrome was signed by Carter in March 1977.

7. It was finally achieved in March 1980.

8. Nor, it should be added, has any been made up to the time of writing—in Laurence Martin's words, 'a strategist's and arms controller's nightmare' (*The Listener*, 10 December 1981).

9. See p. 109 above.

10. Texts in *Survival*, November/December 1975, IISS, London, 1975, pp. 282–5.

11. See p. 136 above, and *Pravda*, 4 August 1974. The Soviet Government accorded the PLO full diplomatic status in October 1981.

12. The text of the statement was published in *Pravda*, 2 October 1977.
13. In his report on the CPSU's 'immediate tasks in home and foreign policy' of 24 February: English text in *Documents & Resolutions, XXVth Congress of the CPSU*, Novosti Press Agency Publishing House, Moscow, 1976, p. 40. Where not otherwise stated, quotations in the remainder of this chapter are taken from this translation. The Russian text of Brezhnev's speech is in L. I. Brezhnev, *Leninskim kursom*, vol. 5, Moscow, *Izdatel'stvo politicheskoi literatury*, 1981, pp. 450 ff.
14. See *The Twenty-Fifth Congress of the CPSU*, Alexander Dallin, Editor, Hoover Institution Press, 1977, p. 67. The corresponding percentages projected in the previous plan were 38.6, 47, 48.6, and 23 per cent.
15. As Nove points out—op. cit., p. 120—the word 'leader' was the Russianized English *lider*, not *vozhd'*, the Russian word applied to Stalin.
16. For the Defence Council, see p. 39 and p. 239n. above. In March Dmitri Ustinov, the Central Committee Secretary responsible for defence industries, joined the Politburo as a full member; and when Marshal Grechko died in April, he succeeded him as Defence Minister, at the age of sixty-eight (his promotion to Marshal followed).
17. *The Times*, 8 June 1976.
18. George Marchais, Secretary-General of the French Communist Party, declined to attend.
19. Text printed in *Za mir, bezopasnost', sotrudnichestvo i sotsial'nyi progress v Evrope: k itogam konferentsii kommunisticheskikh i rabochikh partii Evropy*, Moscow, *Izadatel'stvo politicheskoi literatury*, 1976.
20. See p. 62 above.
21. Communist Ministers participated in the French Government, following the Socialist victory in the elections of 1981.
22. An attempt to mend Sino-Soviet fences was indeed made. At the CPSU Congress in February 1976, Brezhnev had described his Party's struggle against Maoism as 'irreconcilable': Maoist ideology and policy were 'directly hostile' to Marxist-Leninist teaching; and Peking's 'frantic attempts to torpedo *détente*' presented 'a great danger for all peace-loving peoples'. In November, however, the Sino-Soviet border negotiations were resumed after a break of eighteen months. By 9 October 1979, according to the Chinese, they had reached deadlock. On 20 January 1980 (in the wake of the Government invasion of Afghanistan) the Chinese Government postponed the round of negotiations that was to have begun in February of that year.
23. Part of the US President's public reaction to the Soviet invasion of Afghanistan.

17. Nuclear Weapons Negotiations

1. *The Times*, 18 February 1977. In January 1980 Sakharov was sent into internal exile.
2. The argument was, in essence, about whether or not the cruise missile and the *Backfire* bomber had a strategic capability.
3. The summary account offered in this chapter of this proposal and of the subsequent negotiations is indebted to the analysis provided in successive issues of *Strategic Survey*, IISS, London, from 1977 onwards. For SALT II, see Strobe Talbott, *Endgame*, Harper & Row, New York, 1979.
4. *Pravda*, 1 April 1977.
5. For example, see *Pravda*'s article published on 11 February 1978. The English text was reprinted in *Survival*, May/June 1978, IISS, London, 1978.
6. For a description of the 'September Breakthrough' see Talbott, op. cit., pp. 120 ff.
7. Who had succeeded Brandt on the latter's resignation in May 1974.
8. Text reprinted in *Survival*, January/February, 1978, IISS, London, 1978.
9. At Carter's request, following the Soviet invasion of Afghanistan. Several other agreements, under negotiation at the time, were similarly affected. For a list, see *Strategic Survey 1981–82*, IISS, London, 1982, pp. 123–4.
10. The Soviet assessment quoted here is the one given in *Istoriya Vneshnei Politiki SSSR, 1945–1980*, Vol. 2, Nauka, Moscow, 1981, p. 79. The words 'reasonable compromise' repeat a phrase used by Brezhnev at the time. The text of the treaty is in *Survival*, September/October, 1979, IISS, London, 1979.
11. 'Circular error probable' is the radius round a target within which half the warheads aimed at it are expected to fall. For detailed figures, see *Strategic Survey 1980–1981*, IISS, London, 1981, pp. 12 ff.
12. In his speech on US foreign policy, delivered at Harvard on 5 June 1980, in the course of which he urged ratification of SALT II even at that date. The text is in the *New York Times*, 6 June 1980.
13. See p. 35 above.
14. *Pravda*, 7 October 1979.
15. Euromissiles were first defined as Long Range Theatre Nuclear Forces (LRTNF), as distinguished from tactical nuclear weapons, and are now known as INF.
16. *The Times*, 19 November 1981, carried a partial text of the President's 'Declaration of Intent'.
17. *Pravda*, 12 July 1982.
18. *International Herald Tribune*, 1 June 1982.
19. *Pravda*, 22 and 31 December 1982.

20. In the interview given to *Der Spiegel*; see the issue of 2 November 1981, p. 54.

DEFENCE OF THE PERIMETER

18. The Far East

1. Modernization in the fields of agriculture, industry, science and technology, and defence, with the object of enabling China to rank as a modern industrialized country by the end of the century—a policy substantially modified by the subsequent 'Readjustment'.

2. I.e. the period covered by the Cultural Revolution (which—strictly defined—lasted only three years) and its aftermath: see David Bonavia, *The Chinese*, Allen Lane, London, 1980, p. ix.

3. See pp. 22, 112, 248n., 251n. I am indebted to Wolf Mendl for the account of recent developments in the Soviet-Japanese territorial dispute that follows in this chapter. See also his *Issues in Japan's China Policy*, Macmillan for RIIA, London, 1978, pp. 79–80, and the comprehensive treatment in John J. Stephan, *The Kuril Islands: Russo-Japanese frontier in the Pacific*, Clarendon Press, Oxford, 1974.

4. The date of the signing, in 1855, of the Treaty of Shimoda, establishing the Russo-Japanese frontier north of Etoforu.

5. For this clause, see the wording of the Sino-US Shanghai Communiqué of 1972: pp. 113–14. By the end of the decade 'hegemonist' was equated with 'Soviet' in documents of this kind.

6. L. I. Brezhnev, *Leninskim kursom*, op. cit., vol. 7, pp. 374 ff., contains his Minsk speech. For Brzezinski, see Talbott, op. cit., p. 153 and pp. 249–50.

7. The security interests of the US were said in this communiqué not 'to coincide completely'.

8. For a detailed discussion of the state of Chinese defence equipment at this time, see *China's Defence Industries* in *Strategic Survey 1979*, IISS, London, 1980, pp. 67 ff.

9. According to American intelligence sources: see *Strategic Survey 1977*, IISS, London, 1978, p. 130.

10. With the help of efficient artillery, thanks to French Jesuit advisers: see René Grousset, *The Rise and Splendour of the Chinese Empire*, Geoffrey Bles, London, 1952, pp. 288–9.

11. 'Strategic partnership' was Deng Xiaoping's phrase in 1979 and 'parallel strategic outlook' was that used by the US Defence Secretary, Harold Brown, in 1980. A forceful account, from the Soviet viewpoint, of the Sino-Soviet relationship is given in *Istoriya Vneshnei Politiki SSSR 1945–1980*, vol. 2, pp. 594 ff. For the strength of Brezhnev's own feelings about China, see Kissinger's memoirs,

op. cit., *passim*. For the effect of the events of 1978 on Salt II and on Soviet–US relations, see Talbott, op. cit., pp. 250 ff.

12. The interim compromise on US arms sales to Taiwan was announced in a joint communiqué issued in Peking and Washington on 17 August 1982; see the *Financial Times*, 18 August 1982 and *The Economist*, 21 August, pp. 31 ff.

13. *Pravda*, 25 March 1982 carried the text of Brezhnev's speech. For the Chinese response, see *News from Xinhua News Agency*, 27 March 1982.

14. *The Twelfth National Congress of the CPC*, Foreign Languages Press, Peking, p. 59. See also Huan Xiang's article 'Adhere to an independent foreign policy', published in *Xinhua News Agency*, 1 November 1982.

15. See Brzezinski, op. cit., pp. 177 ff, and Kulski, op. cit., pp. 339 ff.

19. The Arc

1. Text published by the International Communication Agency, US Embassy, London, 1978.

2. And, in addition, the Somalis in Djibouti and those in Northern Kenya, all of whom were to be incorporated in Greater Somalia.

3. In August 1980 the US 'inherited' the use of the same facilities in Somalia, in return for the supply of weapons, which were supposed not to be used against Ethiopia. The Soviet Union had already made up for this loss in South Yemen, with air and naval facilities at Aden. A Soviet Treaty of Friendship and Cooperation was signed with South Yemen in 1979.

4. A US State Department estimate at the time. The number of Cuban troops in Ethiopia increased to around 15,000 in the following year: see *Strategic Survey 1978*, IISS, London, 1979, p. 94.

5. Text in *Survival*, November/December 1978, IISS, London, 1978, pp. 271–4.

6. Sadat was assassinated in Cairo on 6 October 1981. He was succeeded as President by Hosni Mubarak.

7. Broadly speaking, the Egyptian aim in these negotiations was to establish an independent Palestinian state, following a transitional period of 'autonomy', whereas the Israelis were willing only to concede Palestinian 'self-administration' in the fields of education and municipal affairs, retaining sovereignty over Gaza and the West Bank themselves.

8. For a contemporary (and sympathetic) account of this bizarre document, see James Reston's 'What did Carter Promise?' in the *International Herald Tribune*, 31 March–1 April 1979.

9. *Istoriya Vneshnei Politiki SSSR, 1945–1980*, vol. 2, pp. 639 ff. For a contemporary view, see Brezhnev's interview given to *Pravda*, 24 December 1977.

10. Unkindly republished by *Le Monde* on 22 February 1979.

11. This inability continued long after the writing was clearly visible on the wall in Teheran: see, for example, *Le Monde* of 12 October 1978, quoting UPI, Reuter, and AFP. On 20 April 1982 *The Times* carried under the heading *Revealed: America's dithering in the Shah's final days*—Robert Fisk's analysis of US documents published by the Iranian Government.

12. General Volnay F. Warner, quoted in the last sentence of John Hackett's Adelphi Paper 'Protecting Oil Suppliers: the military requirements' in *Third World Conflict and International Security*, Part I, IISS, London, 1981, which offers a detailed assessment of the issues involved.

13. The aborted attempt to rescue the US hostages from Teheran. Cyrus Vance resigned as Secretary of State, in protest.

14. *Survival*, November/December 1982, IISS, London, 1982, pp. 277 ff., reprinted extracts from Reagan's statement and reactions to it, Soviet, Israeli, and Arab.

15. Tass declaration, published in *Pravda*, 20 September 1982.

16. The warning to the US was delivered on 18 November 1978, in an interview given to *Pravda* correspondent. For the Soviet recognition of the Iranian Government, see *Pravda*, 13 February 1979. The letters exchanged about the 1921 Treaty between Gotzbadeh and Gromyko, of 14 and 28 August 1980, are quoted by Karen Dawisha in her 'Soviet decision-making in the Middle East: the 1973 October War and the 1980 Gulf War,' *International Affairs*, RIIA, vol. 57, no. 1, 1980–1981, p. 50.

17. Iraq invaded Iran in September 1980, having abrogated the Iraqi–Iranian Treaty of 1975. Brezhnev described this war as 'senseless' both in his speech in Delhi in December 1980 and in his report to the XXVIth CPSU Congress in 1981. The US Government's stance towards the war was also even-handed.

18. The text was carried by *Pravda*, 9 October 1980.

19. The extract from Brezhnev's speech in Moscow was quoted in the *Guardian*, 9 October 1980, by David Hirst. *Pravda* 11 December 1980, carried Brezhnev's Delhi proposals about the Gulf.

CRISIS

20. Afghanistan

1. Text in *Survival*, March/April 1979, IISS, London, 1979, pp. 92–3.

2. These figures are those estimated by *Strategic Survey 1979*, IISS, London, 1980, pp. 48 ff. (Central Asian reservists were soon replaced by troops from other parts of the Soviet Union.) This, taken together

with the same publication for 1980–1, pp. 63 ff., records the basic facts of the invasion and the occupation and also of the internal events in Afghanistan that went before. By the end of 1982 the total number of Soviet troops in Afghanistan was estimated to be in excess of 100,000.

3. See *Pravda*, 29 December 1979; and *Istoriya Vneshnei Politiki SSSR, 1945–1980*, vol. 2, pp. 646–7.

4. At the time, the Soviet invasion received a mixed response even from the Soviet Union's allies. Castro, in his non-aligned role, was embarrassed; Romania publicly demanded a Soviet withdrawal; the GDR, Bulgaria, and Czechoslovakia (predictably) supported the Soviet Union; Poland and Hungary kept as quiet as possible; and India (after Mrs Gandhi's return to power) sought to adopt a middle position between the two super-powers, abstaining on the UN resolution. At the time of writing, the UN plan, for a phased withdrawal, seems to be making some headway: see *International Herald Tribune*, 8 December 1982.

5. See Michael Binyon's 'Russians tell of Horror and Heroism in Afghanistan' in *The Times*, 24 February 1982.

6. The People's Democratic Party of Afghanistan, whose secretary general, Nur Muhammad Taraki, became Prime Minister at the 1978 *coup d'état*.

7. The *Khalq* and the *Parcham* respectively. In the end the *Parcham* came out on top.

8. From April 1978 the victims of the Afghan regime included Muhammad Daud (who had ruled Afghanistan for the previous five years), Adolph Dubs (US Ambassador), Nur Muhammad Taraki (President at the time), and Hafizullah Amin.

9. Vladimir Kuzichkin, whose article 'Coups and killings in Kabul' appeared in *Time*, 22 November 1982, pp. 25 ff.

10. L. I. Brezhnev, *Leninskim Kursom*, op. cit., vol. 7, p. 548.

11. A Russian protectorate was established over Bukhara in the nineteenth century. A Bukhara People's Soviet Republic existed between 1920 and 1924.

12. Op. cit., vol. 2, p. 645.

13. Brezhnev's statement is in *Pravda*, 13 January 1980. Zamyatin's remark was reported by Peter Niewsewand, in the *Guardian*, 10 December 1980.

14. Kuzichkin, op. cit., p. 26.

21. Poland

1. In 1956 Gomulka (detained during Stalin's last years) was returned to power following the Poznan riots. In 1970, following the riots in

the Baltic cities, he was replaced by Gierek, who was expelled from the PZPR in 1981. For the text in translation of the 'Exposition' of the Gdansk Agreement, see *Survival*, September/October 1981, IISS, London, 1981.

2. See Richard Portes, *The Polish Crisis: Western Economic Policy Options*, the Royal Institute of International Affairs, London, 1981, p. 1. Unless otherwise stated, the description in this chapter of the state of the Polish economy at the end of 1980 is indebted to Portes' study.

3. The PZPR—Party of United Polish Workers—is the Polish Communist Party.

4. See Neal Ascherson, *The Polish August*, Penguin Books, Harmondsworth, 1981, p. 201 and p. 271.

5. See *Strategic Survey 1980–1981*, IISS, London, 1981, p. 74. In addition, two Soviet armoured divisions are permanently stationed at Legnica (since 1956, with a low profile). The Warsaw Pact Northern Group Force Headquarters is also at Legnica.

6. *Pravda*, 6 December 1980 and 5 March 1981.

7. The text of this letter was carried by *Pravda* on 12 June 1981.

8. *International Herald Tribune*, 14 December 1981, carried AP's report of translated excerpts from Jaruzelski's broadcast address to the Polish people of 13 December. The Russian translation (in full) of his address was carried by *Pravda*, 14 December 1981.

9. See *Tass* statement, 15 December 1981, p. 1.

10. For accounts of the events in 1981 leading up to and following martial law, see 'A Polish Chronology' in the *International Herald Tribune*, 14 December 1981; Roger Boyes in *The Times*, 13 January 1982, pp. 4 ff.; and the interview with Mieczyslaw Rakowski published in *The Times*, 22 February 1982.

11. Quoted in *The Times* and *International Herald Tribune*, 26 January 1982. By July 1982 about 600 Poles remained in internment: see *The Times*, 23 July 1982.

12. He died in May 1981.

13. In 1981 Walesa visited Rome, where he had talks with the Pope, who had made a triumphal visit to Poland in 1979 (before his election, Cardinal Wojtyla had been Archbishop of Krakow).

14. See tables 1 and 2 in Portes, op. cit., pp. 46–7.

15. The estimate given in *Zycie Warszawy*, 31 December 1980. See, however, Portes' comments, ibid., p. 20.

16. For the Soviet rescheduling, which followed a meeting between Brezhnev and Kania in the Crimea, see *Pravda* of 16 August, 1981. Western governments had already rescheduled about 2.5 billion US dollars in April.

17. A Eurocurrency syndicated loan for Poland in the spring of 1979 was oversubscribed, at 550 million US dollars.

18. See *The Economist*, 11 July 1981, pp. 33 ff., quoting the Polish Minister of Planning.
19. At the close of this Congress, held in Gdansk in September–October 1981, Walesa was re-elected Chairman.
20. Z. Kowalewski, writing in *Le Monde* of 7 January 1982. He left Poland to go on a mission to France just before martial law was proclaimed—a particularly interesting witness.
21. From 1956 onwards, for example, 80 per cent of Polish agricultural land was restored to private ownership. Even in the Stalinist years the regime was less severe in Poland than elsewhere in Eastern Europe. There were no show trials; and in 1956 both Gomulka and Wyszynski were alive and immediately capable of exercising leadership.

22. The Economic Dimension

1. Quotations from Brezhnev's speech to the Congress are taken from the English text in *Documents and Resolutions, the XXVth Congress of the CPSU*, Novosti Press Agency Publishing House, Moscow, 1981. The Russian text is in Brezhnev, *Leninskim Kursom*, vol. 8, Moscow, 1981.
2. In his first press conference as President, in January 1981, Reagan called the Soviet leadership 'immoral' and said that they reserved the right to 'commit any crime, to lie, and to cheat' in order to achieve their aims.
3. At this meeting the EEC Heads of Government recognized the Palestinian people's 'right to self-determination' and the necessity of associating the PLO with any negotiations regarding the Arab–Israeli dispute.
4. This italic is in the official text of Weinberger's address to the Royal Institute of International Affairs, London, 22 October 1981, from which these quotations are taken.
5. Text quoted in *The Economist*, 22 May 1982, p. 67, in an article on 'East–West Trade', which sets out both sides of the American–European controversy.
6. In April 1981, reversing the decision taken by Carter in January 1980. On 30 July 1982 Reagan said that he would allow another one-year extension of the US–Soviet grain agreement: see *International Herald Tribune*, 31 July–1 August 1982.
7. As between the Soviet Government and the Federal German Government, this agreement was signed on 20 November 1981: see the *International Herald Tribune*, 21–22 November 1981. Agreements with the other governments concerned have followed.
8. A convenient list was provided by *The Economist*, 22 May 1982, p. 49,

both of US unilateral measures and of those agreed with other members of Nato.

9. For a summary of this transatlantic 'economic war' (as the French Foreign Minister described it), including the names of the main firms involved, see *The Economist*, 10 July 1982, pp. 63–4. In 1979, high technology exports from the US to the USSR amounted to less than 5 per cent of total American exports to that country (see *The Economist*, 26 December 1981, p. 32), whereas three-quarters of Western European exports to the Soviet Union consisted of manufactured goods. For an assessment of the pipeline project in the light of US Government's decision of June 1982, see the *Financial Times*, 3 August 1982, p. 2; and for the British Government's decision to invoke the (1980) Protection of Trading Interests Act, see p. 1 of the same issue. The developments of November were reported and assessed in the *Financial Times*, 15 November, the *International Herald Tribune*, 15 November, and *Le Monde*, 16 November 1982.

10. The Russian text of the draft plan, published in 1980 before the Congress was held, is in *Osnovnye Napravleniya Ekonomicheskogo i Sotsial'nogo Razvitiya CCCP na 1981–1985 gody*, Izdatel' stvo Politicheskoi Literatury, Moscow, 1980. See also Alec Nove's assessment of the Plan in *The World Today*, vol. 37, no. 5 (May 1981), pp. 168 ff., and in the same issue, pp. 162 ff., an assessment of the political and social aspects of the Congress by Leonard Schapiro, who points out that Brezhnev himself offered a—by Soviet standards—candid account of some of the scourges of Soviet society.

11. Notably, the CIA's *Prospects for Soviet Oil Production*, and its *Prospects for Soviet Oil Production: a Supplemental Analysis*, Washington, DC, April and July 1977 respectively. For a balanced assessment (written before the publication of the Plan), see Philip Hanson's 'Economic constraints on Soviet policies in the 1980s', *International Affairs*, vol. 57, no. 1, 1980–1, pp. 21 ff.

12. The conclusion reached by Jonathan Stern in his 'Soviet energy prospects in the 1980s' in *The World Today*, RIIA, May 1980, which offers a summary both of the statistics and of conflicting opinions (also written before the text of the draft Eleventh Plan were available).

13. See Nove, *The World Today*, p. 169.

14. See *Pravda* 25 May, followed by a leading article in *Pravda*, 26 May. The new measures were described as intended to lead to a simplified and more devolved system of management, an expansion of private plot production, a reduction in agricultural imports from the West, increased procurement prices, enhanced bonuses, and other incentives.

15. This figure of *privelechyonnye* is the estimate given by E. Manevich in

Voprosy ekonomiki, no. 9, 1981, quoted by Nove in *Soviet Studies,* vol. XXXIV, no. 1, January 1982, p. 122.

16. *Naselenie CCCP po dannym vsesoyuznoi perepisi naseleniya 1979 goda,* Izdatel'stvo politicheskoi literatury, Moscow, 1980.

17. Hélène Carrère d'Encausse, *L'Empire Eclaté,* Flammarion, Paris, 1978, pp. 233 ff. offers an assessment based on the 1970 census figures (translated as *The Decline of an Empire,* Newsweek, New York, 1979). For the 1979 census, see Murray Feshbach. 'Between the lines of the 1979 Soviet census' in *Problems of Communism,* vol. 31, no. 1 (January–February 1982), pp. 27–37.

18. *Pravda,* 24 November 1982. See also *Financial Times* of the same date.

23. The Succession Accomplished

1. *Pravda,* 13 November 1982.
2. Ibid., and *The Economist,* 'Brezhnev's legacy', both of 13 November 1982.
3. The diamonds of 'Boris the gipsy' affair and the arrest of the director of the Moscow circus.
4. The simile is mine, but the thought is expounded as the conclusion of the last of Laurence Martin's Reith Lectures: *The Listener,* 17 and 24 December 1981, p. 751.
5. Text in *Pravda,* 28 October 1982.
6. Text in *Pravda,* 23 November 1981.
7. Even those normally inclined to give the US the benefit of the doubt found it hard to do so on this issue: see, for example, *The Economist,* 27 November–3 December 1982, pp. 16–17 and 44–5.
8. *International Herald Tribune,* 23 and 24 November 1982.
9. Brezhnev's statement was reaffirmed by Ustinov in his article published in *Pravda,* 12 July 1982.
10. *Pravda* 7 and 22 December 1982. And if the Soviet Union did develop an ICBM of the MX class, the US might well, in its turn, respond by protecting MX in a way that would mean the end, or the renegotiation, of the ABM Treaty.

THE PROSPECT AFTER BREZHNEV

24. Soviet Options

1. *Le Monde,* 21–22 November 1982 and *Time,* 22 November 1982.
2. In an electoral speech delivered in Moscow on 14 June 1974: *Pravda,* 15 June 1974.

3. To use Ustinov's words, taken from his article published in *Pravda*, 12 July 1982.

4. This obsession, and the repeatedly disastrous consequences that followed, are the subject of Freya Stark's *Rome on the Euphrates*, John Murray, London, 1966.

5. The Appendix, pp. 231–2 above, contains the chapters of the Constitution relevant to foreign policy and defence.

25. An Option for Europe

1. The statement about FBS and the British and French nuclear deterrents, carried in this important statement of Soviet policy, has already been quoted in Chapter 8. See also Ustinov's interview given to Tass, carried in *Pravda*, 20 August 1982.

2. For the views of some distinguished Americans who were very much alive at the time, see McGeorge Bundy, George F. Kennan, Robert S. McNamara, and Gerard Smith, 'Nuclear Weapons and the Atlantic Alliance', *Foreign Affairs*, vol. 60, no. 4 Spring 1982, pp. 735–68.

3. This Soviet commitment was expressed by Gromyko, speaking on Brezhnev's behalf at the United Nations, on 15 June 1982. For an exposition of the Soviet view, see Ustinov's article in *Pravda*, 12 July 1982.

4. Figures quoted by Martin, op. cit. But for an even more deadly range, with the minimum figure set at two million, see the US Congress Office of Technology Assessment's *The Effects of Nuclear War*, Washington, 1979, pp. 83–4.

5. The key passage was 'No one disputes any longer that in the 1980s and perhaps even today—but surely in the 1980s—the United States will no longer be in a strategic position to reduce a Soviet counter-blow against the United States to tolerable levels. Indeed, one can argue that the United States will not be in a position in which attacking the Soviet strategic forces makes any military sense, because it may represent a marginal expenditure of our own strategic striking force without helping greatly in ensuring the safety of our forces.'

    Kissinger's contemporary thoughts on 'Strategy and the Atlantic Alliance' will be found in his article published in *Survival*, September/October 1982, IISS, London, 1982.

6. *Weapons and Peace*: The Annual Memorial Lecture of the David Davies Memorial Institute of International Studies, London, January 1983. For Reagan's remarks, see *The Economist*, 19 March 1983, pp. 45 ff.

7. But I am glad to find myself reaching, though by a different route, conclusions about this that are similar to those of Hedley Bull.

8. In his address to the European Parliament at Strasbourg on 13 November 1973, quoted in the *Glasgow Herald*, 14 November 1973.

9. For a general account of these ideas, see Bridget Bloom's 'Why NATO may think again' in the *Financial Times*, 1 December 1982, for example.

10. The conclusion reached by Gregory Treverton in his lucid Adelphi Paper, *Nuclear Weapons in Europe*, IISS, London, 1981, p. 27.

Select Bibliography

Books

ALLISON, Graham, *Essence of Decision: Explaining the Cuban Missile Crisis*, Little, Brown, Boston, 1971.

AMAL'RYK, Andrei, *Can the Soviet Union Survive until 1984?* Harper & Row, New York; Allen Lane, London, 1970.

ARON, Raymond, *Paix et guerre entre les nations*, Calmann-Lévy, Paris, 1962.

ASCHERSON, Neal, *The Polish August*, Penguin Books, Harmondsworth, 1981.

ASPATURIAN, Vernon V., *Process and Power in Soviet Foreign Policy*, Little, Brown, Boston, 1971.

BONAVIA, David, *The Chinese*, Harper & Row, New York, 1980.

BREZHNEV, L. I., *Leninskim Kursom*, Moscow, 9 vols., Moscow, 1970–82.

BRZEZINSKI, Zbigniew, *The Soviet Bloc*, Harvard University Press, Cambridge, Mass., 1967.

BUCHAN, Alastair, *The End of the Post-War Era*, Weidenfeld & Nicolson, London, 1974.

BUTTERFIELD, M. and WIGHT, M., Diplomatic Investigations, Allen & Unwin, London, 1966.

CARRERE D'ENCAUSSE, Hélène, *L'Empire Eclaté*, Flammarion, Paris, 1979.

CHICHERIN, G. V., *Articles and Speeches*, Moscow, 1961.

CLISSOLD, Stephen, *Soviet Relations with Latin America 1918–68*, Oxford University Press, London, 1970.

CURZON, G. N., *Russia in Central Asia*, Longmans, Green, London, 1889.

DELAHAYE, Yves, *La frontière et le texte*, Payot, Paris, 1977.

Diplomaticheskii Slovar', 2 vols., Moscow, 1964.

Diplomatiya Sotsializma, collective authorship, Moscow, 1973.

DUMONT, René, *Cuba: socialisme et développement*, Editions du Seuil, Paris, 1964.

EDMONDS, Robin, *Soviet Foreign Policy 1962–1973*, Oxford University Press, London, 1975.

ERICKSON, John, *Soviet Military Power*, Royal United Services Institute for Defence Studies, London, 1971.

FORWARD, Nigel, *The Field of Nations*, Macmillan, London, 1971.

FOX, W. T. R., *The Super-Powers—their Responsibility for Peace*, Yale Institute of International Studies, 1944.

FREEDMAN, Lawrence, *The Evolution of Nuclear Strategy*, Macmillan for RIIA, London, 1981.

GITTINGS, John, *Survey of the Sino-Soviet Dispute 1963–67*, Oxford University Press, London, 1968.

GORER, Geoffrey and RICKMAN, John, *The People of Greater Russia*, Cresset Press, London, 1949.

GRIFFITH, William E., *The Sino-Soviet Rift*, Allen & Unwin, London, 1964.

GROMYKO, Antolyi A., *1036 dniei prezidenta Kennedi*, Moscow, 1968.

GROUSSET, Rene, *The rise and splendour of the Chinese Empire*, Godfrey Bles, London, 1952.

HAYTER, William, *Russia and the World*, Secker & Warburg, London, 1970.

HOFFMAN, Erik and FLERON, F., *Conduct of Soviet Foreign Policy*, Aldine and Atherton, Chicago, 1971.

HORELICK, A. L. and RUSH, M., *Strategic Power and Soviet Foreign Policy*, University of Chicago Press, Chicago, 1966.

Istoriya Vneshnei Politiki SSSR 1917–1975, eds. A. A. Gromyko and B. N. Ponomarev, 2 vols., Nauka, Moscow, 1981.

JACOBSEN, Carl, *Soviet Strategy—Soviet Foreign Policy*, Glasgow University Press, Glasgow, 1972.

KARNOW, Stanley, *Mao and China*, Viking Press, New York, 1972.

KENNEDY, Robert, *Thirteen Days, a Memoir of the Cuban Crisis*, Macmillan, New York, 1969.

KHRUSHCHEV, Nikita S., *Khrushchev remembers*, 2 vols., translated and edited by Strobe Talbott, André Deutsch, London, 1974.

KISSINGER, Henry, *The White House Years*, Weidenfeld & Nicolson and Michael Joseph, London, 1979.

KISSINGER, Henry, *Years of Upheaval*, Weidenfeld & Nicolson and Michael Joseph, London, 1979.

KONDRASHEV, E., *Tsenoobrazovanie v promyshlennosti*, Moscow, 1956.

KULSKI, W. W., *The Soviet Union in World Affairs, 1964–1972*, Syracuse University Press, Syracuse, New York, 1973.

LANGE, Oscar, *Socjalizm*, Warsaw, 1973.

LENIN, V. I., *Collected Works*, Foreign Languages Publishing House, Moscow, 1960; Lawrence and Wishart, London, 1960.

MACKINTOSH, J. M., *Strategy and Tactics of Soviet Foreign Policy*, Oxford University Press, London, 1962.

MACMILLAN, Harold, *At the End of the Day*, Macmillan, London, 1973.

MARTIN, Laurence, *The Two-Edged Sword*, Weidenfeld & Nicolson, London, 1982.

MARX, Karl and ENGELS, F., *The Russian Menace to Europe*, ed. Blackstock and Hoselitz, Allen & Unwin, London, 1953.

MEDVEDEV, Roy, *Kniga o sotsialisticheskoi democratii*, Alexander Herzen Foundation, Amsterdam/Paris, 1972.

MEISSNER, Boris, *Die deutsche Ostpolitik 1961–1970*, Verlag Wissenschaft und Politik, Cologne, 1970.

MENDL, Wolf, *Issues in Japan's China Policy*, Macmillan for RIIA, London, 1978.

NOVE, Alec, *The Soviet Economic System*, Allen & Unwin, London, 1981.

SAKHAROV, Andrei, *Progress, Coexistence, and Intellectual Freedom*, Penguin Books, London, 1969.

SALINGER, Pierre, *With Kennedy*, Cape, London, 1967.

SCHAPIRO, Leonard, *The Communist Party of the Soviet Union*, Methuen & Co., London, 1963 and (2nd ed.) 1970.

SCHLESINGER, A. M., *A Thousand Days*, André Deutsch, London, 1966.

SOLZHENITSYN, Alexander, *Archipelag Gulag*, YMCA Press, Paris, 1973; English translation, Collins, London, 1974.

SORENSEN, Theodore, *Decision-Making in the White House*, Columbia University Press, New York, 1969.

SORENSEN, Theodore, *Kennedy*, Hodder & Stoughton, London, 1965.

STARK, Freya, *Rome on the Euphrates*, John Murray, London, 1966.

TALBOTT, Strobe, *Endgame*, Harper & Row, New York, 1979.

TATU, Michel, *Power in the Kremlin*, Collins, London, 1969.

TRISKA, J.F., and FINLEY, D.F., *Soviet Foreign Policy*, Macmillan, New York, 1968.

TROTSKY, Leon, *Moya zhizn'*, Granit, Berlin, 1930.

ULAM, Adam, *Expansion and Coexistence*, Secker & Warburg, London, 1968.

ULAM, Adam, *The Rivals*, Viking Press, New York, 1971.

YORK, Herbert, *Race to Oblivion*, Simon and Schuster, New York, 1970.

ZHDANOV, Andrei, *Essays on Literature, Philosophy, and Music*, International Publishers, New York, 1950.

ZHURIN, V. V. and PRIMAKOV, E. M., *Mezhdunarodnye konflikty*, Moscow, 1972.

ZUCKERMAN, Solly, *Scientists at War*, Harper & Row, New York, 1966.

Periodicals

PUBLISHED IN BRITAIN

Adelphi Papers
The Economist
Encounter
International Affairs
Keesing's Contemporary Archives
The Listener

Military Balance
Strategic Survey
Survey
Survival
The World Today

PUBLISHED IN THE UNITED STATES

Foreign Affairs
Foreign Policy
Problems of Communism

State Department Bulletin
Time Magazine

PUBLISHED IN THE SOVIET UNION

Journal of World Economics and International Relations
Kommunist
Kommunist Vooruzhennykh Sil
Literaturnaya Gazeta
Mezhdunarodnaya Zhizn'

Novoe Vremya
Novyi Mir
SShA
Voprosy Ekonomiki
Voprosy Istorii
The Working Class and the Contemporary World

PUBLISHED IN CZECHOSLOVAKIA

World Marxist Review

PUBLISHED IN CHINA

The People's Daily

Xinhua News Agency

Newspapers

Financial Times
Frankfurter Allgemeine Zeitung
Guardian
Hoy
International Herald Tribune
Izvestiya
Krasnaya Zvezda
Le Monde
New York Times

Observer
Pravda
Rude Pravo
Scotsman
Der Spiegel
The Times
Washington Post
Zycie Warszawy

Index